# RESEARCH METHODS IN ORGANIZATIONAL BEHAVIOR

# Scott, Foresman Series in
# Organizational Behavior and Human Resources

## Lyman W. Porter, Editor

# RESEARCH METHODS IN ORGANIZATIONAL BEHAVIOR

**Eugene F. Stone**

**Department of Psychology**
**Virginia Polytechnic Institute and State University**

**Scott, Foresman and Company**
Glenview, Illinois

Dallas, TX    Oakland, NJ    Palo Alto, CA    Tucker, GA    London, England

**Library of Congress Cataloging in Publication Data**

Stone, Eugene F.
　　Research methods in organizational behavior.

　　(Scott, Foresman series in Organizational Behavior
and Human Resources)
　　Originally published: Santa Monica, Calif.: Goodyear
Pub. Co., c1978.
　　Bibliography: p.
　　Includes indexes.
　　1. Organizational research.　　2. Organizational
behavior—research.　　I. Title.　　II. Series.
[HM131.S8255 1981]　　302.3'5'072　　81-21220
ISBN 0-673-16139-0　　AACR2

## SCOTT, FORESMAN SERIES IN
## ORGANIZATIONAL BEHAVIOR AND HUMAN RESOURCES

　　8-MAL-86 85 84

Printed in the United States of America.

*To my parents,*
*Frank and Josephine Stone*

# CONTENTS

**vii**

# FOREWORD

The Scott, Foresman Series in Organizational Behavior and Human Resources embodies concise and lively treatments of specific topics within the broad area indicated by the Series title. These books are for supplemental reading in basic management, organizational behavior, or personnel courses in which the instructor highlights particular topics in the larger course. However, the books, either alone or in combination, can also form the nucleus for specialized courses that follow introductory courses.

Each book stresses the *key issues* relevant to the given topic. Thus, each author, or set of authors, has made a particular effort to "highlight figure from ground"—that is, to keep the major issues in the foreground and the small explanatory details in the background. These books are, by design, relatively brief treatments of their topic areas, so the authors have had to be carefully *selective* in what they have chosen to retain and to omit. Because the authors were chosen for their expertise and their judgment, the Series provides valuable summary treatments of the subject areas.

In focusing on the major issues, the Series' authors present a balanced content coverage. They have also aimed at breadth by the unified presentation of different types of material: major conceptual or theoretical approaches, interesting and critical empirical findings, and applications to "real life" management and organizational problems. Each author deals with this body of material, but the combination varies according to the subject matter. Thus, each book is distinctive in the particular way in which a topic is addressed.

A final word is in order about the audience for this Series: Although the primary audience is the student, each book in the series concerns a topic of importance to the practicing manager. Managers and supervisors can rely on these books as authoritative summaries of the basic knowledge in each area covered by the Series.

The topics included in the Series to date have been chosen on the basis of their importance and relevance for those interested in management and organizations. As new appropriate topics emerge on the scene, additional books will be added. This is a dynamic Series both in content and direction.

*Lyman W. Porter*
*Series Editor*

# PREFACE

The purpose of this book is to acquaint the reader with a broad sampling of issues relevant to the understanding and application of research methods useful in the study of human behavior in organizational settings. Among the issues covered are: science and the scientific method; elements of the research process; measurement and properties of measures (i.e., reliability and validity); several specific measurement methods (e.g., questionnaires, interviews, and tests); sampling; research design principles; several specific experimental, quasi-experimental, and nonexperimental research designs; a number of specific empirical research strategies (e.g., field study, field experiment, and laboratory experiment); ethical, legal, and other considerations in research; and a few elementary statistical notions. The book deals with all of these topics at an elementary level. Throughout the book, however, the reader is provided with references to works that offer more advanced treatments of various issues.

The book should prove useful to at least three audiences. One is students at both undergraduate and graduate levels enrolled in courses concerning organizational behavior, industrial/organizational psychology, management, behavioral science in administration, organizational sociology, etc. In such courses the book can be used as a supplement to a text whose focus is organizational behavior.

A second audience is students at both undergraduate and graduate levels enrolled in research methods courses in departments of management, psychology, administrative sciences, sociology, political science, etc. At the undergraduate level the book can be used alone. At the graduate level, however, the book should be supplemented by more advanced readings on various topics.

A third audience is practicing managers. An understanding of issues covered in this book should help these individuals in the diagnosis and effective solution of numerous organizational problems.

Readers of this book need no previous training in research methods or statistics. Statistical concepts vital to the understanding of material included in the book are covered in the Statistical Methods Appendix. It should be noted, however, that organizational behavior concepts (e.g., job satisfaction, motivation, and productivity) are used in many examples. As such, previous or concurrent enrollment in a course covering such concepts should make the assimilation of material in the book more interesting.

This book benefited from the generous and helpful involvement of many others. Lyman W. Porter, Howard M. Weiss, Patricia A. Renwick, and Neal Schmitt reviewed the entire manuscript and provided criticisms and suggestions that greatly improved the final product. Daniel Braunstein, Dianna L. Moore, and Laurence R. Takeuchi provided helpful comments on one or more chapters.

I am especially grateful to Lyman W. Porter who has greatly influenced my thinking about research methods and organizational behavior.

Daniel Braunstein deserves special recognition for his contributions to the book: Chapters 1 and 2 were prepared in collaboration with him.

I am also indebted to Margarita P. Estrada who contributed greatly to the completion of this book through her love and encouragement. In addition, she frequently sacrificed the fulfillment of her own dreams so that I could finish the book.

# RESEARCH METHODS IN ORGANIZATIONAL BEHAVIOR

# INTRODUCTION TO ORGANIZATIONAL RESEARCH 1

> Most of our daily activities are carried on without reflection, and it seldom occurs to us to question that which generally passes as true. We cannot, however, always remain in a state of unquestioned belief. For our habitual attitudes are frequently challenged by unexpected changes in our environment, if they are not challenged by our own curiosity or the inquisitiveness of others (Cohen & Nagel, 1934, p. 3).

At some point in your life you have probably been exposed to one or more of the following beliefs about human behavior in organizations:

- Job satisfaction causes job productivity
- Nonmanagerial workers want only money as a reward for work
- Personality tests can be effectively used to select workers for jobs
- A manager's supervisory style remains unchanged across various settings
- The optimum "span of control" of a manager is five
- Professionals are less committed to their employing organizations than nonprofessionals
- Certain traits distinguish leaders or managers from nonleaders

These beliefs have undoubtedly guided the attitudes and behaviors of many organizational members. On the basis of such beliefs organizational structures, reward systems, selection practices, etc., have been established or changed. Yet recent research has shown that these beliefs are not generally valid: Satisfaction may be more the effect of good performance than its cause (Porter & Lawler, 1968; Schwab & Cummings, 1970). The needs of nonmanagerial workers are not limited to money (Centers & Bugental, 1966). Personality tests have, in general, not proven to be effective **1** in personnel selection (Ghiselli, 1966; Guion & Gottier, 1965). A manager's supervisory style is not invariant across different settings, but varies with the productivity of his or her subordinates (Lowin & Craig, 1968). The optimum span of control depends upon the type of technology employed in the manufacture of an organization's product (Woodward, 1958, 1965). There is no necessary relationship between organizational commitment and professionalization (Thornton, 1970). There are no physical traits or personality attributes that show definite and consistent relationships with leadership ability and/or success (Gibb, 1969). In sum, many widely held beliefs about human behavior in organizations have been shown to be invalid when subjected to the test of research.

## IMPORTANCE OF KNOWING RESEARCH METHODS

The above suggests that as organizational members or analysts of organizational phenomena it is important to know not only what is commonly believed to be true about various phenomena, but also the extent to which properly conducted research[1] supports such beliefs. And in order to assess the degree to which beliefs are supported by research we need to understand the research process. Understanding this process enables us to be more effective at (a) solving problems in organizational contexts, (b) understanding and applying the results of research performed by others, (c) assessing the validity of claims made by others concerning the benefits of new practices, equipment, etc., and (d) evaluating the soundness of theory dealing with organizational behavior phenomena.

### Solution of Organizational Problems

Managers are generally faced with a variety of problems: effective recruitment and selection systems must be developed; training programs must be designed and implemented; compensation systems must be designed and effectively administered; work-related attitudes (e.g., job satisfaction) of organizational members must be improved; the performance of organizational members must be improved, and so on. If a manager had no knowledge of research methods such problems might be approached by trial and error. A trial-and-error based solution to problems may or may not work. And, in the absence of knowing how to assess the effectiveness of any given "solution" to a problem, the man-

---

**2**    See definitions of research offered later in this chapter.

ager may end up choosing one that is far from optimal (in terms of relevant criteria).

A manager who, for example, is faced with the problem of improving the performance of his or her subordinates might, using a trial-and-error approach, try such things as differentially rewarding individuals based upon their performance, improving working conditions in the organization, supervising workers more closely, redesigning the jobs of employees, providing the workers with further training, changing work schedules, and improving the general level of job satisfaction among employees. A great deal of time and effort might be expended in the process of trying one or more of these "solutions." In the end, the problem may never be as effectively solved as it could have been if the manager had known and appropriately used research methods in its solution. (The appropriate use of these methods is the focus of this book.)

## Understanding and Applying Research Results

A second reason for studying research methods is to develop a capacity for understanding and applying the results of research done by others. Such research results may provide the manager with valuable information about various organizational behavior-related phenomena. The results of research dealing with organizational behavior are regularly reported in a number of periodicals.[2] Articles in these periodicals deal with issues such as job satisfaction, work motivation, compensation practices, organizational change and development, group processes in organizations, organizational structure, personnel selection, training, employee socialization, job design, performance evaluation, decision making, creativity, organizational commitment, communication in organizations, leadership ,power, influence processes, and interrelationships among these variables.

In the process of trying to solve an organizational problem the manager/researcher[3] should consult the published literature associated with a topic or set of topics to benefit from research that has been done by others. In doing so the researcher may

---

[2] Examples are the *Journal of Applied Psychology, Organizational Behavior and Human Performance, Personnel Psychology,* the *Academy of Management Journal,* the *Journal of Vocational Behavior, Administrative Science Quarterly,* and the *Journal of Applied Behavioral Science.*

[3] Throughout the remainder of this book the term "researcher" will describe any person who uses research methods in the solution of organizational problems. Included in this set of individuals are organizational managers, university-based scientists, employees of consulting firms, and students of organizational behavior in departments of business administration, psychology, sociology, communications, etc.

find, for example, that a solution he or she is contemplating for a given problem has been tried by others and works only under certain circumstances. Or, the researcher may discover that a solution under consideration is less efficacious than others that have been tried. In the best of all worlds, the researcher may find that a solution he or she has proposed for an organizational problem has been extremely effective in a wide variety of contexts in which it has been applied.

In the absence of understanding research methods the reader may find that research reports are difficult, if not impossible, to read and comprehend. One possible outcome of this is that the problem solver will not benefit from the previous efforts of others. Another potential consequence is that the problem solver will inappropriately apply a technique (e.g., participative management) to a problem that would better be solved by another method (e.g., conflict resolution). Still another conceivable result is that the problem solver will use the results of methodologically unsound research as a basis for formulating a solution to a problem. There are yet other deleterious effects of not understanding the results of research done by others. In the interest of brevity these are not elaborated upon here.

### Assessing the Validity of Claims Made by Others

A third reason for studying research methods is to develop skills useful in assessing the validity of claims made by others. Developing such skills is important since organizational managers (and, to a lesser degree, nommanagerial personnel) are often confronted with a myriad of claims made by others about the benefits of various techniques, tools, etc. The manager, for example, may receive a brochure through the mails that extols the virtues of a training program aimed at improving the motivation of sales personnel. Or, the manager may be approached by a representative of a test publishing company and be told about the merits of a package of employee selection tests. Or the manager may, in newspapers, popular magazines, etc., read about the benefits that will accrue to his or her organization and its members if they engage in daily meditation. These examples are but a few of thousands.

What assurance, if any, does the manager have that such claims are correct? What reliance can be placed in such claims, when—as is often the case—the person merchandising a service or product may be more interested in closing a sale than in helping an organization solve its problems? The position taken in this book is that claims made by others should *always* be backed by the
**4**  results of methodologically sound research. It thus becomes

imperative that the potential purchaser or user of ideas, products, or services proffered by others fully understand the research process.

## Evaluating the Soundness of Theory

A fourth reason for studying research methods is to develop a capacity for evaluating the soundness of various theories dealing with organizational behavior phenomena. A theory may be looked upon as a scientifically acceptable principle or set of principles useful in the explanation of some phenomenon (see chapter 2 for a more extensive treatment of theories). In the area of organizational behavior there are theories that deal with job satisfaction,[4] job performance, work motivation, work adjustment, and numerous other phenomena. How sound are such theories? Where there are two or more theories that purport to explain some phenomenon, which theory should be employed? The answers to these and other related questions can be determined using several different criteria (cf. Cohen & Nagel, 1934). One very important criterion in assessing the usefulness of a theory is the extent to which the results of various research studies support the predictions made by the theory. And, such an assessment requires an understanding of research methods: If one does not understand the methods used to test propositions associated with a theory, one cannot determine the degree to which such propositions have been supported by research, and thus the extent of overall support for the theory.

## WAYS OF "KNOWING"

An important consideration in evaluating the soundness of a theory and assessing the validity of claims made by others is the manner in which individuals establish, defend, or change their beliefs about various matters. This is a vital issue, since the confidence that can be placed in the validity of any proposition (e.g., that job productivity causes job satisfaction) is a function of the method(s) a person uses to defend his or her beliefs about the truth of the proposition. In this section we consider four methods for establishing, defending, or changing beliefs about various matters. These four "ways of knowing" (cf., for example, Cohen & Nagel, 1934) are tenacity, intuition, authority, and science.

---

[4] The "need fulfillment theory of job satisfaction," for example, posits that *"Job satisfaction and dissatisfaction are a function of the perceived relationship between what one wants from one's job and what one perceives it as offering or entailing"* (Locke, 1969, p. 316). In this case job satisfaction is "explained" by differences in individuals' needs and perceptions of outcomes associated with the job.

## Tenacity

One method that is used for defending beliefs is tenacity, the tendency to continue to believe a proposition through habit or inertia. We accept a proposition as true simply because we have always believed it to be true. Evidence that contradicts the proposition is discounted (cf. Cohen & Nagel, 1934, p. 193). Tenacity is often the basis for the maintenance of attitudes and opinions about races, languages, and religions.[5] And upon the belief being questioned, the holder may reiterate it as an "act of faith."

Tenacity is a poor method for fixing beliefs, since on any given topic there are likely to be individuals whose beliefs differ from our own. And when differences of opinion surface, there is no satisfactory method for establishing which of several tenaciously held beliefs is to prevail.

## Authority

Another method commonly used to fix and defend beliefs is that of authority: "Instead of simply holding on doggedly to one's beliefs, appeal is made to some highly respected source to substantiate the views held" (Cohen & Nagel, 1934, p. 193). The appeal to authority takes two forms. One form is reasonable, and involves the individual consulting an expert (e.g., a medical doctor, a competent organizational consultant, a lawyer, or a skilled craftsman) when we have neither the time nor the training necessary to solve a problem. We may, if we choose, obtain the opinions of several "experts" before deciding upon a course of action.

The second form of the appeal to authority leads the person to believe that some sources (politicians, philosophers, religious leaders, etc.) are infallible and their opinions on given matters are final. This can have quite deleterious effects because (a) the individual does not go beyond the authority for opinions on a problem, and (b) individuals whose opinions differ from those of the authority may be harassed, punished, etc., to bring about their acceptance of the views of the authority.

Resolving questions through reliance upon authority (whether we are considering the first or the second form) is always a less than optimal strategy. For one, authorities may differ in their opinions about how a problem is to be solved. For example, one consultant may recommend the use of sensitivity training to solve an organizational problem, while another may advocate the redesign of jobs. When the opinions of authorities differ there is no

---

[5] Tenacity may, for example, serve as a basis for the belief that "males are more suited for managerial work than are females." Individuals may subscribe to this opinion even though they lack sound evidence concerning its correctness or truth.

simple way to decide upon the best course of action. A second reason for reliance upon authority being a less than optimal strategy is that authorities are sometimes wrong: Organizational consultants may recommend strategies for solving organizational problems that are ineffective or produce effects opposite those intended. Physicians may prescribe the wrong drug or recommend unnecessary surgery. Vocational counselors may give individuals incorrect advice about the careers they should pursue, and so on. In sum, the method of authority is not, in general, an acceptable "way of knowing."

## Intuition

Intuition is another method for fixing beliefs. This method relies upon the "appeal to 'self-evident propositions'—propositions so 'obviously true' that the understanding of their *meaning* will carry with it indubitable conviction of their truth" (Cohen & Nagel, 1934, p. 194). Some of the propositions considered "self-evident" are "the whole is greater than any one of its parts"; "individuals have an inalienable right to private property"; and "hard work builds character."

Intuition is a poor method for fixing beliefs for at least two reasons. First, many "self-evident" propositions are, in fact, false (e.g., the once "self-evident" proposition that the earth is the center of the universe). Second, there are few propositions for which a claim of "self-evidence" has not been made at some point in time. And if two "self-evident" propositions contradict one another (e.g., "absence makes the heart grow fonder" and "familiarity breeds contempt"), there is no basis for asserting that one is any more valid than the other. In sum, intuition is an inappropriate "way of knowing."

## Science

The methods of intuition, tenacity, and authority are all less than adequate modes of fixing beliefs, because (among other things) there is a high degree of subjectivity in individuals' judgments about what constitutes truth. Unlike the other methods, "Science aims at knowledge that is *objective* in the sense of being intersubjectively certifiable, independently of individual opinion or preference, on the basis of data obtainable by suitable experiments or observations" (Hempel, 1965, p. 141).

Methods of making observations, setting up experiments, etc., constitute the focus of other chapters in this book. We do not, therefore, dwell upon these issues here. Instead, a model of the scientific method is presented and discussed. In addition, the **7** method of science is differentiated from previously mentioned methods for fixing beliefs.

The scientific method consists of: (*a*) the observation of phenomena (facts) in the real world; (*b*) the formulation of explanations for such phenomena, using inductive processes; (*c*) the generation of predictions about phenomena in the real world, using deductive processes; and (*d*) the verification of these predictions through systematic, controlled observation. A model of the method is shown in figure 1. Note that the process depicted in the model is a continuous one. That is, facts produced by one iteration of the induction-deduction-verification cycle become inputs for the next iteration.

FIGURE 1-1    Model of the Scientific Method

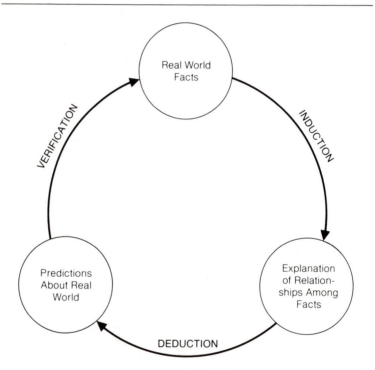

Let's take a closer look at this process. The scientist begins with the observation of facts in the real world. A *fact* is simply a piece of information that has been objectively obtained. By objective we mean that in establishing a fact, the scientist (or person employing the method of science) observes phenomena in such a way that personal feelings or prejudices have a minimum degree of influence on what is observed. For an observation to be considered factual it must be reproducible (replicable). Scientists working independently of one another should be able to observe a given phenomenon and "see" the same thing. For example, if a number of scientists were assembled and asked to count the number of units of product produced by a worker in a given time period (a fact), all should report the same result.

Our confidence in the "truth" of any fact is a function of the degree to which repeated, objective observations of the same phenomenon yield consistent results. It should be noted, however, that no amount of evidence ever establishes a fact as being "true." All we can ever say about facts is that based upon the accumulated evidence a fact is probably true or probably not true.

Having a set of facts that the scientist believes to be probably true, he or she then uses induction (i.e., a process of moving from specifics to generalizations) to develop explanations of such facts.[6] The number of explanations offered to "explain the facts" will vary as a function of the scientist's past experiences, insight, etc. Thus, for example, a scientist observing that a worker's performance has improved over the course of several months may explain this fact or phenomenon by arguing that (a) the individual's ability to do the work has improved, (b) the worker's motivation to do the work has increased, (c) the individual's perceptions of his or her role requirements have become more accurate, or (d) there have been gains in two or more of the aforementioned areas. Each of these represents a possible explanation of the phenomenon. And one or more of these may, at a future point in time, be subjected to critical examination.

It should be noted that under the method of science, facts are not observed or considered in isolation of one another. Rather, an attempt is made to establish some ordering or relationship among facts. Thus, for example, measuring the job satisfaction levels of one group of workers and the degree of occupational identification of another (independent) group of workers would produce two sets of facts which would have little scientific value, since little or no use could be made of such facts. If, however, we measured both the job satisfaction and occupational identification of one or both groups of workers we would have scientifically useful facts, since we might be able to "explain" scores on the occupational identification measure by making reference to scores on the job satisfaction measure. Our tentative explanation might be that "job satisfaction causes occupational identification." Other explanations are possible (e.g., occupational identification causes job satisfaction).

---

[6] It deserves noting that the logical justification for inductive inferences has been questioned (cf., for example, Hempel, 1965; Kaplan, 1964; Popper, 1959; and Sidman, 1960).

Having formulated a tentative explanation of some phenomenon, the scientist then uses deduction (i.e., a process of going from general statements to more specific assertions) to "predict" what should happen in the real world if his or her explanation is a plausible one. If, for example, the general statement (explanation of previously observed facts) is that "job satisfaction causes occupational identification," it follows that if we measure the job satisfaction and occupational identification levels of workers in any particular organization we should find that they are positively related to one another. It should also be the case that if we could somehow alter (e.g., increase) the job satisfaction levels of a given set of workers there should be changes (e.g., increases) in their level of occupational identification. In both cases we deduce what should happen in a particular instance if some more general explanation is valid.

The final step in the method of science is to determine whether or not the predictions that resulted from our deductive reasoning are supported by real world events. Thus, for example, the prediction that job satisfaction and occupational identification should be positively related to one another in a given organization would actually be tested by measuring these two attitudes among members of the organization and examining the degree to which the results or our investigation support our previous prediction.

The process of assessing whether or not our predictions are borne out by the results of real world events is known as hypothesis testing.[7] Such hypothesis testing is one of the major functions of scientific research.[8] It is the process of testing hypotheses in such a way as to allow the facts to discredit them (i.e., show them to be false) that distinguishes the method of science from the methods of authority, tenacity, and intuition. None of these other methods allows for the possibility of currently available facts changing beliefs based upon previously accepted "facts." The cyclical nature of the scientific method, however, assures that erroneous beliefs will be modified when research data fail to support them (cf. Cohen & Nagel, 1934, p. 195).

## Aims of Science

Having described the method of science as a way of knowing, we now consider what are generally viewed as the major aims

---

[7] A hypothesis, loosely viewed, is a conjectural statement about relationships between or among things that vary (e.g., scores on measures of attitudes). The term hypothesis is more fully defined in the following chapter.

[8] As one expert on the philosophy of science (Nagel, 1961) has noted ". . . the deliberate policy of science [is] to expose its cognitive claims to the repeated challenge of critically probative observational data procured under carefully controlled conditions" (p. 12).

or objectives of science and scientific research.[9] The first objective is description. The concern here is with specifying the current state of some system. Description would, for example, be the objective of an organization doing scientific research to answer such questions as: What was the employee turnover rate for last year? What are the levels of job satisfaction among managerial and nonmanagerial employees? How does the productivity of production workers compare with established goals? What percentage of the organization's employees earn more than $3,000 (gross) per month?

The second objective of science is explanation. Having described a system, a scientist may be interested in explaining how it arrived at its present state, how the system currently operates, etc. If, for example, an organization found that managerial employees have a higher level of job satisfaction than nonmanagerial employees, the question might be raised, why are managers more satisfied with their jobs than nonmanagers? Research aimed at answering this question would concern itself with the explanatory purpose of science and scientific research. Such research might investigate factors which the scientist believes are related to and/or responsible for the experienced turnover. Among these might be differences between nonmanagerial and managerial employees' satisfaction with work, pay, promotion prospects, co-workers, or working conditions.

The third and final objective of research is prediction. The scientist makes probabilistic statements about the future state of a system by knowing its present state and any planned changes. For example, a scientist may advance the prediction that if an organization increases the pay offered nonmanagerial employees, the turnover rate for this group will *probably* decrease. Or, the scientist may predict that if individuals in an organization are involved in the setting of production goals, their commitment to reach those goals and hence their productivity will probably increase. Having advanced one or more such predictions the scientist would then do research to assess their accuracy.

## Scientific Research

The term research has been used, without definition, at several points in the preceding text. In order to clarify the meaning of this term, a number of representative definitions follow:

> Scientific research is systematic, controlled, empirical, and critical investigation of hypothetical propositions about the presumed relations among natural phenomena. (Kerlinger, 1973, p. 11)

---

[9] See, for example, Hempel (1965), Kaplan (1964), and Nagel (1961).

[Research is defined as] the careful, diligent, and exhaustive investigation of a specific subject matter, having as its aim the advancement of mankind's knowledge. (Manhiem, 1977, p. 4)

Research is the activity of solving problems which leads to new knowledge using methods of inquiry which are currently accepted by scholars in the field. (Helmstadter, 1970, p. 5)

[Research is] investigation or experimentation aimed at the discovery and interpretation of facts, revision of accepted theories in the light of new facts, or practical application of such new or revised theories or laws. (Woolf, 1975, p. 984)

The common thread that appears to bind all of these definitions together is that scientific *research is the investigation of phenomena via practices consistent with the method of science.* This method for fixing or changing belief was described earlier in this chapter.[10]

It should be noted that the verification of beliefs about various real world phenomena involves what is known as empirical research. An empiricist is one who believes that "all knowledge must originate in experience" (Kemeny, 1959, p. 127). Stated somewhat differently, facts are made known to us through our senses (hearing, seeing, smelling, touching, and tasting). And for a fact to be considered "real" it must be capable of being sensed by others; that is, it must have objective reality. Empirical research, then, is research which deals with facts that have objective reality.

## IMPORTANCE OF STATISTICS IN RESEARCH

In the process of conducting a scientific investigation a researcher often collects quantitative data or facts about real world phenomena. Among such data or facts may be scores of job applicants on preemployment tests, production figures for a group of workers during a given time period, ratings of performance obtained from the supervisors of a set of workers, and scores of organizational members on various measures of job-related attitudes. If the researcher is dealing with large quantities of data it may be difficult, if not impossible, to "make sense" of them or communicate their meaning to others. Statistical methods are of considerable value in summarizing and communicating the essence of large quantities of data. Statistical methods are, in addition, vital to the understanding of some topics (e.g., reliability and validity of measures) that are considered in future chapters.

---

[10] Additional descriptions of science and scientific research are available in Cohen and Nagel (1934), Hempel (1965), Kaplan (1964), Kemeny (1959), Nagel (1961), and Popper (1961).

We recommend, therefore, that the reader who is unfamiliar with basic statistical methods study the statistical Appendix of this book prior to reading the succeeding chapters. Those who have had an introductory course in statistical methods may find a review of the Appendix useful.

## OVERVIEW OF BOOK

The purpose of this book is to acquaint the reader with a number of techniques and issues useful in the conduct and analysis of research. Toward this end, the research cycle is described in some detail in chapter 2. In addition, the chapter focuses on the definition of a number of terms commonly used in the discussion of research.

Scientific research requires that phenomena in the real world be systematically observed. It requires the measurement of various attributes of individuals, groups, organizations, etc. Chapter 3 of the book, therefore, concerns itself with measurement and properties of measures (e.g., reliability and validity). In chapter 4 a number of measurement methods, such as observation, questionnaires, interviews, and tests, are described.

It is often the case in research that facts or data are collected from less than the total number of individuals, groups, or organizations that might have participated in a study. The degree of confidence we have in the data from such a subset of cases (i.e., a sample) being representative of the entire set of cases (i.e., the population) is a function of the way in which members of the sample were selected from the population. Various procedures for selecting such subsets (i.e., sampling procedures) are discussed in chapter 5. In addition, the chapter covers a number of other issues associated with sampling.

The manner in which a study is planned and executed (i.e., research design) has implications for the confidence that may be placed in a study's results and their applicability to individuals, groups, or organizations other than those who actually participated in the study. The design of research is, therefore, the focus of chapter 6. Several experimental and quasi-experimental research designs are described and evaluated. In addition, factors which tend to make the internal and external validity of research results suspect are discussed.

There are a number of strategies the researcher may employ to study any given phenomenon. Among such empirical research strategies are field studies, laboratory experiments, field experiments, sample surveys, and case studies. These and other strat- **13** egies are described in chapter 7. Advantages and disadvantages of each strategy are also considered.

In chapter 8 the reader is exposed to a potpourri of issues aimed at supplementing the technical material in other chapters of the book. Among the topics considered are ethical and legal considerations in research, and competing values that face the researcher.

# THE RESEARCH PROCESS

In the preceding chapter it was noted that the scientist employs empirical research to verify his or her beliefs about various real world phenomena. The overall strategy for conducting such research is elaborated in this chapter. In addition, a number of important terms associated with empirical research are presented. Before this, however, a hypothetical organizational study is described. The study will be referred to throughout this chapter to facilitate the reader's understanding of various issues associated with empirical research.

## A FICTITIOUS EMPIRICAL STUDY

The vice president of marketing of the XYZ Tool Company, which manufactured and distributed small hand tools, was dismayed by the performance of the firm's sales force. A review of the organization's records revealed that while individuals in the sales force would generally meet established sales quotas, they would seldom exceed such quotas. Perplexed by this situation, the vice president engaged the services of an organizational consultant who claimed to have expertise in solving sales problems such as those facing the XYZ Tool Company.

In discussing the sales problem with the vice president of marketing, the consultant learned that: (a) the lackluster performance of the sales force could not be explained by a lack of demand for small hand tools; (b) members of XYZ Tool Company's sales force, when compared to members of the sales forces of similar firms, did not differ meaningfully on age, sex, race, educa- **15** tion, etc.; (c) sales personnel with the XYZ Tool Company received a monthly salary (assuming they met the sales quota) that was equal to the average earnings figure for salespeople employed by other manufacturers and distributors of small hand tools; and (d) when salespeople exceeded the quota by at least 10% they were "rewarded" with a free dinner at one of several local restaurants. The sole owner and president of the firm sponsored these dinners and made it a point to attend each one. During the course of the meal the president would congratulate all present for the fine job they had done during the previous sales period. He firmly believed that this was a fair reward for above average sales performance. (Neither the president nor vice president of marketing had, however, polled members of the sales force on their reactions to these dinners.)

A number of explanations of the sales problem were considered by the consultant. One was that the XYZ Tool Company's salespeople were less experienced than salespeople employed by other similar companies. Another was that members of the XYZ Tool Company's sales force did not have a high level of motivation to sell the firm's products. Still another was that the tools produced by the firm were in some way less marketable than the tools manufactured by the company's competitors.

Conversations with members of the sales force and other available evidence led to rejection of all but the explanation of insufficient motivation. The consultant suspected that the firm's compensation practices were responsible for this hypothesized motivational problem. The only reward for sales above the quota was a free dinner. And talks with members of the sales force revealed that this was not considered a sufficient inducement to warrant selling more than the quota.

To remedy the situation the consultant recommended that the firm pay its salespeople on a straight commission basis: the more a person sold, the greater the amount he or she would earn. Anxious to improve the performance of its salespeople, the XYZ Tool Company agreed to let the consultant empirically test the merits of this recommendation. The test would proceed as follows: Members of the sales force would be randomly assigned to one of two groups. Members of one group would continue to receive a salary for meeting or exceeding the established sales quota. Members of the other group would be paid on a straight commission basis. At the end of a specified period the sales data for the two groups would be compared. If the sales volume for the group paid on a commission basis exceeded that of the other group by a certain percentage (agreed upon by the consultant and managers of the XYZ Tool Company), the firm would then pay all members of the sales force on a commission basis. If,

**16**

on the other hand, the sales data revealed either extremely small differences or no differences, the company would revert back to a policy of paying all members of the sales force on a salary basis.

## A MODEL OF THE RESEARCH PROCESS

Figure 2-1 shows the basic steps that must be followed in any empirical study of a phenomenon.

FIGURE 2-1    The Empirical Research Cycle

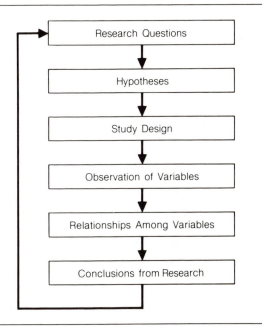

Briefly, empirical research requires that the researcher first recognize a problem and/or formulate a question or set of questions that will be addressed by a study. Next, the researcher develops hypotheses that he or she plans to empirically test. A specific strategy or study design is then developed to assess the validity or truth of the hypotheses. The researcher next implements the strategy and observes the values of relevant variables (see definition later in this chapter). The resulting data are then analyzed (e.g., statistically) to determine whether or not they provide support for hypothesized relationships among variables. Finally, the study's results are examined by the researcher and used as a basis for conclusions about studied phenomena. In-depth coverage of each of these steps is contained in the following paragraphs.

## Problem Statements and Research Questions

It has been argued that research can never get under way until and unless a researcher perceives a problem (either theoretical or applied). It is the researcher's perception or recognition of a problem that motivates research. And the goal of such research is the solution of the problem (Cohen & Nagel, 1934).

A *problem statement* or *research question* may be looked upon as "an interrogative sentence or statement that asks: What relation exists between two or more variables?" (Kerlinger, 1973, p. 17). In the hypothetical study introduced earlier, the problem —as perceived by the consultant—was: What is the relationship, if any, between the manner in which salespeople are paid (i.e., salary or commission) and the level of their performance (i.e., sales volume)?

How are such research questions or problem statements formulated? What can the researcher do to help arrive at a researchable problem statement? First of all, it should be noted that the determination of a research question is often a lengthy process involving a progressive narrowing of the scope of a researcher's interest in some phenomenon. While initial formulations of research questions are likely to lack a clear focus, there is generally a high degree of focus in the research question finally selected for study. In the XYZ Tool Company study, for example, the initial focus of the researcher was rather general: Why don't salespeople continue to sell the firm's products once they've reached the established quota? The final research question was, however, much more specific. Moreover, while the initial definition of the research issue suggested little, if anything, about a strategy for developing information that would be useful in solving the problem, the final research question was specific enough to be of value in this regard.

Second, in arriving at a problem statement the researcher generally does not "start from scratch." There are several sources of information that might be useful in the development of research questions (Selltiz, Wrightsman, & Cook, 1976). These include extant theory related to the phenomena of interest, reports of previously conducted research dealing with such phenomena, beliefs of others who have an interest in and/or knowledge about the phenomena, and one's own beliefs and insights about the phenomena. In the case of the sales problem at the XYZ Tool Company, for example, the researcher could have done such things as examine theories about the determinants of job performance;[1] review the existing body of empirical research associated

---

[1] Among such theories are those presented by Georgopoulos, Mahoney, and Jones (1957), Locke (1968), and Porter and Lawler (1968).

with job performance and its correlates; discuss the productivity problem with other individuals who might have knowledge or insights about the problem, such as employees of the XYZ Tool Company and the researcher's colleagues; and draw upon his or her own knowledge about productivity problems. Doing one or more of the above might greatly facilitate the formulation of a "good" problem statement or research question.

These are the criteria for assessing whether or not a research question or problem statement is a "good one" (Kerlinger, 1973): (a) The problem statement should deal with the relationship between two or more variables. The research question finally developed by the consultant engaged by the XYZ Tool Company meets this standard in that it asks if there is a relationship between the manner in which individuals are paid and the level of their performance. (b) The research question should be as clear and unambiguous as possible. In our hypothetical study, for example, the consultant's final formulation of the research question meets this criterion. Initial statements of the problem (e.g., that offered by the vice president of marketing) were deficient in this respect. (c) The problem should be stated in such a way as to imply the possibility of its solution through empirical research. The final problem statement of the consultant is acceptable in this regard.

In general, the formulation of good problem statements is not an easy task. The reader should not, therefore, become discouraged if initial efforts aimed at the development of good research questions prove unsuccessful.

## Hypotheses

Having formulated a problem statement or research question, the researcher's next task is to develop a hypothesis (or set of hypotheses). A *hypothesis* may be viewed as a tentative explanation about the relationship between two or more variables. In the case of our contrived study, for example, a plausible hypothesis is, "Salespeople who are paid on a commission basis will have a higher level of performance (i.e., sales) than will those paid on a salary basis."

The reader should note that there are at least three important differences between a problem statement and a hypothesis. First, whereas a problem statement raises the *question* of how variables are related to one another, a hypothesis provides a tentative answer to such a question. Second, while a problem statement should be phrased in such a way as to suggest its resolution through empirical research, it does not provide as specific a guide for such research as does a hypothesis. In the case of our hypothetical study, for example, the hypothesis suggests a specific **19** strategy for solving the problem (i.e., pay salespeople on a commission basis). Third, and finally, unlike a research question, a hypothesis can be shown to be "false" through research. In the fictitious study, for instance, evidence from an empirical study could lead to rejection of the hypothesis that individuals paid on a commission basis will sell more than those paid on a salary basis. No evidence, however, would lead to rejection of the problem statement, since whatever the results of a study, the question raised by the problem statement is answered. In sum, assertions or hypotheses can be shown to be incorrect, questions or problem statements cannot.

There are a number of criteria for assessing the merits of any given hypothesis (cf., for example, Cohen & Nagel, 1934; Kerlinger, 1973). First, the variables referenced in a hypothesis should all have empirical referents; that is, there should be a mode for observing or experimentally "creating" each such variable.[2] The hypothesis associated with our contrived example is acceptable in this regard since the level of sales can be directly observed, and we can (experimentally) vary the manner in which salespeople are compensated.

Second, a hypothesis should provide an answer (albeit tentative) to the question raised by a problem statement. The hypothesis connected with our fictitious study certainly meets this criterion.

Third, a hypothesis should not only explain presently known facts, but should also predict future facts. A hypothesis must, therefore, always be stated *in advance* of collecting evidence aimed at its testing. If and only if a hypothesis is stated in advance of collecting facts aimed at its testing will such facts be useful in the verification or refutation of the hypothesis. The reason for this is that if a hypothesis is stated in advance of observing data aimed at its testing, there is the possibility that such data will not provide support for the hypothesis. If, on the other hand, the hypothesis being "tested" is developed by first observing the data aimed at its "testing," it will always be supported by such data. There is no guarantee, however, that the same hypothesis will be supported by data collected at some future point in time (cf. Cohen & Nagel, 1934, p. 210).

Fourth, and finally, a hypothesis should be as simple as possible. One hypothesis is simpler than another if it makes reference to a smaller number of independent elements. The hypothesis associated with our contrived example is a relatively simple one in that it contains only a small number of independent elements (i.e., salespeople, performance, and compensation bases). One

---

[2] More precisely, each variable should be capable of being operationalized in some way. Operationalization of variables is discussed later in this chapter.

hypothesis is also simpler than another if it is more general. A general hypothesis is one that can explain a phenomenon across a wide variety of situations without qualifications. The hypothesis associated with our contrived study is not as simple as, for example, the hypothesis that "people who are paid on a commission basis will have a higher level of performance than those paid on a salary basis." The latter hypothesis is simpler in that (*a*) it references all people, not just salespeople, and (*b*) it considers general performance, not just sales performance.

## Overall Study Design

Once the researcher has an empirically testable hypothesis, his or her next task is to formulate a strategy for testing it, i.e., a research design. A *research design* is nothing more than a plan for conducting research in such a way as to answer research questions. In the case of our hypothetical study, for example, the research design (plan) called for the assignment of salespeople to two groups via a random process (cf. chapter 6), the payment of one group on a salary basis and the other on a commission basis, and the determination of whether or not the level of sales differed for the two groups after a specified period of time.

In designing an empirical study a number of questions must be answered by the researcher. These include: Who or what shall be the focus of the study? What attributes (e.g., behaviors, attitudes, and physical characteristics) of individuals, organizations, systems, etc., shall be observed? In what contexts (laboratories, organizations, etc.) shall the observations be made? and, What methods shall be employed to analyze the data produced by a study?

In answering these questions, two points should be considered. First, a researcher is always faced with constraints on the resources (people, time, money, etc.) available to do a study. A prime consideration, therefore, is to be cost effective in designing research. Second, there are *numerous alternatives* to measuring variables and assessing the reliability and validity of measures (cf. chapters 3 and 4), choosing individuals, groups, organizations, etc., for participation in research (cf. chapter 5), the conditions under which and the contexts in which observations are to be made (cf. chapters 6 and 7), and resolving ethical, legal, and value-related issues in research. Two researchers asked to test the same hypothesis might develop very different research designs. And any single researcher in the course of carrying out a research program centered upon a single phenomenon may use a number of quite dissimilar research designs. Put simply, there are many different ways to design a study. More importantly, **21** there is no one right design for the study of a given phenomenon. Any given design has associated with it certain costs and certain benefits (cf., for example, chapters 5, 6, and 7). In designing a study, therefore, the researcher should consider (a) the amount and type of previous research related to the phenomenon of interest, (b) the resources available to conduct the research in question, (c) the extent to which the results of a given study will be believed and used by organizational managers, and (d) numerous other factors dealt with in subsequent chapters of this book. The guiding question, however, in evaluating the merits of any given design is: Will the results of research done in accordance with a given design provide suitable data with which to test a given hypothesis?

## Variables

Having a study design, the researcher's next step is to implement it and observe the values of relevant variables. A *variable* is a symbol which takes on differing values. Among the variables that are commonly referred to in organizational research are sex, age, income, job satisfaction, organizational commitment, and motivation. Note that each of these symbols can take on at least two values. Sex can assume the values male and female. Age can assume the values 1, 2, 3, etc. The remaining symbols can all assume a number of different values. In our hypothetical study there were two variables. One was compensation basis (which assumed the values "salary" and "commission"). The other was performance (which assumed the value of the dollar amount of a person's sales).

*Other Terms.* The term "variable" is frequently encountered in discussions of empirical research. Two other terms found in such discussions are "concept" and "construct."

A *concept* is "an idea which combines several elements from different sources into a single notion" (Chaplin, 1975, p. 105). It is a generalization formed from the observation of various particular instances of things, events, etc. Roundness is a concept familiar to most people. The concept is formed by observing numerous things with round shapes, such as balls, oranges, ball bearings, circles, and wheels, and generalizing from such experiences the property of roundness. Concepts referenced in organizational behavior research include satisfaction, commitment, identification, productivity, motivation, achievement, performance, work, and job.

A *construct* is a concept that has been "deliberately and consciously invented or adopted for a special scientific purpose" (Kerlinger, 1973, p. 129). Such concepts are called constructs because they are "something that the scientist puts together from his own imagination, something that does not exist as an isolated observable dimension of behavior" (Nunnally, 1967, p. 85). An example of a construct used in organizational behavior research is "equity"—the perception that a person is getting his or her "fair share of rewards." More precisely, equity exists when the ratio of one's outcomes (pay, praise, etc.) to one's inputs (effort, skill, etc.) equals that of some comparison other (e.g., a co-worker with the same job title and duties). Note that equity is not something that can be directly observed. Rather, equity must be inferred from asking an individual such questions as: Compared to others you know who are doing work similar to yours, do you feel you are getting your fair share of rewards? All in all, how satisfied are you with the levels of pay, praise, and other rewards you get from doing your job? Are you getting as much in the way of rewards from your job as you deserve?

Another example of a construct employed in organizational behavior research is "organizational commitment." An individual would be considered highly committed to an organization to the extent that he or she (a) expressed a willingness to exert high levels of effort in the service of organizational goals, (b) manifested a strong desire to remain a member of the organization, and (c) subscribed strongly to the organization's values and goals (cf., for example, Stone & Porter, 1975). It should be noted that one cannot directly observe the level of an individual's organizational commitment. Instead, it is inferred, for example, from responses an individual gives to questionnaire items aimed at assessing this construct.

The reader should note that constructs are the basic elements used in the construction of scientific theories. More precisely, "all theories in science mainly concern statements about constructs rather than statements about specific observable variables" (Nunnally, 1967, p. 85). As noted, the function of observable variables is to provide empirical referents for constructs (values of the former employed to infer values of the latter).

A researcher, for example, could not directly test a theory asserting that organizational commitment is at least in part "caused by" job satisfaction. Rather, empirical referents (e.g., scores from questionnaire measures) of these constructs would be used in evaluating the validity of the assertion.

The reader should observe that any given term (motivation, satisfaction, achievement, performance, etc.) may be alternately referred to as a concept, construct, or variable. For example, consider the term "motivation." A person may observe several instances of purposeful behavior in individuals and generalize from this that the individuals so behaving are "motivated." In this con-  **23** text the term is used as a concept. The term motivation might also be used as a label for a construct. It would assume the role of a construct as soon as it became en element in a theory. Motivation serves as a construct in a theory of work behavior (cf. Vroom, 1964) that relates "performance" to "motivation" and "ability" (more specifically, $P = f$ [M $\times$ A]). "Motivation" might, finally, assume the status of a variable if a researcher develops a measure of the "motivation" construct and labels the values produced by the measure as "motivation scores." A number of researchers have used scores from questionnaire measures of "motivation" in the prediction of work effort or performance (cf. Hackman & Porter, 1968). And, "motivation" has been referred to as a variable in theoretically oriented discussions dealing with the phenomenon (cf. Mitchell & Biglan, 1971; Steers & Porter, 1975).

As the usage of a term may vary from one context to the next, the reader should not be disconcerted if he or she finds a given term referred to as a concept in one context, a construct in another context, and a variable in still another context.

*Independent, Intervening, and Dependent Variables.* In discussions of organizational behavior theory and research the reader is likely to encounter not only the term variable, but also more specialized terms such as independent variable, intervening variable, and dependent variable. These terms are introduced and defined below.

An *independent variable* is a variable which when varied is assumed to be the cause of changes in another variable (i.e., the dependent variable). A *dependent variable* is a variable that varies as a consequence of changes in the values of its assumed cause (i.e., the independent variable). An *intervening variable* is an unobservable process and/or state associated with an organism (e.g., a person) that helps to explain linkages between an independent variable and a dependent variable.[3] For examples of independent, dependent, and intervening variables, consider the fictitious study introduced earlier in this chapter. In that study it was hypothesized that those paid on a commission basis would outsell those paid on a salary basis. The independent variable in this study is compensation basis (salary or commission). The dependent variable is sales performance. A simple model of the assumed causal connection between compensation basis and sales performance is shown in part *a* of figure 2-2. This simple model shows that changes in sales performance are caused by changes

---

[3] Intervening variables are also commonly referred to as hypothetical constructs. See, however, MacCorquodale and Meehl (1948) for distinctions between the two terms.

in compensation basis. What the model does not show is *why* changes in one variable produce changes in the other.

FIGURE 2-2

*a.* Simple model of causal link between "compensation basis" and "sales performance"

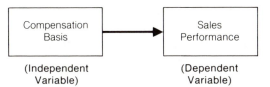

(Independent          (Dependent
Variable)             Variable)

*b.* More elaborate model of causal links between "compensation basis" and "motivation," and "motivation" and "sales performance"

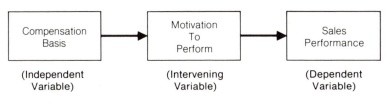

(Independent     (Intervening     (Dependent
Variable)        Variable)       Variable)

It is here that the intervening variable comes into play. It offers an explanation of why changes in compensation basis result in changes in sales performance. In the case of our contrived study, an intervening variable that appears useful in explaining why compensation basis influences sales performance is motivation. The assumption is that paying individuals on a commission (as opposed to salary) basis will lead to increases in motivation to sell, and this increased motivation will, in turn, result in higher sales. A model depicting this is shown in part *b* of figure 2-2.

The reader should note that while the values of both independent and dependent variables can be directly or indirectly observed, the values of intervening variables cannot. Instead, they must be inferred from the values of observables. In our hypothetical study, for instance, the values of the independent variable are observable—a person is paid on either a "commission" or "salary" basis. Similarly, the values of the dependent variable are observable—a person sells *X* dollars worth of the company's tools in a given period. The values of the intervening variable, motivation, are not observable. Instead, we *infer* that those individuals who sold the most had the highest level of motivation.

Before closing this subsection on independent, intervening, and dependent variables, it is important to note that a variable **25** labelled as independent in one study may be designated as dependent in another, and vice versa. Moreover, within the same investigation the same variable may serve as both an independent variable (for one analysis) and a dependent variable (for another analysis). To help clarify the above see figure 2-3. In Study 1, job satisfaction has been given the status of a dependent variable. Changes in job satisfaction are assumed to be caused by changes in the autonomy individuals have on their jobs. In Study 2, on the other hand, the role of job satisfaction is that of an independent variable. Changes in employee absenteeism are presumed to be caused by changes in job satisfaction.

FIGURE 2-3   The Differing Status of a Variable Across Two Investigations

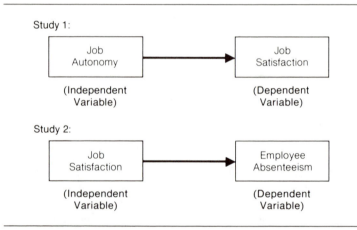

The status of a variable can also change for different analyses within the same study. For example, the model in figure 2-4 shows that job effort causes job performance, and job performance in turn causes the individual to receive organizational rewards (e.g., pay and recognition). Note that a researcher could perform two separate analyses with measures of these three variables. In the first analysis job effort could be correlated with job performance; in this instance the status of job performance is that of a dependent variable. In the second analysis job performance could be correlated with received organizational rewards; the role of job performance would be that of an independent variable.

*Moderator Variables.* A moderator variable is any variable which when systematically varied "causes" the relationship between two other variables to change. Stated somewhat differently, the relationship between two other variables will differ depending upon the level of the moderator variable. The moderator variable notion is clarified in figure 2-5. The figure shows that the relationship between job effort and job performance differs

FIGURE 2-4    The Differing Status of a Variable in Two Analyses of the Same
Investigation

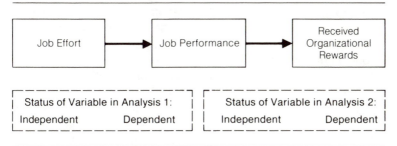

for different levels of the moderator variable, "level of job knowledge." For individuals who have a low level of job knowledge,
increases in job effort lead to only minor changes in the level
of job performance. For individuals who have an average level
of job knowledge, increases in job effort lead to moderate increases in job performance. And, for individuals who have a high
level of knowledge, increases in job effort lead to rather substantial
increases in job performance.

FIGURE 2-5    The Moderating Effect of Job Knowledge on the Relationship
Between Job Effort and Job Performance

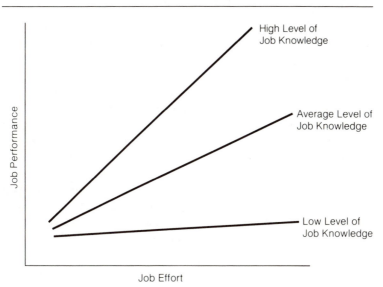

The moderator variable phenomenon is important in a number
of organizational research contexts, one of which is where the
relationship between a preemployment test and job performance
differs among groups formed on the basis of such variables as    **27**

age, sex, race, etc. (The moderator variable in such instances is group membership.) A variable that predicts job success for one group may not predict it for another. While it would thus be appropriate to use the test in the selection of employees belonging to one group, its use in selecting employees in the other group would be less justifiable (perhaps even illegal). (For more on the moderator variable and its role in organizational research, see Saunders, 1956, and Zedeck, 1971.)

*Predictor and Criterion Variables.* A great deal of research in organizations is concerned with the discovery and applications of tests, employment applications, biographical information blanks, and other devices useful in the selection of individuals for jobs, promotion, participation in training, etc.[4] In reports of such research the reader is very likely to encounter the terms "predictor variable" and "criterion variable." These terms are also used in chapter 3 of this book. Their definitions are presented below.

When scores on one variable are used to predict scores on another variable, the variables function, respectively, as *predictor* and *criterion* variables.[5] For example, scores on the Graduate Record Exam are frequently used to predict how well students will do in graduate school. In this case scores on the examination serve as the predictor variable while success in graduate school (e.g., grade point average) serves as the criterion variable.

This is but one of many examples that could have been cited involving predictor and criterion variables. For additional examples the reader should consult any one of a number of published works.[6]

*Operational Definitions of Variables.* An *operational definition* of a variable is a statement which specifies the procedures that are to be used in establishing an empirical referent for a construct. For examples of operational definitions, consider the hypothetical study involving compensation bases and sales performance. In that study operational definitions of both of these constructs were needed. The researcher used the type of compensation plan (commission vs. salary) as an operational definition of the compensation base construct, and the dollar volume of sales during a given time period as an operational definition of sales perfor-

---

[4] For additional information on such devices see Dunnette (1976), Landy and Trumbo (1976), and Schneider (1976).

[5] The term prediction is used here to mean "correlate with." As is noted in chapter 3, there is no need for scores on a predictor variable to be obtained prior to those on a criterion. The most important standard is that scores on the predictor correlate with scores on the criterion.

[6] See, for example, Dunnette (1976), Ghiselli (1966), Landy and Trumbo (1976), McCormick and Tiffin (1974), and Miner (1969).

mance. Note that a number of other operational definitions of these two variables might have been used. In the case of sales performance, for example, some other operational definitions are (a) the number of calls made during a given time period, (b) the number of hours the salesperson spent in trying to sell the firm's products, and (c) the number of sales that were of a "repeat business" nature.

It has been argued that "the starting point of any science is, basically, a set of phenomena which have been operationally defined" (Underwood, 1957, p. 52). A requirement of the scientific method is that the researcher empirically test predictions about real world phenomena (cf. chapter 1). Such testing cannot be accomplished unless and until the scientist establishes empirical referents for the constructs associated with these predictions. For example, there is no way to test the prediction that increased "job autonomy" results in increased "job satisfaction" without operationally defining both of these constructs. Similarly, it is *impossible* to verify or falsify any hypothesis unless the constructs referenced by it can be operationally defined.

There are two basic procedures that a researcher can employ in establishing an operational definition of a variable. One is to specify the measure that will be used to provide an empirical referent for a construct. Thus, for example, one could operationally define job satisfaction as the scores produced by a number of commonly used questionnaire measures of this construct (e.g., the Job Descriptive Index, the Minnesota Satisfaction Questionnaire, and the Job Satisfaction Index).

The second method for establishing an operational definition is to experimentally produce various levels of a variable. In our hypothetical study, for example, two levels of the compensation basis variable were created by paying some salespeople on a commission basis and others on a salary basis. (For a more extensive treatment of methods for establishing operational definitions of variables see Underwood, 1957, chapter 3.)

### Relationships Among Variables

Having implemented a research strategy and observed the values of relevant variables, the researcher's next task is to assess the extent to which the data produced by a study support previously stipulated hypotheses. There are numerous techniques for establishing the degree to which two or more variables are related to one another.[7] In this section nontechnical descriptions of several such techniques are presented.

---

[7] See, for example, Cohen and Cohen (1975); Cooley and Lohnes (1971); and Hays (1973).  **29**

One method of determining whether or not variables are related to one another is to assess the extent to which mean levels of the variable differ between or among groups.[8] In the case of our hypothetical study, for example, the degree to which compensation basis was associated with sales performance could be established by comparing the mean levels of sales for groups paid on commission and salary bases. A graphical display of the results of such a comparison is shown in figure 2-6. As can be seen in the figure, the group paid on a salary basis had an average level of sales of $1500. The range of sales for individuals in this group was $500 to $2,400. The group paid on a commission basis, on the other hand, had an average level of sales of $3,500. The range for this latter group was $2,600 to $4,400. The data indicate that there are clear and important differences between the average levels of sales for the two groups: the average level of sales for those in the commission group is more than 2.3 times that of those in the salary group. The data appear to provide clear support for the researcher's hypothesis that compensation basis is related to sales performance.[9]

FIGURE 2-6    Comparison of Sales Performance for Groups Paid on Salary and Commission Basis

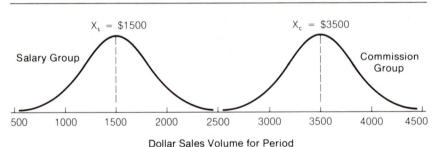

$X_s = \$1500$       $X_c = \$3500$

Salary Group                               Commission Group

| 500 | 1000 | 1500 | 2000 | 2500 | 3000 | 3500 | 4000 | 4500 |

Dollar Sales Volume for Period

Note: $X_s$: Mean level of sales for "salary" group
$X_c$: Mean level of sales for "commission" group

Another technique for assessing the extent to which variables are related to one another is to examine the degree to which they correlate with one another (correlation is described in the

[8] A statistical technique called analysis of variance would actually be used in testing for differences between mean levels of a variable among groups. For treatments of analysis of variance see Edwards (1968), Hays (1973), Kirk (1968), and Winer (1962).

[9] In an actual study the researcher would, generally, not only make "eyeball" comparisons of means differences among groups, but would also assess whether or not such differences were statistically reliable (i.e., statistically significant). The confidence placed in the results of such a statistical comparison would be inversely related to the probability that the observed means differences could have been chance-based. See Glass and Stanley (1970), Guilford and Fruchter (1973), Hays (1973), Marascuilo (1971), and Winer (1962) for additional information on such statistical comparisons.

statistical Appendix). If two variables are correlated then changes in the level of one variable will be accompanied by *systematic* (i.e., nonrandom) changes in the level of the other variables.

Figure 2-7 shows the results of a hypothetical study in which scores of 30 students on the "Quantitative Ability" subscale of the Graduate Record Examination were used to predict their performance in a graduate-level program in Physics. Performance was, in this case, operationally defined as the student's grade point average for all graduate level courses. As can be seen in the figure, there appears to be a relatively high degree of association between these two variables. The correlation coefficient for these data is, in fact, .76.[10]

FIGURE 2-7    Relationship Between "Quantitative Ability" Scores and Grade Point Average

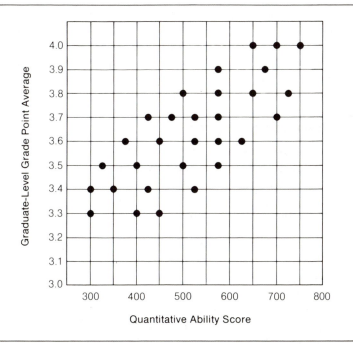

In the examples just cited the relationships examined were between one independent and one dependent variable. There are however, many research situations in which there are several in-

---

[10] Apart from knowing the magnitude of a correlation coefficient, a scientist would also want to know whether or not the relationship was one that was statistically reliable (i.e., statistically significant). Again, the confidence placed in results of a correlational analysis would be inversely related to the probability that the observed correlation coefficient could have resulted from chance. See Glass and Stanley (1970), Guilford and Fruchter (1973), Hays (1973), Marascuilo (1971), and Winer (1962) for additional information on the confidence placed in the results of correlational analysis.

dependent and/or dependent variables. In such instances it may be necessary to use techniques other than those described. Among such techniques are factorial analysis of variance, multiple correlation, discriminant function analysis, canonical correlation, and multivariate analysis of variance. Those interested in learning more about these and other data analytic methods are referred to any one of a number of works.[11]

An important point (more fully developed in chapter 6) deserves mention prior to closing this section on relationships among variables; it is that correlation is a necessary but insufficient condition for establishing a causal relationship between two variables. Causality implies correlation, but correlation does not imply causality. Thus, for example, the research finding that (empirical referents of) ''job satisfaction'' and ''job performance'' are correlated with one another does not justify the conclusion that job satisfaction causes job performance. Nor does it justify the conclusion that job performance causes job satisfaction. The only conclusion that is justified by an empirical finding of a correlation between two variables is that a hypothesis asserting a causal connection between them has survived one chance of being discredited by real world data.

## Conclusions from Research

Having assessed the extent to which relationships exist between (or among) variables considered by a particular study, the researcher is then faced with the task of determining what, if any, conclusions are justified by the study. A number of issues associated with research conclusions will now be considered.

*Strategy-Related Constraints.* The truth or falsity of any given hypothesis can never be established by a *single* study, because in any single study strategy-related factors (the way in which variables are operationalized, the context in which a study is executed, etc.) may have a profound influence on the study's results. One investigator may, for example, find a strong relationship between two variables using one set of operational definitions of them. Another researcher, using a different set of operational definitions, may find the variables to be uncorrelated with one another. Future chapters in this book cover other strategy-related features (artifacts, confounding variables, etc.) that may lead to the support of a hypothesis in one study and its nonsupport in another.

*Decision Errors.* In the investigation of any phenomenon a researcher often studies only a limited subset of the individuals, groups, organizations, etc., in which he or she is interested. Data

---

[11] See, for example, Cooley and Lohnes (1971), Hays (1973), Overall and Klett (1972), and Tatsuoka (1971).

from the subset (i.e., sample) are used as a basis for making inferences about the entire set of individuals, groups, organizations, etc. (i.e., the population). Data from a sample may, for example, be used to infer the existence of a correlation between two variables in a larger population.

Whenever statistical techniques are employed to make inferences about the existence of a relationship between two variables in a population using sample statistics (e.g., mean, variance, and correlation), errors of two types can be made (reasons for this are explained in Hays, 1973). First, data from the sample may lead to the conclusion that a relationship (difference between means, correlation, etc.) exists when this is in fact not the case. This is known as a Type I error. Second, the researcher may conclude on the basis of sample statistics that there is no relationship in the population when, in fact, one exists. This is known as a Type II error. In any given study there is always some probability of making both types of errors. The results of any single study must always be interpreted in this light. Moreover, the possibility of these types of errors suggests the need for multiple studies aimed at the testing of any given hypothesis.

*Research Results and Theory.* One purpose of scientific research is to investigate whether or not real world facts support theory-based predictions about real world phenomena.[12] The reader should note that theories, per se, are never either verified or falsified through research. Rather, propositions deduced from theories are subjected to empirical tests. And, the greater the number of theory-based propositions that are supported by empirical research, the greater our confidence in the ability of the theory to explain and/or predict real world phenomena. One implication of this is that the results of any single study never verify or falsify a theory. Instead, such results speak to the probable truth of various empirically testable propositions derived from a theory. (Note, however, that if the results of numerous empirical studies fail to provide support for theory-based propositions, a scientist may choose to revise or abandon a theory.)

## Closing Comments

The reader has now been exposed to all of the basic steps associated with the conduct of empirical research. Recapitulating, these are: developing research questions, formulating empirically testable hypotheses, generating an acceptable study design, ob-

---

[12] A theory may be looked upon as *"a set of interrelated constructs (concepts), definitions, and propositions that present a systematic view of phenomena by specifying relations among variables, with the purpose of explaining and predicting the phenomena"* (Kerlinger, 1973, p. 9). For more elaborate treatments see Hempel (1965), Nagel (1961), and Popper (1959). **33**

serving the values of relevant variables, testing for relationships among variables, and drawing conclusions from research results. Before bringing this chapter to a close·two important points deserve mention.

First, the conclusions from one iteration of the research cycle serve as inputs for the formulation of research questions dealt with by the next iteration of the cycle. This "feedback" is represented by the linkage between the "conclusions from research" and "research questions" elements in figure 2-1.

Second, the results of one iteration of the process depicted in figure 2-1 raise a number of questions that should at some point be addressed by an investigator. One is: could such results be replicated (i.e., reproduced) in another study employing the same design, measures, etc.? Another is, would such results be obtained if crucial parameters of the study (e.g., operational definitions of variables, participants, and study contexts) were varied?[13] As will be made clear in subsequent chapters, our confidence in the existence of any phenomenon increases when a number of investigations (involving different measures, participants, etc.) all produce consistent results.

---

[13]Repeating a study with modified parameters leads to what are called "extensions" of a study.

# MEASUREMENT AND PROPERTIES OF MEASURES 3

Assume that as a manager in an organization you are interested in testing the hypothesis that "job satisfaction" is inversely related to "employee absenteeism." In order to empirically investigate the credibility of this hypothesis you have to do several things, including: (1) operationally defining each of the variables of interest, (2) measuring the levels of the two variables for a given group of employees, (3) performing statistical analyses of the data, and (4) judging the truth value of the hypothesis in light of your study's results.

As should be obvious, the measurement of variables is critical in any empirical study. If variables cannot be operationally defined and measured, hypotheses involving such variables can never be empirically tested. Simply put, measurement is the *sine qua non* of all empirical research.

A number of key issues associated with measurement are considered in this chapter. These include the measurement process, levels of measurement or scaling, scale construction techniques, the value of standardized measures, and the reliability and validity of measures. The discussion of measurement concludes in chapter 4 where several measurement methods are described.

## THE MEASUREMENT PROCESS

*Measurement* is nothing more than the process of assigning symbols (e.g., labels, numbers, etc.) to objects or events according to rules (Nunnally, 1967, p. 2; Stevens, 1968, p. 854). In some instances the symbols we assign to objects or events have **35** no quantitative meaning. For example, in the measurement of eye color we may assign the labels brown, blue, green, and other to individuals depending upon their eye color. In other instances the symbols we assign do have quantitative meaning. For example, in the measurement of a worker's productivity we may count the number of units the worker produces per day.

Both examples involve a process called *mapping* (Kerlinger, 1973, p. 428; Stevens, 1968, p. 854) in which a rule of correspondence indicates how items in one set (the domain) are to be assigned to symbols or numbers in another set (the range). In the case of eye color the rule of correspondence provides a basis for assigning people (members of the domain) to eye-color-based categories (members of the range). In the case of employee productivity the rule of correspondence gives us a means for assigning people (members of the domain) to numbers associated with productivity levels (members of the range). Measurement, then, always involves a process through which items in one set are matched with (or mapped into) items in another set. As Stevens (1968) has so aptly stated: "If you would [want to] understand the essence of a given measuring process you should ask what was matched to what" (p. 854).

We should point out here that in reality, people or events *are not* the object of measurement; attributes of people, items, events, etc., *are* the object of measurement. In the case of measuring a person's "job satisfaction," for example, we are measuring one of a multitude of attributes of the person—not the person. As Nunnally (1967, p. 3) points out, this distinction, while important, is often not made. For example, when a person's height is measured it is often incorrectly assumed that the person has been measured. In actuality what has been measured is an attribute of the person (height). The attribute and the person (possessor of the attribute) are not the same and should not, therefore, be confused.

## LEVELS OF MEASUREMENT OR SCALING

A *scale* may be looked upon as any measuring instrument (questionnaire, interview, test, thermometer, observation, etc.) composed of one or more "items" (question, observation, etc.) that have logical or empirical relationships with one another (cf., for example, Selltiz, Wrightsman, & Cook, 1976, p. 580). That is, a scale may be looked upon as a set of "items" so constructed that entities (people, things, events, etc.) being measured (i.e., scaled) can be systematically assigned scores on the scale, the

**36** assignment of such scores being related to the "amount" of the measured attribute the entity possesses (cf., Kerlinger, 1973, p. 492).

Scales are created by the formulation of rules for assigning numerals or symbols to aspects (i.e., attributes) of objects or events (Stevens, 1958, 1968, 1971). For example, the meter stick is a scale which tells us what symbol to assign to an attribute of an object (i.e., the object's length).

While hundreds of thousands of scales probably exist for measuring the various attributes of people, things, objects, events, etc., all scales can be assigned to one of four basic types: (a) nominal, (b) ordinal, (c) interval, and (d) ratio (Stevens, 1958, 1968, 1971). Each of these basic types of scales is considered below.

## Nominal Scales

In nominal scaling, symbols (e.g., labels, numerals, etc.) are applied to attributes of objects, people, events, etc., for the purpose of simple categorization. No ordering among categories is implicit in such scaling. The measurement of sex, for example, involves nominal scaling. Individuals are assigned one of two labels (male or female) depending upon their sex. Another example of nominal scaling is the measurement of organizational role. Here individuals are assigned one of a given number of labels (e.g., assembler, secretary, machinist, carpenter, electrician, typist, accountant, etc.) according to their role in an organization (see figure 3-1).

FIGURE 3-1    Nominal Scaling Example: Mapping Workers into Job Title-Based Groups

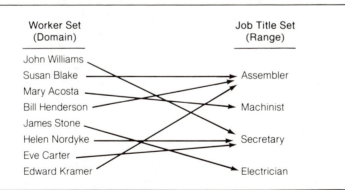

Note that while the labels associated with organizational roles (i.e., job titles) may relate to other variables that are ordered (that is, job title may be associated with prestige ratings of occupations), the job titles alone give us no information about how jobs are ordered.

## Ordinal Scales

In ordinal scaling, objects, persons, events, etc., are ranked (least to most, smallest to largest, low to high, etc.) with respect to the measured attribute. Ordinal scaling would result if, for example, one of the workers listed in figure 3-1 had been asked to rank the other workers in terms of a "liking" dimension. Assume that John Williams had been asked to perform this task and that the ordering shown in figure 3-2 resulted. The ranks shown in figure

FIGURE 3-2   Ordinal Scaling Example: Mapping of Co-Workers into a Set of Liking Ranks

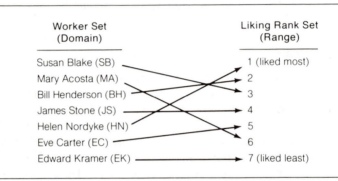

| Worker Set (Domain) | Liking Rank Set (Range) |
|---|---|
| Susan Blake (SB) | 1 (liked most) |
| Mary Acosta (MA) | 2 |
| Bill Henderson (BH) | 3 |
| James Stone (JS) | 4 |
| Helen Nordyke (HN) | 5 |
| Eve Carter (EC) | 6 |
| Edward Kramer (EK) | 7 (liked least) |

3-2 indicate that with respect to the liking construct HN > BH > SB . . . MA > EK. These data tell us *only how* John Williams has ordered his co-workers, *not how much* each is liked. Thus, while HN and EK have the most extreme rankings (1 and 7, respectively), it is possible that (*a*) JW likes both HN and EK quite a bit, (*b*) JW likes HN quite a bit and dislikes EK intensely, (*c*) JW intensely dislikes both HN and EK, or (*d*) JW has some other set of attitudes about these workers. It should be apparent, therefore, that while ordinal scaling tells us how things are ranked with respect to some measured attribute we know nothing about the distances between the ranked items on the measured attribute.

## Interval Scales

In the case of interval scales, objects are not only ordered with respect to some measured attribute, but the intervals between adjacent points on the measurement scale are equal. It is possible, therefore, to determine distances among objects with respect to the measured attribute. The measurement of temperature by a (centigrade) thermometer is an example of interval scaling. We know that the difference between any two adjacent scale points on the thermometer (e.g., 5° and 6°) equals the distance between

**38**

any other two adjacent scale points (e.g., 6° and 7°, 7° and 8°, etc.).

Let us *assume* that an interval scale exists for the liking construct we have been dealing with in this chapter. Individuals are asked, "How much do you like [name of person]?" Their responses are recorded on a five-point scale with the following anchors[1]:

| _____ | _____ | _____ | _____ | _____ |
|---|---|---|---|---|
| Very little | Some | A considerable amount | A great amount | An extra-ordinary amount |

Assume also that JW was asked to respond to this question about his co-workers, and the mapping shown in figure 3-3 resulted.

FIGURE 3-3   Interval Scaling Example: Mapping Workers into a Set of Liking Scale Points

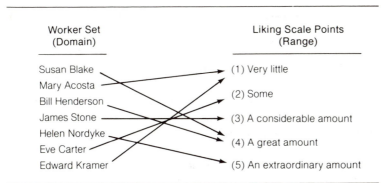

The data in figure 3-3 indicate that, in terms of liking, HN > SB = BH > JS > EC > MA = EK. Moreover, the data tell us that the difference in liking between MA and EC, for example, equals the distance between SB and HN (or the distance between any other two adjacent scale points).

## Ratio Scales

Ratio scales have all of the properties of interval scales. In addition, a logical or absolute zero point for the scale exists. Measures such as for length, weight, and many other physical measures have ratio scale properties. The result of any counting operation also results in ratio scaling, since there may be 0, 1, 2, 3, . . . or N objects. For example, consider the data shown in figure 3-4.

[1] The reader should note that these scale anchors have been shown to reasonably approximate the characteristics of interval scales (see Bass, Cascio, & O'Connor, 1974).

These data resulted from counting the number of times the individuals under consideration had been absent from work during a given year. Note that MA has been absent 0 times. (The scale has a logical zero point!)

FIGURE 3-4   Ratio Scaling Example: Mapping Workers into a Set of Absence Frequency Scale Points

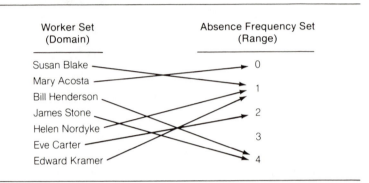

## SCALE CONSTRUCTION METHODS

Four types of scales have been described in the preceding paragraphs. We have not thus far considered the matter of how such scales are actually developed. In the case of nominal scaling there is little or no problem, since we need merely set up rules for assigning items to one category or another of our scale. Similarly, the development of ordinal scales presents few, if any, problems since scaling on an ordinal basis requires only rules for ranking items with respect to a measured attribute. The development of interval and ratio scales (especially where such scales are used in the measurement of psychological, sociological, and sociopsychological variables) is, however, not at all simple.[2]

## STANDARDIZED MEASURES

Good scales (in terms of reliability and validity criteria discussed later in this chapter) often take considerable time, effort, and expense to develop. Once such measures are developed they are often widely used.

---

[2]For additional information on the development and use of various types of scales see Fishbein (1967), Guilford (1954), Gulliksen and Messick (1960), Manning and Rosenstock (1968), Nunnally (1967), Romney, Shepard, and Nerlove (1972), Stevens (1958), and Torgerson (1958).

In the case of the measurement of length, for example, the meter stick is used in almost all countries. The centigrade thermometer is also used on an almost universal basis. These and other measures have become what are called (Nunnally, 1967) "standardized measures." Such standardized measures have a number of properties (Nunnally, 1967, pp. 4-7) that deserve mention here.

First, standardized measures result in *objectivity*. The measurement of a variable by one researcher can be objectively verified by any other researcher. If the same scale is used and the value of the measured variable does not change, all persons who measure the variable should get the same result.

Second, standardized measures, in the case of many commonly used scales, give us *quantitative information* about the measured attribute. This allows us to report the results of measurement in far greater detail than we could in the absence of the measure (e.g., we can weigh a person to the nearest gram—or even more precisely if necessary—rather than saying the person is either heavy or not heavy). Moreover, quantification of the measured attribute allows us to employ mathematical methods (e.g., descriptive and inferential statistics) in analyzing the results of measurement.

Third, measurement with standardized measures allows for the accurate and economical *communication* of research results. A scientist in the United States, for example, can measure some variable and report the results to another scientist in the Soviet Union with accuracy and relative ease (by phone, mail, telegram, etc.). In the absence of a standardized measure the Soviet scientist would first have to determine how the variable under consideration was measured, develop a scale comparable to that used by the American scientist, and then try to replicate the measurement. As you can well imagine, this would be quite costly in terms of time, money, and other resources.

Fourth, and finally, once a standardized measure of some attribute has been developed it can often be reproduced and used in a relatively *economical* fashion by interested users. Scales such as meter sticks are mass-produced and relatively inexpensive. Scales for the measurement of psychological, sociological, and sociopsychological variables are also often capable of mass production and economical use. (This is especially true in the case of paper-and-pencil-type measures.)

As can be seen, standardized measures have many advantages over nonstandardized measures. We recommend, therefore, that if an acceptable (in terms of reliability and validity criteria discussed later in this chapter) standardized measure of a con- **41** struct exists, the researcher employ it rather than develop a totally new measure.[3]

In the physical and life sciences standardized measures are developed and employed to a much greater extent than in the social sciences. This is especially true of scales designed for behavioral research in organizations. In fact, Barrett (1972) blames the lack of standardized measures for many of the difficulties organizational researchers face in interpreting the results of the multitude of studies that have been performed on job satisfaction and related attitudes. He notes that "Industrial Psychologists have been slow to perfect and use sophisticated instruments and other hardware" (p. 5). While the critique was aimed at industrial psychologists in particular, it also applies to researchers from many other academic disciplines (cf. Scott, 1965, p. 294).

While the use of standardized measures may be less pervasive in the behavioral than in the physical and life sciences, there are a number of measures employed in organizational behavior research that are considered more or less standardized. These include: (a) the Job Descriptive Index (Smith, Kendall, & Hulin, 1969) used in the assessment of job satisfaction; (b) the Leader Behavior Description Questionnaire (Stodgill & Coons, 1957) used in the measurement of two dimensions of leader behavior (i.e., initiating structure and consideration); (c) the Minnesota Satisfaction Questionnaire (Lofquist & Dawis, 1969) used in the assessment of numerous facets of job satisfaction; (d) the Strong Vocational Interest Blank (Strong, 1938) employed in the indexing of occupational interests; (e) the Personality Research Form (Jackson, 1967) used for the nonclinical assessment of personality; (f) the Thematic Apperception Test (McClelland, Atkinson, Clark & Lowell, 1953) employed in the measurement of motives; and

---

[3]There is, however, at least one important caution concerning the use of standardized measures: the chronic use of any single measure may, over time, lead individuals to equate the operational definition of a construct with the construct itself. For example, if organizational researchers always use a particular questionnaire to operationalize the construct of job satisfaction, over time the researchers may come to believe that the measure is equivalent to the construct itself. If the measure actually is a perfect reflection of the construct there is no problem. This is probably never the case with measures employed in organizational behavior research.

Virtually all measures employed in such research are fallible. The scores yielded by any given measure may not be dependable, accurate, or stable (cf. discussion of reliability later in this chapter). For example, even though a person's true standing with respect to some construct remains unchanged, measuring the construct at two points in time with the same measure may yield inconsistent results. In addition, the scores yielded by a measure may be incomplete or inappropriate reflections of the underlying construct (cf. discussion of validity later in this chapter). For example, a questionnaire measure of overall job satisfaction may not have items dealing with one or more facets of satisfaction (e.g., work itself, pay, or promotion prospects).

Since any single operationalization of a construct is likely to produce fallible scores, it has been suggested (Campbell, 1960; Webb, Campbell, Schwartz, & Sechrest, 1966; etc.) that constructs be operationalized in a number of ways (i.e., multiple operationalism). For example, operationalizing a construct with not only a questionnaire, but also with an interview, observation, etc. (cf. chapter 4 for more on these measurement methods).

(g) numerous other measures of abilities, attitudes, interests, etc.[4]

## PROPERTIES OF MEASURES:
## RELIABILITY AND VALIDITY

In the labels given tests, in statements of intent and descriptive material, many explicit and implicit claims are made. These claims amount to assertions of empirical laws between the test and other possible operations. Requirements for evidence as to reliability and validity are requirements that some of these laws be examined and confirmed. Our insistence on the importance of such evidence comes from our cumulative experience, in which test constructors and uses have frequently been misled. (Campbell, 1960, p. 546)

Two extremely important properties all measures should possess are reliability and validity—irrespective of the particular measurement techniques the researcher chooses to use. By way of introduction, we offer the following definitions of reliability and validity. *Reliability* reflects the degree to which the results of measurement are free of error, that is, are attributable to systematic sources of variance (Guilford, 1954; American Psychological Assn., 1973). *Validity* reflects the degree to which a measure actually measures what it purports to (Nunnally, 1967, p. 75).

Consider the following hypothetical situation. You go to your family physician because you have not been feeling well; for the past few days you've felt nauseated, feverish, and weak. The physician takes your temperature with a thermometer that (unbeknownst to him) is defective. He reports that your temperature is normal and sends you on your way with reassurances that there's nothing wrong with you. Two days later, you die from a disease that went undiagnosed because of the poor quality of the measure used to assess your body's temperature. Consider a second hypothetical example. While on a business trip you rent an automobile. For each mile that you actually drive the car, the car's odometer registers 1.5 miles. When you return the car you pay 150% of what your mileage charge actually should be. Finally, consider this third hypothetical example. You have been hired to manage a claims processing division of a large insurance company. Under your control are ten claims processing units. Each unit has 20 claims processors and a supervisor. The company is very concerned about employee effectiveness and efficiency. To promote these ends you ask each supervisor to provide you with performance ratings of individuals in their respective units.

---

[4]See Bonjean, Hill, and McLemore (1962), Buros (1961, 1974), Chun, Cobb, and French (1975), Miles and Lake (1967), Miller (1964), Patchen, Pelz, and Allen (1966), Robinson, Athanasiou, and Head (1969), Robinson and Shaver (1973), and Shaw and Wright (1967). In addition to presenting the measures themselves, many of these sources also provide reliability and validity data on the various instruments. Some even give references to studies in which the measures have been used.

The ratings are submitted to you a short time later. You use these data as a basis for determining the amounts of merit increases for the 200 claims processors. Some weeks after pay changes have been made you meet with your unit supervisors. In the meeting you discover that the performance ratings given you by the various supervisors were made with a number of different criteria in mind. One supervisor considered only the quantity of work each person turned out. Another looked only at the quality of processed claims. Still another gave "high" ratings to his attractive female subordinates and "low" ratings to the others in his unit. The remainder used several other bases for determining the ratings of their subordinates. Instead of promoting efficiency and effectiveness, the performance ratings led to dissatisfaction and turnover among some of those who were truly the top performers, role ambiguity and dissatisfaction among others, and incorrect perceptions about what the company expected from its workers, in the case of still others.

These examples should suffice in terms of demonstrating the importance of using reliable and valid measures. In some instances the adverse effects of an unreliable and/or invalid measure may be relatively slight and inconsequential. In other instances, however, the use of an unreliable and/or invalid measure may lead to catastrophic outcomes.

As was pointed out earlier in chapter 2, all empirical research is aimed at providing data upon which to base decisions. Such data result from whatever measures the researcher happens to employ in a particular study. If we want to make "correct" decisions based upon a study's findings then it is imperative that reliable and valid measures be employed in the data collection phase of the study.

Reliability and validity are explained more fully in the remainder of this chapter. Since, as we shall point out later, reliability is a necessary but not sufficient condition to assure validity we begin the coverage of these two concepts with a discussion of reliability.

## Reliability

One way of viewing reliability is from the standpoint of the degree to which measurement of any attribute contains error. To the extent that scores yielded by some measure are error-free, to that extent the measure is reliable. Some synonyms for reliability (Kerlinger, 1973, p. 442) are dependability, stability, consistency, predictability, and accuracy.

**44**   Looking at reliability as measurement that is relatively error-free stems (according to Tryon, 1957) from the seminal work of Spearman (1910) and Yule (1922).[5] These early theorists asserted that whenever we measure some attribute an observed score ($X_O$) results. This observed score has two components: A true score ($X_T$) component and an error ($X_E$) component.[6]

The observed score is simply the result of measurement. The true score is the score that would result if we had a perfect (i.e., error-free) measure of the attribute. While we never actually know the value of $X_T$, it can be estimated by measuring an attribute a large number ($N$) of times and computing the mean of all observed values (i.e., $X_{O1}$, $X_{O2}$, $X_{O3}$, . . . ., $X_{ON}$).[7] The average of all such observed scores ($\overline{X}_O$) equals $X_T$. The reason for this is explained below.

First, in averaging the $N$ observed scores the error component of scores approaches zero. Error variance is virtually eliminated from $\overline{X}_O$ because of the fact that this type of variance is nonsystematic in nature: If on one occasion measurement results in an overestimate of $X_T$ (i.e., $X_E$ is positive), it is assumed that on some other occasion measurement results in an underestimate of $X_T$ (i.e., $X_E$ is negative). The end result is that the mean of error scores ($\overline{X}_E$), given repeated measurement of an attribute, is zero (cf. Ghiselli, 1964, p. 224).[8]

Second, it is known from elementary statistical theory that if the distributions of $X_T$ and $X_E$ components are independent, then the expected value of observed scores, $E(X_O)$, equals the sum of the expected values of true scores, $E(X_T)$, and error scores, $E(X_E)$.[9]

And since the expected value of error scores, $E(X_E)$, equals zero, it follows that the expected value of true scores, $E(X_T)$, equals the expected value of observed scores, $E(X_O)$.[10]

From elementary statistical theory it is also known that when true scores ($X_T$'s) and error scores ($X_E$'s) are statistically independent of one another then the variance of observed scores ($\sigma_O^2$) equals the sum of the variances of true scores ($\sigma_T^2$) and error scores ($\sigma^2$).[11]

The reliability ($r_{xx}$) of a measure can be expressed using these terms. Specifically, reliability is true score variance divided by ob-

---

[5] This discussion of reliability uses several assumptions of ''classical test theory'' (cf., for example, Spearman, 1910, and Yule, 1922) that have recently been questioned by a number of psychometricians (cf., for example, Lumsden, 1976, and Campbell, 1976). In the interest of brevity the problems associated with these assumptions are not elaborated here.

[6] $X_O = X_T + X_E$　　[7] $X_T = (X_{O1} + X_{O2} + X_{O3} + \ldots + X_N)/N = X_O$

[8] $\overline{X}_E = (X_{E1} + X_{E2} + X_{E3} + \ldots + X\ EN)/N$　　[9] $E(X_O) = E(X_T) + E(X_E)$

[10] $E(X_O) = E(X_T) + E(X_E)$; and since $E(X_E) = 0$; it follows that, $E(X_O) = E(X_T)$

[11] $\sigma_O^2 = \sigma_T^2 + \sigma_E^2$

served score variance.[12] Through simple algebraic manipulations it can be demonstrated that reliability can also be expressed in terms of error and observed score variances.[13]

As was indicated earlier, values of true scores and the variance of these scores are never actually known. There are procedures, however, for determining total and error variances for any given set of scores. Using these values the reliability of measure can thus be assessed (see footnote 13).

A number of different procedures may be used to empirically assess the reliability of a measure. Among these are the parallel forms, test-retest, and internal consistency methods.[14] Each of these is briefly described below.

*Test-Retest Method.* If there is only one form of measure (e.g., one version of a test) we can assess its reliability by the test-retest method. To do so the measure would be applied to a set of individuals at two different points in time and the resulting scores correlated. A high correlation coefficient (i.e., one near 1.0) would suggest high reliability, while a low coefficient (i.e., one near 0) would suggest low reliability.

If a physical attribute is being measured and the measurement process does not affect the measured property then the test-retest estimate of reliability is often satisfactory (e.g., in such sciences as physics, chemistry, etc.). In the case of many behavioral and attitudinal measures, however, the test-retest method often presents problems. First, if the time period between measurement is relatively short, then the subject's memory of responses to the first test may be a factor in spuriously inflating the correlation between scores on the "test" and the "retest." The resulting correlation will thus be an overestimate of the test's true reliability. Second, if the time period between measurement is relatively long, the value of the measured attribute (e.g., individuals' self-reports of job satisfaction) may change. For some persons scores on the attribute may increase while for others they may decrease. To the extent that this occurs and results in a different ranking of individuals on the attribute for the two time periods, the correlation between scores for these periods will be attenuated or lowered in value. In such a case, the test-retest coefficient will be an underestimate of the measure's true reliability.

These problems have led some psychometricians (e.g., Kuder & Richardson, 1937; Nunnally, 1967) to recommend that the test-

---

[12] $r_{xx} = \dfrac{\sigma_T^2}{\sigma_O^2}$    [13] $r_{xx} = 1 - \dfrac{\sigma_E^2}{\sigma_O^2}$

[14] The reader should note that the test-retest, parallel forms, and internal consistency methods of estimating reliability differ in terms of what they consider to be systematic (e.g., true) and error variance. For discussions of how the methods differ in this regard see Cronbach (1947), Guion (1965a), or Thorndike (1967).

retest method not be used to assess a measure's reliability. This is sound advice concerning the measurement of many attributes of people (attitudes, opinions, abilities, etc.). It would appear that the only reasonable uses of the test-retest method are in situations where the attribute being measured does not change over time and is not perceptibly altered by the measurement process. This would appear to restrict the test-retest method to assessing the reliability of measures of attributes of nonliving entities (i.e., length, mass, electrical current, radioactivity, etc.). It should be noted that although the assessment of a measure's reliability via the test-retest technique is problematic, this reliability index still appears in some research reports. The reader should thus be familiar with the index and problems associated with it.

*Parallel Forms Method.* The assessment of reliability via the parallel or alternate forms method takes place in three stages. First, two (or more) separate measures of a construct are developed. These should have equal mean scores, equal variances, etc. (cf. Gulliksen, 1950b, for a complete list of requirements associated with the assessment of reliability via the parallel forms technique). Second, the two forms of the measure are administered to a set of subjects. The temporal spacing of these administrations varies from one study to the next. In some cases the two forms are completed in the same administration session. In other instances several months may come between administering the two forms. The third and final step is to determine the degree of correlation between scores on the two measures. The resulting correlation is the parallel forms reliability estimate.

Estimating reliability with the parallel forms method can be useful in several instances. One is where the researcher wants to determine the impact of a change-oriented organizational intervention (i.e., a program to increase knowledge, change attitudes, alter values, etc.). To assess the amount of change that has taken place, the variable that is the target of the intervention might be measured before and after individuals are exposed to the change program.

If an identical test were used as a pre- and post-intervention measure any changes detected between the two periods would, because of "carry-over effects" (Ghiselli, 1964, pp. 277–279), be difficult to interpret. With the use of parallel forms, however, the effects of "carry-over" are lower than with test-retest procedures since the content of two (or more) exams is not precisely the same (Ghiselli, 1964, p. 280). (Prior to their use in an applied context the equivalence of the parallel forms should be assessed by having one group of individuals complete both forms. Then, correlate the resulting scores.)

Another instance where parallel forms of a measure may be **47** useful is when numerous individuals are administered achievement or aptitude tests in group settings. Multiple forms of a test allow the individual in charge of testing to reduce the possibility of cheating by giving contiguously seated test-takers different forms of the test. (Prior to their use in an applied context the equivalence of these forms should be established again in the manner outlined above.)

A third instance where the parallel forms method is useful is in assessing the reliability of judges' ratings of others. Examples are ratings of employment interviewers on the acceptability of job applicants for a given position and ratings of supervisors on the performance of their subordinates. The judges (interviewers, supervisors, etc.) may be looked upon as parallel forms of a measure. The degree of intercorrelation between the ratings of two or more judges is known as inter-judge or inter-rater reliability. (See Ebel, 1951, for the assessment of inter-rater reliability when there are more than two raters.)

*Internal Consistency Method.* Another technique for assessing a measure's reliability—assuming that only one form of the measure is available—is through the determination of its internal consistency. A test, questionnaire, etc., is internally consistent to the extent that there is a high degree of intercorrelation among items that comprise the measure.

A number of computational methods exist for determining a measure's internal consistency. One such method is the split-half technique. To use this technique the researcher measures some attribute with a multi-item measure. After measurement the test's items are divided so as to create two subsets of items. Total scores for the two subsets are then correlated. To the extent that the test is internally consistent, the correlation between total scores for the two subsets will be high.

One technique for splitting a test into two subsets is to create one subtest using all of the original measure's odd-numbered items and another subtest using the even-numbered items. Another technique involves the random assignment of test items to two groups. For tests of even moderate length the number of possible "splittings" and resultant split-half reliability estimates can be quite large. Computation of all such split-half reliability estimates can be quite a lengthy and tedious process. And, for almost all of the multi-item measures used in the social sciences the split-half coefficient based upon one halving of a test often would not equal that resulting from another splitting of the test. It would therefore be difficult, given a group of differing split-half coefficients for a test, to assess its "true" internal consistency. While it would be difficult to compute (in the case of measures

**48**   with large numbers of items), a useful index of a measure's "true"

internal consistency would result from averaging the reliability co-efficients of all possible test splittings.

Fortunately, this is not necessary to get an unbiased estimate of a test's "true" internal consistency. A number of relatively simple techniques exist for arriving at such an estimate. (See Cronbach, 1951; Ghiselli, 1964; Guilford, 1954; Hoyt, 1941; or Tryon, 1957, for various internal consistency reliability formulas. The Tryon, 1957, paper provides an excellent review of several methods for estimating internal consistency reliability.)

The internal consistency estimate should be employed whenever the researcher wishes to assess the degree to which the items in a measure are homogeneous (i.e., indices of a common construct). Therefore, likely candidates for reliability analysis via the internal consistency method are multiple-item measures purporting to be measures of a single dimension. Most paper-and-pencil type measures of job satisfaction, job involvement, role-conflict, etc., should probably be subjected to an assessment of their internal consistency reliability.

*Increasing Reliability.* A test can be made more reliable by increasing its length and/or improving its internal consistency. If a test has a known reliability level and its length is increased by some amount, the reliability of the lengthened test can be easily estimated.[15] Suppose, for example, that the reliability of a 10-item test is .60 and we increase test length by a factor of two. The 20-item test will have a reliability of .75. It is assumed here that the items added for increasing the original test length are from the same content domain as the test's original items; and that average intercorrelation of the added items does not differ from the average intercorrelation of the original items.

The other mechanism for improving the reliability of a test is to increase internal consistency. If a test has a relatively large number of items that have varying inter-item correlations, then removing those items that have relatively low correlations with other test items will improve internal consistency. The removal of such items results in what is known as a "purified" test.[16]

*Predictor-Criterion Correlations: Importance of Reliability.* In many programs of research, especially those concerned with human behavior in organizations, we are not as concerned with the absolute scores that result when we measure some variable

---

[15] Assuming that the reliability of the original test is $r_{xx}$ and that test length is increased by a factor of $k$, reliability of the lengthened test, $r_{xx}^*$ is given by:
$$r_{xx}^* = \frac{k\, r_{xx}}{1 + (k - 1)\, r_{xx}}$$

[16] The reader should note that the purification of tests, while leading to increased reliability, may have an adverse effect on validity; that is, by increasing the internal consistency of a test we may decrease the ability of scores on it to predict scores on another measure. For explanations of this phenomenon see Ghiselli (1964, p. 352), Guilford and Fruchter (1973, pp. 435–436), and Loevinger (1954).

**49**

as we are with their ability to predict scores on other measures. For example, if we were to measure the job satisfaction levels of a group of employees it may be more important to know how well these predict some criterion (e.g., turnover or absenteeism) than simply to know what the absolute levels of satisfaction happen to be.

The reliability of a measure places an upper limit on the degree to which it will correlate with any other variable. Specifically, the correlation between variables *X* and *Y* (assuming that *Y* has been measured by a perfectly reliable instrument) can never exceed the square root of the reliability of variable *X*.[17] Suppose, for example, that a measure of job satisfaction having a reliability of .64 is used to predict a perfectly reliable criterion (e.g., job tenure). The correlation between these two variables can never exceed .80.

It is also worth noting that if both variables *X* and *Y* are measured with instruments having less than perfect reliability, the observed correlation between the two variables will equal the product of: (*a*) their true correlation and (*b*) the square root of the product of their respective reliabilities.[18] The "true" correlation between variables *X* and *Y* is the value that would be obtained if each variable were measured with a perfectly reliable instrument. Assume, for example, that the true correlation between variables *X* and *Y* is .70, and that each variable has been measured with an instrument having only .60 reliability. The observed correlation between the two variables will be .42, which is considerably lower than their true correlation (i.e., .70). As should be obvious from this example, measurement of variables with instruments having less than perfect reliability will lead to an observed relationship that is often considerably lower than the true relationship. In the extreme case where the reliability of either variable is zero, the observed relationship will be zero—no matter how strong the true relationship happens to be.

If we have an observed relationship between two variables and reliability estimates for their measures, we can easily determine the relationship that would exist between them if perfectly reliable measures had been used in measuring both. To do so we would simply divide the observed correlation between the two variables by the square root of the product of their respective reliabilities.[19] This procedure "corrects" an observed correlation between two variables for attenuation caused by less than perfect

---

[17] $r_{XY} \leq \sqrt{r_{XX}}$; where $r_{XX}$ is the reliability of the measure of variable *X*.

[18] $r_{XY} \text{(obs.)} = r_{XY} \text{(true)} \sqrt{r_{XX} \cdot r_{YY}}$; where $r_{XX}$ and $r_{YY}$ are, respectively, the reliabilities of measures of variables *X* and *Y*.

[19] $r_{XY} \text{(true)} = \dfrac{r_{XY} \text{(obs.)}}{\sqrt{r_{XX} \cdot r_{YY}}}$

reliability of either or both of the measured variables. The use of this "correction for attenuation" should not be attempted, however, until the reader becomes familiar with the problems that may result when it is applied (see Guilford, 1954, pp. 400–402, or Nunnally, 1967, pp. 217–219).

## Validity

The concept of reliability and its importance have just been discussed. Reliability is a property every measure should possess. In addition, every measure should possess another equally important property—validity. It is to the discussion of this latter concept that we now turn.

In assessing a measure's reliability we concern ourselves with such factors as its internal consistency, stability over time, etc. In assessing a measure's validity our concern is with determining the extent to which it measures what it purports to measure. To assess this, the developer and/or user of the measure may be concerned with one or more of several specific types of validity: (a) content validity, (b) construct validity, (c) criterion-related validity, (d) face validity, (e) incremental validity, (f) convergent and discriminant validity, and (g) synthetic validity. Each of these is considered in the paragraphs that follow.

*Content Validity.* A measure has content validity to the extent that items making up the measure are a representative sample of the domain of items associated with the variable being measured (Ebel, 1956; Gulliksen, 1950a; Lennon, 1956; Nunnally, 1967). Content validity suffers when the measure contains items aimed at measuring variables outside the domain of interest. For example, a questionnaire measure of job satisfaction would lack content validity if it contained items designed to assess strength of religious beliefs, alienation from society, etc. Content validity also suffers when the items in a measure underrepresent the relevant domain. A test of typing proficiency that required the test-taker to type only numbers would lack content validity since typing generally involves the use of almost all typewriter keys, not just those associated with numbers.

In order to demonstrate that a test has content validity a universe of items must be defined, and items from this universe must be chosen in such a way as to insure that the measure finally created has a representative sample of these items. For example, an investigator interested in the study of job satisfaction might write a large number of items for a questionnaire measure of job satisfaction and then have a group of judges assess the extent to which the items represent the relevant universe.

The degree to which a test has criterion-related validity or **51** construct validity can be assessed quantitatively. Quantitative statements on the content validity of a measure are often difficult (if not impossible) to make (Lennon, 1956, p. 296). As one writer has noted, establishing the content validity of a measure "rests heavily on expert judgment and more or less subjective impressions about the behavior associated with responses to the items or statements of the test . . . [and] this armchair approach to test validation is, at best, only a starting point [in establishing the validity of a test]" (Dunnette, 1966, p. 124).

It should be noted that attempts have been made to develop a quantitative index of content validity (cf. Lawshe, 1975). The utility of this quantitative index has not, however, been determined.

*Construct Validity.* Some variables can be observed directly (e.g., the number of units a worker produces in a certain time period). Other variables cannot be directly observed (e.g., a worker's motivational level). The values of such variables must be inferred from other observable variables.

Variables that are abstract (e.g., motivation) are known as constructs (Nunnally, 1967, p. 85). One construct we are all familiar with is "intelligence." We cannot directly assess intelligence, but instead must infer intelligence levels from scores on "intelligence tests." These are our operational definitions of the "intelligence" construct.

The construct validity of a measure is established by showing that it is an appropriate operational definition of the construct it purports to measure (American Psychological Association, 1974). Demonstrating this is often a lengthy process requiring a series of empirical studies.

Initially, the researcher must develop an operational definition (measure) of the construct being studied. The researcher must then establish hypotheses about how scores on this measure relate to one or more directly observable variables. The investigator may also indicate how the particular construct being studied relates to other constructs. This set of hypotheses about how the variables relate to one another is known as a "nomological network" (Cronbach & Meehl, 1955).

After the nomological network has been specified the researcher must then, through one or more empirical studies, demonstrate that the operational definition of the construct being validated relates in hypothesized ways to the other variables in the network. To the extent that it does, the construct validity of the measure (i.e., the operational definition of the construct) is supported.

Two sets of relationships are important. First, the construct being validated should correlate with other observables and/or **52** constructs that extant theory and research suggest should be related to it. (Included here are other operational definitions of the construct being validated.) Second, the construct undergoing evaluation of its validity should *not* correlate with other constructs and/or observables that existing theory and research suggest are unrelated to it. To the extent that the researcher's hypotheses are verified by empirical research, the construct validity of the measure (i.e., operational definition of the construct) is supported. (More will be said about this in the section "Convergent and Discriminant Validity.")

Consider the following example. A researcher hypothesizes that some individuals have greater degrees of "commitment" to their employing organization than others. The investigator reasons that people who have high levels of organizational commitment (OC) will (*a*) express a willingness to exert high levels of effort in the service of organizational goals, (*b*) have a strong desire to remain a member of the organization, and (*c*) internalize the organization's values and goals. With these thoughts in mind the researcher develops a questionnaire measure of the OC construct. In addition, a nomological network involving the OC construct is established. The researcher hypothesizes that OC will be positively related to such variables as job satisfaction, job involvement, productivity, and organizational level. It is further hypothesized that OC will relate negatively to absenteeism and turnover. Finally, the researcher predicts that there will be no relationship between OC and sex.

Data on these variables are collected in one or more empirical investigations. If the data support the predictions inherent in the nomological network, support for the validity of the OC construct is provided. To the extent that the data resulting from such studies do not support hypotheses of the nomological network the researcher must either modify the operational definition of the construct, reformulate portions of the network, or, in the extreme case, abandon the construct entirely.[20]

*Criterion-Related Validity.* We are dealing with the question of criterion-related validity when we use scores obtained from one measure, the "predictor," to infer an individual's probable standing on some other variable, the criterion. The criterion may be either a behavior or an attitude. For example, many organizations administer occupational aptitude and interest measures to prospective employees. Scores on these measures may be used to infer future job performance (a behavior) and/or job satisfaction (an attitude).

Criterion-related validity can be approached from three dif-

---

[20] For additional information on this validational strategy see APA Standards (1974), Bechtoldt (1959), Campbell (1969), Campbell and Fiske (1959), Campbell (1976), Cook and Campbell (1976), Cronbach and Meehl (1955), or Nunnally (1967).

ferent perspectives, depending upon when the predictor and criterion variables are measured. One possibility is to measure the predictor variable at one point in time and the criterion at some future point. For example, scores college students obtain on the Graduate Record Examination or the Admissions Test for Graduate Studies in Management are often used to infer who will succeed in graduate school. We are dealing with *predictive validity* in this instance.

It is also possible to measure the predictor and criterion variables at the same point in time. The present levels of pay organizational members receive may, for example, be used to infer their "satisfaction with pay." In this case, we are dealing with what is called *concurrent validity.*

Finally, it is possible for the criterion measure to be measured at one point in time and the predictor to be measured at a later point. Evidence gathered in autopsies is often, for example, used to infer what caused an individual's death. Here we are dealing with what is called *post-dictive* validity.

Whether our concern is with post-dictive, concurrent, or predictive validity the basic validational technique is identical: We measure both the "predictor" and criterion variables and correlate the two. The resulting correlation coefficient ($r$), also commonly called a *validity coefficient,* indicates the criterion-related validity of the "predictor." Validity coefficients vary from $-1.0$, indicating a perfect inverse relationship between the "predictor" and the criterion, through 0, indicating no relationship between the predictor and the criterion, to $+1.0$, indicating a perfect positive relationship between the predictor and the criterion. (Figures depicting relationships of various strengths are in *a* through *f* of figure A-2 of the Appendix.)

Criterion-related validity is undoubtedly the form of validity of greatest interest to the organizational manager. The success of virtually all personnel selection techniques (e.g., testing, interviewing, etc.) rests upon their criterion-related validity. And recent federal and state activities designed to insure equal employment opportunities to various minority groups, such as blacks, Chicanos, women, the aged, and the physically handicapped, make it almost imperative that the organizational manager understand what is implicit in criterion-related validity. (For more on the validity of tests for minority groups see Einhorn & Bass, 1971, or Guion, 1966.)

*Face Validity.* A measure has face validity to the extent that it "appears to measure" whatever it purports to be measuring (Nunnally, 1967; but, see Mosier, 1947, for other interpretations of face validity). Note that a measure may "appear" to be a valid index of some variable, but lack construct and/or criterion-related validity. Conversely, a measure may lack face validity, but be an excellent predictor of some criterion.

One of the primary reasons face validity is important is that if measures are to be successfully employed in research and/or applied contexts, they should be "acceptable" to both those who will employ them and those subject to measurement. For example, an individual applying for a job as a telephone installer/repairman would probably not object to a preemployment test aimed at his or her ability to use hand tools and read simple wiring diagrams. The individual, though, would probably seriously question the requirement that he or she pass an examination aimed at assessing knowledge of how charged electrical particles behave in electromagnetic fields—even if performance on such an examination very accurately predicted the degree to which test takers would succeed on the job.

We conclude our treatment of face validity with the following excerpt from a recently published work on test standards: " 'Face' validity, the mere appearance of validity, is not an acceptable basis for interpretive inferences from test scores" (American Psychological Association Standards, 1974, p. vii).

*Incremental Validity.* It has been argued (Sechrest, 1963) that before a measure is used in applied contexts, evidence should be provided as to its incremental validity (see also Landy & Trumbo, 1976). A measure has incremental validity to the degree that it provides "some increment in predictive efficiency over the information otherwise easily and cheaply available" (Sechrest, 1963, p. 154).

To illustrate the concept of incremental validity we employ a fictitious example involving the prediction of "academic success" in a graduate school of management. Operationally, the school defines academic success as successful completion of the degree program. For years the school used undergraduate grade point average as its sole predictor of success. With the use of these data the school could correctly predict success 60% of the time.

At some point in its history the school began using a second predictor, scores of students on the Admissions Test for Graduate Studies in Business (ATGSB). When data from the ATGSB were used in conjunction with undergraduate grade point average the school found that it could correctly predict success 80% of the time, the increase in prediction accuracy being attributable to the incremental validity of the ATGSB scores. (For an actual example of the use of ATGSB scores in predicting academic success see Srinivasan & Weinstein, 1973.)

Given the rapid rate with which measures of various types are being developed in the social sciences it would appear that not **55** as much attention is being paid to the concept of incremental validity as it deserves.

*Convergent and Discriminant Validity.* Often in the process of developing a measure of some variable the researcher provides evidence as to the measure's convergent validity: the extent to which scores on the measure correlate with scores on other independent measures of the variable (Campbell & Fiske, 1959). For example, a researcher interested in measuring job characteristics could obtain ratings of these both from incumbents in various jobs and from their supervisors. To the extent that the ratings provided by job incumbents correlated highly with those supplied by supervisors there would be evidence in support of the convergent validity of the job characteristics measure.

In addition to being concerned with the convergent validity of a measure, the researcher should also pay attention to its discriminant validity: the extent to which strong correlations are absent between a given measure and measures of other variables from which it is assumed to differ (Campbell & Fiske, 1959).

Assume that you are interested in the study of a construct called job involvement (JI). You develop a questionnaire measure of JI and then have judges assess both its content and face validity. The measure of JI is now used, along with measures of job satisfaction, organizational commitment, and several other variables you believe to be conceptually distinct from JI. The data are analyzed and you find that each of your measures is highly reliable. The measure of JI does not correlate over .30 with any of the other measures you've used in the study. These data would support a conclusion on your behalf that discriminant validity exists for the. JI measure. Had the JI measure been highly correlated (e.g., $r = .80$) with the organizational commitment measure or the job satisfaction measure the discriminant validity of the JI measure would be called into question.

The mechanics of establishing convergent and discriminant validity are described in an excellent paper by Campbell and Fiske (1959). We recommend that the reader consult this reference for additional details. In addition, the reader may want to refer to a recent paper by Kalleberg and Kluegel (1975) that discusses some limitations of this validational technique.

*Synthetic Validity.* In selecting individuals to fill job openings, organizations often use one or more preemployment tests. The criterion-related validity of such tests is generally established via a concurrent validational strategy. Validation of a test by this means requires that test scores and criterion measures be available for relatively large numbers of individuals, since concurrent validities do not often exceed .40 and to be statistically reliable a validity **56** coefficient of .40 must be based on a sample of at least 25 cases.

(Zedeck & Blood, 1974, suggest that 50 to 60 cases are required to make feasible correlational analyses associated with criterion-related validational studies. A more recent paper by Schmidt, Hunter, & Urry, 1976, argues that in many criterion-related validity studies sample sizes of even 50 to 60 may be inadequate.)

In many organizations, however, there are relatively few jobs that have 25 or more incumbents. Validating selection tests for jobs with relatively small numbers of employees per job (i.e., 25 or less, assuming predictor-criterion validities of .40) thus requires a different strategy. A procedure that can be used in validating a test or battery of tests for jobs with few incumbents is synthetic validity.

Synthetic validity (also called job component validity) is "the inferring of validity in a specific situation from a logical analysis of jobs into their elements, a determination of test validities for these elements, and a combination of elemental validities into a whole" (Balma, 1959, p. 395). An example should clarify the process of establishing the synthetic validity of a test battery. Assume that we are faced with the task of developing a battery of selection tests for the job of electronics assembler. The organization we are developing the test battery for has only five incumbents in the job, making a criterion-related validity study inappropriate. We decide to use a synthetic validational strategy and proceed in the following manner: First, the key elements or requirements of the electronics assembler job are identified. Then an attempt is made to find a set of other jobs for which the key elements found for the electronics assembler position are critical in terms of job success,

For example, finger and manual dexterity may be key elements in the jobs of both electronics assemblers and mechanical assemblers. If there were a sufficiently large number of mechanical assemblers we could develop a battery of selection tests for this job using a criterion-related validational strategy. We could then use the same battery to select individuals for the electronics assembler position—operating on the assumption that the two assembler positions have key elements (finger and manual dexterity) in common. What predicts job success for the mechanical assembler's job should also predict job success for the electronics assembler's job.

In our example we only considered one job other than the job for which we ultimately hoped to develop a selection battery via the synthetic validity method. In many cases, not one but several other jobs would be involved in developing the test battery, since there are often several key elements or requirements associated with the job for which we want to establish a selection battery, and it may not be possible to find any other single job **57** having all these key elements or requirements. (For additional information on this technique see Balma, 1959; Guion, 1965b, and Lawshe & Steinberg, 1955.)

*Predictor-Criterion Relationships: Influence of Range Restriction.* As was pointed out earlier in this chapter, the correlation coefficient (*r*) is used to index the degree to which a measure has criterion-related validity. We also noted that to the extent that our measures of the predictor and the criterion variable are unreliable, the observed predictor-criterion correlation will approach zero. Thus, if we conduct a study and observe a low predictor-criterion correlation we should always consider the possibility of less than optimal reliabilities for the measures being used.

Low predictor-criterion correlations may, however, also be the result of a problem known as "restriction of range." This condition exists when the variability of one or more variables upon which a sample correlation coefficient is based is lower in the sample than in the population. Figure 3-5 illustrates how this may come about.

FIGURE 3-5   Scatter Diagram Showing Effects of Restriction of Range on
Correlation

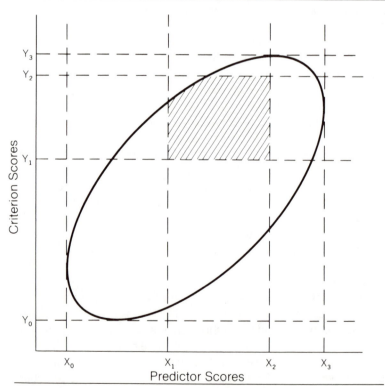

Assume that we are interested in the relationship between a predictor of job success (e.g., scores on an aptitude test) and a criterion measure (e.g., supervisory ratings of job performance) and that the ellipse in figure 3-5 represents the relationship that would obtain between the predictor and the criterion if we were to secure predictor and criterion data from all members of the relevant population. In this case assume that the relevant population is the set of all persons who would apply for the job if an opening existed.

The relationship depicted by the ellipse is based on the assumption that all those applying for the job would be hired—regardless of how they scored on the predictor measure. It is also assumed that those hired would still be holding the job (i.e., not have been discharged or quit) when criterion data were collected. Note that the predictor-criterion correlation for this set of individuals appears to be relatively strong.

From the standpoint of establishing criterion-related validity the testing and hiring of all persons in the relevant population would be ideal. There would be a great deal of variance for both the predictor and the criterion variable. This is quite important since all else constant, the greater the variability of two variables the greater their correlation.

Having unrestricted variability for both the predictor and the criterion variables is a situation seldom seen in reality. Several factors are responsible for this. First, organizations generally do not hire all job applicants. Those with scores below an organizationally established predictor cutoff level ($X_1$ in figure 3-5) are frequently not hired. Second, a number of persons who take the test and get relatively high scores (above $X_2$ in figure 3-5) may decide to work for other organizations. Third, of the individuals the organizations actually hire, a number will either quit or be fired at some later date because their performance is below the organizationally established cutoff-level for acceptable performance ($Y_1$ in figure 3-5). Fourth, and finally, of those initially hired, those with exceptionally high performance (above $Y_2$ in figure 3-5) may either quit to take better jobs elsewhere or be promoted out of the job. The net result of the above is that when we actually go about determining the criterion-related validity of our predictor we will have only the data points in the shaded portion of the ellipse. The range of predictor scores, which in the population is $X_0$ to $X_3$, has been restricted and now includes only the data points between $X_1$ and $X_2$. The range of criterion scores has also been restricted. This range includes scores from $Y_0$ to $Y_3$ in the population, but only scores between $Y_1$ and $Y_2$ in the sample. Were we to compute a predictor-criterion correlation based upon **59** the restricted set of points we would find it to be much lower than the original population-based correlation.

In practice, the effects of restriction of range on predictor-criterion validity and other correlations are often quite marked. For example, in one study (Thorndike, 1947, cited by Guilford & Fruchter, 1973) it was reported that while a composite aptitude score correlated .64 with a criterion measure for an unrestricted sample, the predictor-criterion correlation for a sample with restriction of range problems was only .18. The results of this study provide clear evidence on the effects of restriction of range on the correlation coefficient.

The organizational researcher should always give consideration to the possibility of observed correlations being influenced by restriction of range—especially in the case of concurrent criterion-related validities.

# MEASUREMENT METHODS 4

Based on our discussion of the basics of measurement and properties of measures, we can now consider the ways in which data are actually collected. Among the various methods that might be used to collect data in organizations are observations of behavior, interviews, objective measures (questionnaires, aptitude tests, achievement tests, etc.), projective measures, sociometry, Q-sorting, and a variety of unobtrusive measures. In any given organizational study one or more of these techniques may be employed to collect data.

## QUESTIONNAIRES

Questionnaires are probably the most frequently used data-gathering device in terms of behavioral research in organizations (see, for example, the data reported by Schoenfeldt & Gatewood, 1974). Questionnaires are written collections or sets of items (questions) to which the subject is asked to respond. Any given questionnaire may measure one or more of the following things: (a) attitudes, (b) opinions, and (c) demographic characteristics of the subject.

Given the wide variety of variables questionnaires can measure, we might expect there to be a great number of questionnaires for various purposes. This is the case. In the areas of organizations and organizational behavior alone there are thousands of questionnaires for measuring variables such as job satisfaction, need fulfillment, company satisfaction, alienation from work, job stress, job tension, job motivation, occupational values, leadership style, **61** vocational interests, occupational status, etc. In the area of job satisfaction alone, dozens of measures have been developed (Robinson, Athanasiou & Head, 1969).

There are several important dimensions along which questionnaires vary. Among these are degree of structure, scales and scale anchors, method of administration, etc. To illustrate how the structure of questionnaire items may vary, consider the measurement of job satisfaction. At one end (structured) on the structure continuum we could measure satisfaction by asking: "Are you satisfied with your job?" Each subject would respond by checking either (a) yes or (b) no, the two alternatives provided the subject. This would be a highly structured item. A somewhat lesser degree of structure would exist if the subject were asked to indicate the extent to which he or she agreed with the statement: "I find my job quite satisfying," using the following response alternatives: (a) strongly disagree, (b) moderately disagree, (c) neither disagree nor agree, (d) moderately agree, and (e) strongly agree. At the other (unstructured) end of the structure continuum, job satisfaction could be assessed by asking the subject to respond in whatever manner he or she chose to the question: "What things do you like and/or dislike about your job?"

Not unrelated to the matter of structure are the scales and scale anchors associated with individual questionnaire items. A variety of questionnaire items with different types of scales are shown in figure 4-1. Note that for any given questionnaire item several things may vary:

- *Number of Scale Points.* An item may provide the subject with two response possibilities (scale points), as in the case of question number 1, or the number of scale points may take on some larger value as in the case of items numbered 2 through 5.
- *Continuity of Scale.* An item may have what appears (to the subject) to be a continuous scale, as in the case of item number 4, or the scale may have discrete steps, as in the case of item number 3.
- *Scale Anchors.* The labels associated with scale points are called anchors. These anchors may be words, numbers, or combinations of the two. In some cases all points on a particular scale may have anchors (e.g., item 3), while in others only a portion of the scale points may have anchors (e.g., item 5).

The decision to employ a questionnaire in any given study is one that must be made by the researcher in charge of the study itself. Such factors as the study's budget, the purpose of the study, the nature of the subject population, and a number of other factors must be taken into account in such a decision.

There are both advantages and disadvantages to using questionnaires to collect data (Selltiz, Jahoda, Deutsch & Cook, 1959). **62** Among the advantages are:

FIGURE 4-1   Sample Questionnaire Items for the Assessment of Job Satisfaction

1.  All things considered, are you satisfied with your job?

    _____    _____
    Yes         No

2.  How often do you feel satisfied with your job?

    _____   _____   _____   _____   _____
    Never      Rarely    Sometimes   Often     Always

3.  All things considered, I'm satisfied with my job.

    _____   _____   _____   _____   _____   _____
    Strongly   Moderately   Slightly   Slightly   Moderately   Strongly
    Disagree   Disagree    Disagree   Agree      Agree        Agree

4.  What percentage of the time do you feel satisfied with your job?

    |____|____|____|____|____|____|____|____|____|____|
    0%   10%  20%  30%  40%  50%  60%  70%  80%  90%  100%

5.  All things considered, I'm satisfied with my job

    1       2       3       4       5       6       7
    Not at                  Somewhat                Totally
    All True                True                    True

a.  The questionnaire is a relatively inexpensive mode of data collection. The per subject cost of data is likely to be far less than what it would be with the use of several alternative data collection techniques (e.g., interviews).

b.  Questionnaires can be administered by a relatively unskilled individual. Participant observation, .interviewing, and several other techniques for collecting data often require far greater degrees of competence on the part of the individual who is actually collecting data. Williams, Seybolt, and Pinder (1975) point out, however, that there are numerous problems that must be solved concerning the administration of questionnaires in organizational settings. For example, where to administer them, what type of "atmosphere" to create, introduction of the questionnaire, hecklers, inquisitive respondents, and anonymity.

c.  Questionnaires can be mailed to respondents. Thus it is possible to obtain data from wide geographical locations at a relatively low cost per subject.

d.  Questionnaires can be administered to groups of individuals. Interviewing, on the other hand, generally involves dealing with each individual separately.

e.  The questionnaire presents a uniform stimulus to all subjects (i.e., each subject receives an identical questionnaire). When data are collected via an interview, on the other hand, each subject may get a slightly different version of each item, since as the interviewer may tire, the subject may pick up subtle cues given by the interviewer, etc.

f.  The anonymity that often accompanies the questionnaire may lead subjects to be more open and truthful (especially on sensitive or controversial topics) than they would, for example, be if they were in an interview situation.

**63**

In terms of disadvantages, the questionnaire as a data collection technique may result in one or more of the following:

a. Missing data may be more of a problem with the questionnaire than with the interview, since the interviewer can clarify questions the respondent does not understand. The subject can obtain no such clarification from a questionnaire. This may cause some individuals to not respond to many items. In some cases items may be omitted so frequently that the entire questionnaire will be discarded by the researcher.

b. If questionnaires are mailed to potential respondents the percentage of returned questionnaires (i.e., the response rate) may not exceed 50%.[1] Low response rates are a problem in that there are often important differences between the attitudes, opinions, demographic characteristics, etc., of those who return questionnaires and those who don't. To the extent that response rates are low, the results of a study may not be generalizable to the entire set of potential respondents (cf. chapter 5 and section on external validity in chapter 6).

c. The questionnaire cannot be used with illiterates or with individuals who have reading problems. To the extent that individuals cannot cope with the reading demands placed upon them by questionnaires, the researcher can expect one or more of the following problems: (1) low return rates, (2) missing data, and (3) random responses.

d. Most questionnaires are inflexible in that individuals must respond to items of a relatively structured nature. As a result, people may feel unable to explain fully their attitudes, values, opinions, etc. In an interview, on the other hand, the subject is often free to respond to a given question in the manner he or she chooses, or first answer in terms of fixed alternatives and then indicate why the chosen alternative was actually selected. The structured nature of many questionnaires may thus limit the amount of information that might be obtained from research subjects.

There are a number of other types of objective data-gathering techniques besides questionnaires. Among these are tests (intelligence, aptitude, achievement, etc.), personality measures, interest inventories, measures of values, biographical information blanks, and several other lesser used methods. Given the wide variety of these other methods and the scope of this book, we offer but brief descriptions of these other techniques.

## TESTS

One method of introducing the reader to the wide variety of tests in use today is to mention the general purposes that tests serve. Two commonly reported dimensions tests assess are achievement and aptitude.

- *Achievement.* These tests are designed to measure a person's current level of skill or ability in some area, as opposed to measuring a person's potential level of attainment in the area. Achievement tests may measure mental, motor, or psychomotor performance dimensions. All students have been exposed to achievement tests of various types in their course work. Such

---

[1] For factors influencing response rates in mail surveys see Dillman (1972), Kanuk and Berenson (1975), Linsky (1975), and Selltiz, Wrightsman, and Cook (1976, p. 297).

tests commonly measure achievement in relatively narrowly defined areas.

- *Aptitude.* Ability or aptitude tests are designed to measure a person's potential in a given area rather than what a person has already learned in that area. Tests in this area may tap mental, motor, or psychomotor dimensions. Examples are the General Aptitude Test Battery, Employee Aptitude Survey, Differential Aptitudes Test, Scholastic Aptitude Test, MacQuarrie Test for Mechanical Ability, Minnesota Spatial Relations Test, Minnesota Paper Form Board Test, Minnesota Mechanical Assembly Test, Bennett Test of Mechanical Comprehension, Purdue Pegboard Test, and Crawford Small Parts Dexterity Test (Blum & Naylor, 1968; Miner, 1969).

An important point for the reader to grasp is that while a given test may be called an aptitude test, very rarely if ever is it devoid of achievement-oriented content. Thus the same test may be used in one instance to index aptitude and in the other to index achievement.[2] As Nunnally (1972) notes: "Even with the best of efforts, it presently is not possible to measure aptitude apart from achievement" (p. 346). (An interesting way of contrasting achievement and ability tests is offered by Cleary, Humphreys, Kendrick & Wesman, 1975.)

One way of distinguishing between the two types of tests is how they are used by an organization. If the test is used to predict future performance on a job then it can probably be thought of as an aptitude or potential ability measure. If, on the other hand, the test measures the degree to which a person has mastered certain specific job-related skills, then the test can be looked at as an achievement or present ability measure.

## PERSONALITY MEASURES

There are many different objective measures of personality traits. A trait (i.e., an attribute or characteristic) is simply a dimension of behavior (or the tendency to behave in one fashion as opposed to another) that is measurable. There are three broad classes of traits that are assessed by personality measures (Nunnally, 1967, p. 470):

- *Social Traits.* These relate to behavior that is characteristic of a person in his or her dealings with others. Among the traits that can be considered as social are shyness, dominance, gregariousness, aggressiveness, etc.
- *Motives.* These involve individual differences in needs or desires for aggression, affiliation, power, dominance, self-abasement, etc.
- *Adjustment.* The object of measurement here is to assess the degree to which a person is free from emotional distress and/or behavior that is socially disruptive in nature. Adjustment implies the absence of neuroses and psychoses.

There is one important dimension in which personality mea-

---

[2] See, for example, Blum and Naylor (1968), Maier (1973, p. 122), Nunnally (1972, p. 345), and Schneider (1976).

sures differ that deserves mention here: the principal use of an instrument. Some measures are used principally in the diagnosis and monitoring of psychopathology (e.g., the Minnesota Multiphasic Personality Inventory, developed by Hathaway & McKinley, 1943). Others are used primarily for measuring the traits of individuals with no known adjustment problems (e.g., the Personality Research Form developed by Jackson, 1967). Whereas research in work organizations might at times involve the use of the latter type of measure, the use of instruments aimed at the assessment of psychopathology is extremely rare. And, even where personality measures of a nonclinical nature have been used in organizational research, their utility in predicting organizationally relevant variables (e.g., job performance) has not been impressive.[3]

## INTEREST MEASURES

There are several relatively well known and widely used measures of interests (e.g., the Strong Vocational Interest Blank developed by E. K. Strong, 1938, and the Kuder Preference Record developed by G. F. Kuder, 1934 and 1956). These forms are commonly used in vocational guidance and counseling. The rationale underlying their use is that a person is far more likely to succeed in an occupation if he or she finds the activities associated with the occupation to be interesting. As with personality measures, interest measures have had mixed success in predicting various organizationally relevant variables (cf. Ghiselli, 1966). Moreover, the extent to to which interest inventories are subject to faking and the degree to which this is an important concern (in terms of their validity) is an open question.

## VALUES INVENTORIES

A number of instruments exist for the assessment of values, i.e., peoples' preferences for "life goals" and "ways of life" (Nunnally, 1967, p. 515). There are measures of general values (e.g., the "Study of Values" developed by Allport, Vernon, & Lindzey, 1951) and measures of more specific values (e.g., the "Survey of Work Values" scale of Wollack, Goodale, Wijting & Smith, 1971). The interested reader is directed to any of several interesting articles on general and work-related values.[4]. A number of scales for the measurement of occupational values are presented in Robinson et al. (1969).

---

[3] See, for instance, Ghiselli (1966), Guion and Gottier (1965), Hedluise (1965), and Schneider (1976).

[4] See, for example, the works of Dukes (1955), Hyman (1966), Kohn and Schooler (1969), and Pittel and Mendelsohn (1966).

## INTERVIEWS

Interviews are "meetings" in which the interviewer directs questions at the interviewee and records the obtained responses. The meetings themselves often involve face-to-face interaction between the interviewer and the interviewee. Interviewing by other means (e.g., over the telephone) is also possible. The major difference between data collection via the questionnaire and the interview is that in the case of the former technique the *respondent* reads the questions and records his responses to the questions, while in the case of the latter method the interviewer both presents the questions to the subject *and* records the elicited responses.

Interviews differ in terms of the degree of structure present in (*a*) the questions asked by the interviewer and (*b*) the responses evoked from the interviewee. A typology of interview strategies, using unstructured and structured categories for both questions (i.e., interview items) and response possibilities is shown in figure 4-2.[5]

FIGURE 4-2   A Typology of Interview Strategies

| | | Interview Items | |
|---|---|---|---|
| | | Unstructured | Structured |
| Response Possibilities | Unstructured | Unstructured Interview | Semi-Structured Interview-I |
| | Structured | Semi-Structured Interview-II | Structured Interview |

The unstructured, informal, nondirective, or clinical interview is one in which the interviewer often does little more than keep the interviewee's comments focused on some topic. The respondent generally has complete control over the length and content of such comments. The structured, directive, limited response, or formal interview, on the other hand, is one in which both the interview items (i.e., questions) and response possibilities available to the respondent are predetermined. The interviewer presents the interviewee a "standard" set of questions during the interview. Responses to these questions are made by the interviewee selecting one (or more) of the several "standard" alternatives that accompany each item in the interview schedule. (An interview schedule is a set of interview items that, depending upon the interview strategy, may or may not be accompanied by a set of response possibilities for each item.)

[5] Adapted from Bouchard (1976, p. 371).

There are two types of semistructured interviews. The first type allows the respondent to answer a predetermined set of questions in any manner he or she chooses. Open-ended and free-response interviewing are labels that have also been used to identify this strategy. The second type of semistructured interview requires the interviewee to respond in a structured fashion to unstructured interview items. There are no known uses of this semistructured interviewing strategy. (See Bouchard, 1976, for at least one potential application of this strategy.) Whether an interview is unstructured, semistructured, or structured is something that should be dictated by the purpose of the study being conducted, the study's subjects, and other constraints associated with the study itself. Whatever the strategy ultimately selected by the researcher, however, there are a number of advantages and disadvantages of collecting data via interviewing that should be considered.

Among the advantages or benefits associated with data collection via interviewing are (Selltiz et al., 1959):

a. Interviews can be used with illiterate subjects or subjects with reading deficiencies. Questionnaires, as the reader will recall, are difficult, if not impossible, to use with such subjects.
b. Often a far greater proportion of the subjects contacted by an interviewer will participate in a study compared with the proportion of subjects who will return a mailed questionnaire.
c. Interviews—especially those that tend toward the unstructured variety —are quite flexible. The interviewer can approach the discussion of the interview topic in a wide variety of ways. Even in interviews that tend toward the limited-response type, the interviewer can often clarify questions in the interview schedule that the interviewee does not fully understand. In addition, even with the limited-response interview the interviewee may often have the opportunity to go beyond the mere selection of one of a number of given response alternatives (e.g., the interviewee may indicate what motivated the choice of a particular response, then qualify the response to any given question).
d. The validity of an interviewee's response may be assessed to some extent. The interviewer may, for example, "probe" the interviewee on questions where such efforts appear necessary. In addition, the interviewer can observe and record details about the behavior (nervousness, hesitation in responding, etc.) of the interviewee in responding to items in the interview schedule.
e. The interview, especially the free-response type, is often a more appropriate means of collecting data in early phases of a study, where the objective lies more in the development of hypotheses than in their testing.

In terms of disadvantages associated with the use of interviews as a data gathering technique, the following are worthy of note:

a. The interview is generally more costly than other techniques (e.g., the questionnaire). In some instances interviews conducted over the telephone are less costly than mailed questionnaires.

b. The interview has the potential of being a more "reactive" technique for collecting data than, for example, the questionnaire. In addition to an interview assessing a particular attitude, for example, the interpersonal nature of the interview process may actually lead to changes in the attitude. While questionnaires are also considered to be reactive measures (Webb, Campbell, Schwartz, & Sechrest, 1966), the "impersonal" nature of the questionnaire may result in less such reactivity than an interview.

c. The training of interviewers is often a long and costly process (see, for example, Hyman, Cobb, Feldman, & Stember, 1954). The more nondirective the interview, the greater the need for highly skilled interviewers. Consider, for example, the skill differences that might be found between an individual whose job it was to administer a questionnaire that measured some dimension of personality to groups of individuals versus an individual doing nondirective interviewing to assess the same construct. A clerk might suffice for the former task, while a clinical psychologist with graduate-level training might be needed for the latter task.

d. The interviewer may (because of fatigue, decreased task interest, etc.) alter the manner in which questions are put to interviewees, the fidelity with which responses are recorded from one interview to the next, etc. As a consequence, the validity and reliability of obtained data may suffer.

e. Characteristics of the interviewer, the interviewee (e.g., sex, race, socioeconomic status, etc.) and their combination may influence the measured variables.[6]

f. The interview, even if it is of the nondirective variety, may not lead to as thorough an understanding of the phenomenon under investigation as alternative data collection methods (e.g., participant observation [Becker & Geer, 1957]).

## OBSERVATIONS OF BEHAVIOR

In research using the observation of behavior as a data-gathering technique the researcher serves as the measuring instrument. The behavior of individuals and/or groups is observed by the researcher-observer, whose responsibility is to record relevant aspects of such behavior. There are several ways in which such observation may vary from one research situation to the next.

First, the observation may vary along a structure continuum (Selltiz et al., 1959). In *structured observation* the observer knows the aspects of individual and/or group behavior that are relevant to the study being conducted. As a result, he or she may often have a relatively well-developed plan for recording what is observed. The lesser the degree of structure, the less carefully are such plans made in advance of actual data collection.

Second, the observer may or may not participate in the social setting he or she is observing. In what is called *participant observation* the observer participates in the activities of the system under study. At the other extreme on the participation continuum is the case where the observer has no interaction with the system under

---

[6] For more on these potential influences see Bouchard (1976), Hyman et al. (1954), Schmitt (1976), Smith and Hyman (1950), and Williams (1964).

study. (Becker & Geer, 1957, make a strong case for participant observation.)

Third, the observer may or may not be "hidden." A hidden observer is one who is not "visible" to the individual and/or group under study. There are advantages and disadvantages to "hiding" the observer that the prospective researcher should be familiar with (see Runkel & McGrath, 1972, pp. 189–191; Becker & Geer, 1957; or Williams & Raush, 1972).

Fourth, the behavioral units being observed may vary on a molecular-molar dimension (Heyns & Zander, 1953). The more molecular the approach taken in observing behavior, the smaller the units of behavior that the observer is responsible for observing and recording. In general, the more molecular the observed behavioral units the greater the reliability (see the discussion of inter-rater reliability in chapter 3) of the obtained measures. Validity, however, may suffer somewhat as the observed units of behavior become more and more molecular (Kerlinger, 1973, pp. 541–544). Consider, for example, observation of the work behavior of a secretary. An observer might be able to reliably observe and record the number of minutes the secretary is engaged in typing. If, however, the purpose of the observation is to measure the general effectiveness of the secretary, then the "number of minutes spent typing" index is less than adequate in terms of validity since such behaviors as filing, answering the telephone, etc., are not represented in the measure (i.e., the measure lacks content validity).

Fifth, and finally, the sampling of behavior may take place on a "time" or "event" basis. In *event sampling* the observer is concerned with the observation and recording of only certain types of predetermined behaviors. In *time sampling* observation takes place at specified time intervals and concerns itself with whatever behavior is being exhibited by the subject(s) at the scheduled observation periods (Arrington, 1943; Heyns & Zander, 1953, etc.).

Like other methods of data collection, the observation of behavior has advantages and disadvantages. Among the advantages are:

   a. The observer can often obtain data about behavior that subjects may be either unwilling or unable to report themselves (Becker & Geer, 1957).
   b. In addition to observing and recording the behavior of subjects, the observer can often make (with varying degrees of accuracy) inferences about what caused the behavior.
   c. Behavior is observed as it occurs. Thus, retrospective reports by subjects (which are often incomplete) are avoided.

These advantages should be viewed in combination with the following disadvantages:

**70**

a. Observers are "fallible" measuring devices. They may provide incomplete reports of what they observe. In addition, observers may fatigue as a study progresses and adversely affect the reliability and validity of data they collect.

Ʈ. The observation of behavior (especially if it is of the non-hidden, participant variety) may be a more reactive method of measurement than, for example, questionnaires.

c. Observers often require considerable training. Such training can be expensive and time consuming.

d. The observation of behavior may be extremely costly since an observer must be present when the behavior under study is actually exhibited by the subject(s). In some instances the behavior of interest may be exhibited very infrequently. Thus, the proportion of irrelevant sampled behavior to total sampled behavior (i.e., the "dross rate") may be quite high (Webb, Campbell, Schwartz & Sechrest, 1966, pp. 32–33).

## PROJECTIVE MEASURES

Measurement using what are known as projective techniques is accomplished by having the subject describe or interpret a stimulus "object" other than himself. Projective techniques are "based on the hypothesis that an individual's responses to an 'unstructured stimulus' are influenced by his needs, motives, fears, expectations, and concerns" (Nunnally, 1972, p. 481). A stimulus with an agreed-upon public meaning is said to be structured. An unstructured stimulus, on the other hand, has no agreed-upon public meaning (Nunnally, 1967, pp. 494–495).

Undoubtedly all readers of this book have heard or read about the Rorschach (ink-blot) technique for the assessment of personality. This is but one of many projective measures in use today. In addition to ink blots, cloud pictures, art media of various types, dramatic play (e.g., psychodrama), incomplete sentences, pictures, and numerous other stimuli have been used in the projective measurement of various dimensions of individual differences. (cf., for example, Sargent, 1945; Lindzey, 1959).

The techniques themselves have been grouped (Lindzey, 1959) on the basis of the type of response required of the subject being measured. The five types of responses are: (a) *Association:* the subject is presented a stimulus and responds by indicating the first word, image, or percept that is evoked by the stimulus; (b) *Construction:* the subject is asked to produce a product of some type (a story, picture, sculpture, etc.). The final product is used in evaluating the subject; (c) *Completion:* the subject is provided with an incomplete product (story, picture, etc.) and is required to complete it; (d) *Choice or Ordering Techniques:* the subject is required to choose a fixed number of items from a pool of available alternatives or to order the available alternatives in terms of some criterion (liking, repugnance, relevance, etc.); and **71**

(e) *Expressive:* the subject is asked to combine stimuli in such a way as to produce a novel product. In addition to evaluating the subject on the basis of the product that results, the evaluation also focuses on the manner in which the product was produced.

While projective techniques were originally developed for the clinical assessment of personality by psychiatrists, clinical psychologists, etc. (cf. Sargent, 1945), recently their use for non-clinical purposes appears to be increasing (Korman, 1971). McClelland, Atkinson, Clark, and Lowell (1953) have used one projective technique (the Thematic Apperception Test) extensively to measure achievement motivation and other motives of possible interest to the organizational researcher.

One of the reasons advanced to support the use of projective measures is their supposed nonsusceptibility to "faking" (i.e., the conscious manipulation of a test score by a subject designed to make the subject appear to the examiner to have either more or less of a measured attribute) and other types of "response styles" (see, for example, the arguments of Schultz, 1973, p. 154). The literature (reviewed by Murstein, 1963) is not unequivocal with regard to the merits of projective measures in reducing or eliminating response styles of various types. As concerns their use in industry (see Kinslinger, 1966, for a review), the evidence on these techniques is not as strong as it should be to recommend them for other than basic research purposes. Miner (1969) writes that "there is no question that more must be learned about the various ways people reveal themselves through their test responses before projective tests can achieve their full potentiality as personnel selection techniques" (p. 191). A stronger position is taken by Barrett (1963) who argues that the best known of the projective tests (i.e., the Rorschach test) "has accumulated such a high record of failure as a [personnel] selection test that . . . using it for such purposes is a complete waste of time" (pp. 139–140).

## Q-SORTING

Q-Sorting (Stephenson, 1953) is a technique for sorting cards with names of stimuli into a number of categories (piles) in terms of some specified criterion (e.g., liking, worth, attractiveness, etc.). The number of cards that must go into various piles is fixed by the researcher so that a distribution (often near normal in shape) of stimuli on the relevant dimension results. A subject might, for example, be given names of 100 different jobs and asked to place jobs on different piles based upon whether or not the subject would like to hold the job. The sort might be done in terms of a distribution such as that specified in figure 4-3. The resulting distribution would tell us the relative degree of liking the subject has for the various jobs.

FIGURE 4-3.  Distribution of Stimuli in a Q-Sort

| Pile Number: | 1 | 2 | 3 | 4 | 5 | 6 | 7 |
|---|---|---|---|---|---|---|---|
| Number of Jobs: to Be Placed in Pile | 5 | 10 | 20 | 30 | 20 | 10 | 5 |

Note that in performing a Q-sort the subject is doing the equivalent of rank-ordering stimuli (with respect to some attribute) with the restriction that there be a specified number of ties at each scale point. In the limiting case (where the number of piles equals the number of stimuli), Q-sorts are identical to the simple ranking of stimuli.[7]

## SOCIOMETRY

Sociometry is a data-gathering technique useful in the study of such things as communication, interaction, and choice patterns among members of social groups. Sociometry data are usually collected by questionnaires, but other means such as observation may be employed.

In a sociometric study the subject is presented with a list of names and asked who he or she would most like to interact with (work, live, or talk with, etc.). The subject is allowed to select one or more individuals for such interaction. Once analyzed, the data show preferred interaction patterns among group members.

Results of a hypothetical sociometric study are shown in figure 4-4. The arrows indicate choices made by group members in responding to the research question, "Who would you most like to have as a member of a work group of which you are to be a member?"

In figure 4-4 the data show, for example, that Peter Graves has been chosen by three individuals, Carmen Williams has been chosen by two individuals, etc. These data would be useful to us if, for example, we were interested in the formation of a maximally cohesive work group.[8]

---

[7] The Q-sorting technique is described and/or critiqued by Block (1956), Jones (1956), Kerlinger (1972), Nunnally (1967), Stephenson (1953), Sundland (1962), and Wittenborn (1961). The prospective user of Q-sorts is advised to consult one or more of these publications for additional information on the technique.

[8] The reader may obtain additional information on sociometry from such sources as Lindzey and Borgatta (1954), Lindzey and Byrne (1968), Moreno (1953), Northway (1952), or Proctor and Loomis (1951).

FIGURE 4-4   Hypothetical Data from a Sociometric Study of Co-Worker Preferences

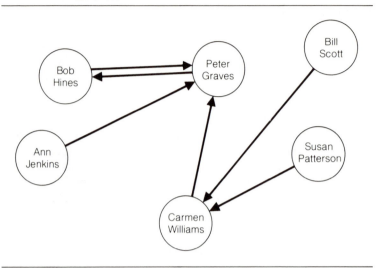

## UNOBTRUSIVE MEASURES

A final set of methods for obtaining data fall under the heading of "unobtrusive measures" (Webb et al., 1966). Looked at broadly, unobtrusive measures are those which (1) do not require the cooperation of a respondent to obtain and (2) do not, through the process of measurement, contaminate the measured variable (Webb et al., 1966, p. 2).[9] Among the types of measures which Webb and co-authors consider unobtrusive are:

- *Physical Traces*. Here we look for signs of "erosion" or "accretion." The popularity of displays in a museum, for example, was measured in one study by the rate of tile replacement around exhibits (an erosion index). The consumption of various types of liquor was, in another study, assessed by combing through the trash containers in a city (an accretion index).
- *Archives*. Archival data can be placed in one of two major categories. One is what Webb et al. (1966) call "the running record" (consisting of the records of a society that are kept on an ongoing, continuous basis). Among the possible sources of data in this category are actuarial records, political records, judicial records, voting patterns, budget figures, etc. The second category of archival data consists of what are called "episodic and private records" (p. 88). Among such records are sales records of various organizations, industrial and institutional records of various types (e.g., records of employee productivity and absenteeism), written documents of a private nature, etc. These, while often more difficult to obtain than "running records," may be of greater use to the researcher because of lower dross rates.

[9] The reader should note that there may be ethical problems with the use of unobtrusive measures. A number of these are covered in chapter 8.

- *Simple Observation*. This class of measures includes all instances where the observer is hidden and the researcher has had no part in structuring the situation in which the observation is taking place. Observation has already been dealt with in this chapter. The important distinction separating observation, in general, from what Webb et al. include in their discussion of unobtrusive observation is that in the latter case the observer is hidden from the subjects being observed.

Webb et al. (1966) lament the fact that the dominant mass of social science research is based upon the collection of data via interviews and questionnaires. "Overdependence" on these two "fallible methods" of collecting data is objectionable in their opinion since:

Interviews and questionnaires intrude as a foreign element into the social setting they would describe, they create as well as measure attitudes, they elicit atypical roles and responses, they are limited to those who are accessible and will cooperate, and the responses obtained are provided in part by dimensions of individual differences irrelevant to the topic at hand (p. 1).

What Webb et al. argue for is not abandoning interviews and questionnaires as measuring devices, but using other measures to confirm the results produced by interviews and/or questionnaires. To the extent that the results produced by a questionnaire or interview agree (i.e., have convergent validity) with those of other methods, our confidence in the validity of our measures is increased.

Why are measures such as questionnaires or interviews often insufficient when used alone to measure a variable or a set of variables? Webb et al. point to three general threats to the valid interpretation of results produced by these measures:

1. "Reactive measures" often produce error from a study's subjects. (A reactive measure is one which influences what it is intended to measure in addition to simply measuring it.) Errors may result if subjects are aware they are being measured in some fashion (the "guinea pig effect"). Errors may also result if in responding to an interview the respondent believes that a special role (other than the one he or she would normally take in the absence of measurement) should be assumed during the measurement process (role selection effects). Still another source of error associated with reactive measures is that the initial measurement of some variable may cause real changes in it that will appear when the variable is measured at some later point in time (measurement as change agent effects). Finally, when interviews or questionnaires are used to measure a variable, the subject may adopt some pattern in responding to individual items (agreeing with all statements, marking only right-hand or left-hand scale points, etc.) that results in the subject's *observed score* differing from the subject's *true score* on the variable (response-set effects). **75**

2. The investigator may also influence a study's results when questionnaires or interviews are used for data collection. Characteristics of the interviewer (age, race, sex, etc.) may cause subjects to respond differently to questions they are asked (interviewer effects). Error may also be introduced if, over time, the researcher's ability to observe and record some phenomenon changes (instrument change effects) for one reason or another (the investigator may loaf, become bored or tired, etc.).

3. The manner in which a study's sample is selected may influence the study's results (sampling error). One cause for concern here is that certain data collection methods can only be used with limited subsets of the population (population restriction effects). For example, questionnaires may only be used with literate subjects, while the investigator may want to generalize to the entire population (literate and illiterate) in some region. Another potential problem associated with sampling is that successive samples taken from some population may vary in critical ways from day to day (instability of population effects). For example, the average level of job satisfaction for workers in any given organization may differ if measured on Monday or Tuesday of any given week because many of the less satisfied workers may regularly not come to work on Mondays. A final problem associated with sampling arises when the samples of populations that could be measured by a specific technique change over geographical areas (population instability over areas effects). For example, the feasibility of studying attitudes of farm workers using a self-administered questionnaire may vary from one region of the United States to the next since workers in various regions may differ in terms of literacy, fluency in English, etc.

These are some of the problems that might present themselves in a study where obtrusive measures (questionnaires, interviews, etc.) are employed. Given the potential for obtaining invalid data using obtrusive measures, the use of multiple measures, including possibly those of the unobtrusive variety, should be considered in studies where their use is feasible.[10]

The literature on data collection techniques is vast. In this chapter we have been able only to introduce the reader to some of the issues associated with this very important aspect of research. This information should place the student of organizational behavior and/or the practicing manager in a better position to understand the research that has been conducted by others on human behavior in organizations.

---

[10] For more on the use of multiple measures see Bouchard (1976), Campbell and Fiske (1959), Cook and Selltiz (1964), Cook and Campbell (1976), and Webb et al. (1966).

# SAMPLING 5

Earlier in this book it was noted that one of the things a researcher must do in carrying out an empirical study is decide who or what shall be the study's focus. The researcher must determine the individuals, groups, organizations, events, etc., that will be observed, interviewed, etc., in "getting the facts" associated with a study.

If the focus of a study is restricted to a relatively "small" number of individuals, groups, organizations, etc., then collecting data from or about all of them is *generally* not costly (in terms of time, costs, etc.). If, on the other hand, a study involves a relatively "large" (e.g., thousands) number of individuals, groups, organizations, etc., then the costs of obtaining data from or about all of them is often quite costly.

If we were to conduct an interview study of job satisfaction levels among all employees of a firm having about 50 workers, a single interviewer could probably do all the required interviews in a week or less. If, on the other hand, we were to conduct an interview study of job satisfaction levels of all members of the civilian labor force in the United States (approximately 93 million people), an army of interviewers would have to devote a considerable period of time and effort to obtain the data. If, for example, a thousand interviewers were to work at the task and each complete 8 interviews per day, it would take 11,625 days (about 31.8 years!) to do the necessary interviewing. The costs of such a study would be "astronomical" and the data from most individuals would be so aged by the time the study was completed that data value would be highly questionable. In sum, a study in which all **77** members of the civilian labor force were interviewed would not be very feasible.

How, then, might we estimate the average level of job satisfaction for this set of individuals without doing 93 million interviews? One possibility would be to interview only a subset (i.e., a sample) of these individuals and use data from the sample to infer the average level of job satisfaction of the larger set (i.e., the population). The manner in which we selected the subset of workers would greatly influence the degree to which our prediction (based upon the sample's data) would mirror data obtained from all members of the population. If the subset of workers interviewed had been "appropriately selected" (i.e., via random sampling) the average job satisfaction level of 93 million individuals could accurately be predicted using data from a sample of just a few thousand.

## PURPOSE OF SAMPLING

The purpose of *sampling* is to obtain data on a subset of some population so that at a later point in time inferences can be made about the *population* (i.e., the whole set) based on the data from the *sample* (i.e., the subset). In the example cited above, all registered voters in the United States constitute the population. In other studies the population might be all male college students in the nation, all tool and die makers working in organizations with over 50 employees, all housewives who have part-time jobs, all individuals who were in the armed services between 1964 and 1966, etc. The precise criteria employed by the researcher to define the population varies from study to study. For any given study the criteria can be determined by simply answering the following question: "To what set of people, events, or things do I want my study's conclusions to apply?"

Having defined the population of interest, the researcher must then determine the number of elements (i.e., single members of the population) from which data are to be obtained. If the population in question is relatively small in size and easily accessible for participation in the study the researcher may choose to obtain data from all members of the population. A questionnaire study involving "all members of the United States Senate" might not present problems. An interview study involving "all employed males in the United States" would be quite difficult, if not impossible, to execute. In the latter case, the researcher would probably limit the number of individuals (elements) in the population from

which he or she would secure data; that is, the study's sample would be smaller than the population. Several methods might be used by the researcher to select the study's sample. These are described in the paragraphs which follow.

## SAMPLING TYPES

### Random Sampling

If a sample is selected in such a manner as to insure that (*a*) every member of the population is available for inclusion in the sample, (*b*) every member of the population has an equal opportunity to be included in the sample, and (*c*) every subsample of a given size, lower than that of the population, has an equal probability of being selected, the sample is known as a *random sample*.

Suppose, for example, that we were interested in obtaining a random sample of all blue-collar workers in a particular organization. We might proceed as follows. First the names of all such workers are written on individual slips. These slips are then placed in a huge drum and thoroughly mixed. Following this, slips of paper are drawn from the drum until the specified sample size is reached.

There are many other techniques for drawing random samples from populations (see Cochran, 1963; Kish, 1953, 1965; and Warwick & Lininger, 1975). More important than the mechanics of drawing random samples, however, is the rationale for sampling on a random basis. Let's briefly consider why it is important to work with random samples.

We noted above that quite often data from a sample are used to infer or deduce something about the population from which the sample was drawn. The statistics (sample mean, sample standard deviation, etc.) we derive from sample data are our basis for inferring the values of population parameters (population mean, population variance, etc.). In order for us to make inferences about population parameters from sample statistics we need to know that our sample is representative of the population from which it was drawn. A sample is *representative* of a population if it has approximately the same characteristics as the population. While we generally never know whether or not our sample actually does have the same characteristics as the population from which it was drawn, we know that if our sampling was done on a random basis the probability of our sample being representative is greater than it would be with other than random sampling. Viewed strictly, unless we have samples that are representative of the population from which they are drawn, statistical inferences about population characteristics cannot be made using sample data.

**79**

## Systematic Sampling

In systematic sampling we employ a list of the population. A random starting point on the list is then chosen. After this every *n*th person on the list is chosen for inclusion in the sample.[1] To maximize the probability of the selected sample being representative of the population from which it is drawn, the initial assignment of population elements to positions on the list should be done on a random basis.

## Stratified Sampling

Stratification is often the first step in a two-stage sampling effort. The population is first divided into strata using one or more criteria that serve as a basis for assigning population elements to mutually exclusive categories. In the second stage of the process samples are selected from each of the strata.

An example should serve to make stratified sampling clearer. Suppose we were interested in studying the job satisfaction levels of employees in a certain organization. We might want to first assign workers to one of two mutually exclusive categories: (*a*) white-collar workers and (*b*) blue-collar workers. Subsequent to the creation of these two strata we could then randomly select a given number of individuals from each stratum. Those selected from the two strata would then comprise the study's sample. Through stratified random sampling we could, for example, include a larger number of white-collar workers in the final sample than would have resulted from simple random sampling.

## Cluster Sampling

In cluster sampling the sample unit (i.e., the cluster) contains more than one population element. The cluster may be a workgroup, the set of employees in one branch of a multi-branch service organization, members of a church congregation, or any other multi-element subset of the population.

The logic of cluster sampling may be easier to grasp through illustration. Suppose we were interested in finding out whether or not employees of "small-sized" outlets of a national retailing chain had higher levels of job involvement than employees of "large-sized" outlets in the same chain. To assess the relative levels of job involvement we might select a number of small- and large-sized stores for participation in the study. Each such selected store (and its employees) would represent a cluster.

Cluster sampling may be the first phase of a two-stage sampling plan. Subsequent to selecting clusters in the first stage of

[1] The value of *n* is determined by dividing the population size by the sample size.

sampling, some other sampling strategy (e.g., random sampling) may be used in the second stage.

## Quota Sampling

In quota sampling the objective is to select fixed numbers of elements from each of several distinguishable subsets of some population. To illustrate what is involved in quota sampling consider the following example. An organizational researcher is interested in discovering the features of jobs that workers in a certain organization value. He feels that variables such as age and sex may be important correlates of values. Rather than getting a random sample of workers in the organization, the researcher decides that he will interview at least fifty persons in each of four groups: "young" males, "old" males, "young" females, and "old" females. He interviews workers until data have been obtained from each group (in accord with the established quotas).

## Purposive Sampling

The rationale underlying purposive sampling is that if a researcher uses "sound judgment" and an "appropriate" sampling strategy, it is possible to "hand pick" elements for inclusion in a study's sample in such a way as to develop a sample that is satisfactory in view of a study's needs (Selltiz et al., 1959). A researcher may, for example, be interested in finding out how various members of an organization perceive its "climate." The sampling plan developed by the researcher involves assessing the perceptions of a number of organizational members who the researcher believes have organizational roles that should result in maximally different views of the organization's climate.

The reader should note that purposive sampling does not involve the random selection of elements from a given population. As such, results obtained from a study in which the sample has been "hand picked" cannot be generalized to *any* population. Purposive sampling should only be employed where the representativeness or external validity (cf. chapter 6) of a study's results is not a concern.

## Convenience Sampling

Convenience sampling is a term used to describe sampling of a nonrandom nature in which the researcher collects data from one or more elements of the population simply because they're available at the time. This method of sampling has also been labelled *accidental sampling* and *incidental sampling*.

**81**

Convenience sampling is probably the most frequently used sampling strategy in organizational behavior research. The reason for this is that organizational researchers are often placed in a position of using a convenience sample or doing no research whatsoever. For example, a researcher conducting a study in a given organization may be told by management that certain individuals can be included in the sample while others cannot, even though those excluded from the sample may be part of the relevant population for the study.

As was mentioned earlier, to the extent that a researcher's sampling strategy differs from random sampling, to that extent will the generalizability of the study's results suffer. Thus the generalizability of most organizational research is probably open to debate. Does this mean that the findings of studies employing convenience samples are of no value whatsoever? We think not. For even though the results of any particular study may not allow the researcher to generalize beyond the study's sample, the cumulative results of many different studies of some phenomenon may provide some basis for assessing the merits of any given hypotheses or set of hypotheses.

## SAMPLING ISSUES

In addition to being familiar with the several sampling strategies discussed above, the reader should also be aware of a number of sampling-related issues that are covered in the following paragraphs.

### Sampling and Generalizability

After conducting a study every researcher is faced with the question, "To what population may I reasonably generalize the results of my study?" The answer to this question is very much a function of the sampling procedure used by the researcher.

Let us consider two extreme sampling strategies: random sampling and accidental sampling. In the case of random sampling the researcher has a well defined population in mind and elements of the population have been sampled in such a way as to maximize the probability of the sample mirroring the population in all significant respects. The findings of a study based on this type of sampling can probably be safely generalized to the relevant population. That is, we are probably safe in assuming that a certain finding obtained for the sample would be obtained for the population.

In the case of convenience sampling, on the other hand, we
**82** generally have no idea as to what constitutes the relevant popula-

tion. Where convenience sampling has been used the researcher cannot safely generalize sample-based results to *any* population. Consider the following examples: Results of a study of the determinants of job satisfaction using a convenience sample of unemployed housewives could not reasonably be generalized to the population of employed males and females. A program to allow greater degrees of employee participation in decision making may produce satisfactory results for workers with certain need complexes but yield opposite results for individuals with different needs. Attitudes about contraception gathered from students in an undergraduate management course will not be representative of attitudes held by the public.

Implications of these examples are clear. First, the results of a study based on a sample drawn from any one population may not be generalizable to any other population. And second, the results of a study employing a nonrandom sample (from a known or unknown population) may not *safely* be generalized to any population whatsoever.

## Sample Size

An important concern of every researcher is the size of his or her sample. Sample size is a key concern for two reasons, the cost of conducting a study and the implications of sample size for statistical size.

Let us first consider the costs associated with a study. As sample size increases the total costs of conducting a study increase. In some instances the cost of an additional observation may be negligible (e.g., interviewing an additional person in a national opinion poll). In other instances, however, the cost of an additional observation may be great (e.g., in the quality-control-related testing of a product where such testing leads to the destruction of the tested item).

A researcher's budget may often set an upper bound on the number of elements of the population that may be included in the sample. The presence of liberal amounts of resources, however, should not lead a researcher to sample all elements of the population, since in many instances such extensive sampling is not needed to answer the research questions associated with a study. Where resources are extremely limited, the researcher may not be able to obtain data from enough elements in the population to answer a study's questions.

Where possible, sample size should be based not on the resources available to conduct a study, but on the ability of any given sample size to yield data that are capable of answering the research questions associated with a study. This leads to our **83** second consideration in the determination of sample size: the relationship between sample size and the power of statistical tests.

As we mentioned earlier in this chapter, data from samples yield statistics (sample mean, sample variance, etc.) that are used to infer population parameters (population mean, population variance, etc.). As the size of the sample increases the degree to which a sample-based statistic approximates its associated population parameter increases. That is, the reliability or precision of the sample statistic increases as sample size increases (Cohen, 1969). Whatever the population parameter happens to be, the larger the value of the sample used to estimate it the more precise will be the estimate. Precise estimates of population parameters are highly desirable since the detection of some phenomenon (a difference between the mean values of a variable for two or more groups, a non-zero relationship between two variables, etc.) we believe exists in some population is intimately related to the precision of sample statistics.

Let us consider the following example to clarify what we've been talking about thus far concerning sample-based statistical tests. Assume that the sample correlation between two variables we are studying is .60 (i.e., the two variables are fairly strongly related to one another). As the size of the sample upon which this correlation coefficient is based increases, the width of the confidence interval about the coefficient decreases (see Hays, 1973, pp. 661-665). Stated differently, as the sample size increases the range of values that we can be relatively certain includes the population correlation coefficient (i.e., the width of the confidence interval) decreases. The nature of this decrease is shown in table 5-1. The table shows the 99% confidence interval for a sample correlation coefficient of .60 and various sample sizes.

As can be seen from the data in table 5-1, when the sample size equals 20 our confidence interval is quite wide. The interval decreases in width as the sample size increases so that for a sample of 2,000 the interval is relatively narrow.

The data presented in table 5-1 are for the correlation coefficient. Similar data could be presented for other estimators of population parameters. Such data would all show that as the size of the sample increases, the accuracy with which we can estimate any given population parameter increases. What this implies is that if we want our statistical tests to be relatively powerful (i.e., have a low probability of Type II error) we should use "large" samples in our research. All else equal, the larger the size of our sample the more powerful is any statistical test we perform

**84**    (Cohen, 1969).

TABLE 5-1   The 99% Confidence Interval About a Sample Correlation
Coefficient ($r$) of .60

| Sample Size | Lower Limit of $r$ | Upper Limit of $r$ |
|---|---|---|
| 10 | −.27 | +.93 |
| 20 | +.06 | +.81 |
| 40 | +.26 | +.80 |
| 60 | +.33 | +.77 |
| 80 | +.38 | +.75 |
| 100 | +.40 | +.74 |
| 150 | +.44 | +.72 |
| 200 | +.46 | +.70 |
| 250 | +.48 | +.69 |
| 300 | +.49 | +.68 |
| 500 | +.52 | +.67 |
| 1,000 | +.54 | +.65 |
| 1,500 | +.55 | +.64 |
| 2,000 | +.56 | +.63 |
| 3,000 | +.56 | +.63 |
| 5,000 | +.57 | +.62 |
| 10,000 | +.58 | +.61 |

It should be noted here, however, that as the power of a statistical test increases, so does the probability of detecting an effect (e.g., a difference between the mean value of a variable for two groups or a correlation coefficient that differs from zero) that is statistically reliable (i.e., statistically significant). For example, with a sample size of 1,000, a correlation coefficient of .052 would be considered statistically significant (using a one-tailed test with an alpha level of .05 [cf. Cohen, 1969]). A correlation of this size, however, implies that less than a third of one percent (.0027 precisely) of the variability in one variable can be "explained" by knowing values of the other variable. Looked at somewhat differently, 99.73% of the variance is left unexplained. The correlation of .052, while statistically significant, would be of virtually no practical importance.

The lesson to be learned from the above is that there is a nontrivial distinction between statistical significance and practical importance. For any given effect size (cf. Cohen, 1969)—no matter how small it is in practical terms—a large enough sample will always guarantee that the effect will be one that is statistically significant. A naïve interpreter of research results might believe that just because an effect is statistically reliable it is also important. Nothing could be farther from the truth. For one to impute importance to a research finding, not only should the effect be statistically reliable, but it should also be of relatively large magnitude (cf. Hays, 1973, pp. 413–424).   **85**

A researcher must weigh the gains in precision associated with increasingly large samples against the costs such large samples may entail. The final decision to use one particular sample size as opposed to another should probably be left to a statistician or an experienced researcher who fully understands the statistical implications of changes in sample size.

# RESEARCH DESIGN

The design of research generally follows the statement of a research problem and the specification of one or more empirically testable hypotheses. A *research design* is simply a plan for conducting research in such a way as to allow the results of a study to be interpreted with a minimum degree of equivocality.

This chapter introduces the reader to a number of issues associated with the design of research. Among these are assessing the validity of claims made by others, controlling variance as a research strategy, basic research designs, and the internal and external validity of research findings.

## VALIDITY OF CLAIMS MADE BY OTHERS

In the course of your life you will hear numerous claims made by others concerning the benefits that will accrue to you as a consequence of using one product vs. another, buying one service vs. another, or adopting one behavioral mode vs. another. Consider the following examples: A manufacturer of toothpaste reports that using its brand will result in you having greater "sex appeal" than if you had used competing brands. A fast-food chain claims that if you patronize their outlets you can "have it your way," implying that such individualized treatment of patrons may not be available elsewhere. A management theorist contends that if you redesign jobs so as to provide individuals with more job autonomy, the job satisfaction levels of individuals affected by such changes will increase.

How could you as the potential user of various goods, services, and ideas offered by others assess the validity of claims associated with them? One method, consistent with the model of scientific inquiry presented in this book, would be to actually do empirical research aimed at testing the validity of the hypotheses implicit in the various claims. Consider the claim concerning job redesign. The theorist's claim suggests at least two empirically testable hypotheses: First, if we take an existing job and redesign it to allow job incumbents more autonomy, their level of job satisfaction should increase. Second, if we looked at incumbents in jobs that varied only in terms of the amount of autonomy offered job incumbents, the greater the level of autonomy associated with the job the greater should be the level of job satisfaction. Testing the first hypothesis would require that we conduct an experiment in which we actually manipulated autonomy, the study's independent variable. The second hypothesis could be tested by the concurrent measurement of autonomy and satisfaction levels of individuals in various jobs.

In conducting both of these studies, however, we would want to take every reasonable precaution to insure that it was increased job autonomy that accounted for increased job satisfaction and not some other factor or set of factors. For example, if we looked at incumbents on existing jobs and found that job autonomy was positively related to job satisfaction, one possible competing hypothesis would be that jobs high in autonomy also tend to be high in pay; and, it's pay that is actually influencing satisfaction levels—*not autonomy*. This is but one of many competing hypotheses that could be generated to "explain" the observed positive relationship between autonomy and job satisfaction.

In order to rule out the many rival hypotheses that can often be generated to explain the results of any given study, the researcher must properly design his or her study. A *research design* is nothing more than a plan for conducting research so that research questions associated with a study can be answered.

## DESIGN AND THE CONTROL OF VARIANCE

The adequacy of any given research design is a function of the extent to which the researcher can control variance. In the case of a well-designed study, the researcher is in a position to conclude that the variability of scores for the study's dependent variable is a function of the variability of scores for the study's independent variable(s), and not a function of the variability of scores for one or more other independent and/or intervening variables. For example, in the case of the job design study just

**88**

discussed, the researcher would like to be able to conclude that the variability in job satisfaction scores was a function of the variability in job autonomy scores and not a function of variability of other variables (e.g., pay levels for the various jobs).

In order to conclude that the variability in scores for a study's dependent variable is a function of variability in scores for the independent variable(s), the researcher must control several types of variance: (a) the variance associated with the independent variable(s); (b) the variance connected with other variables that may cause dependent variable scores to vary in a systematic fashion; and (c) the variance attributable to measurement error. Controlling each of these three sources of variability is accomplished in the manner described below.

## Independent Variable Variance

Before indicating how we influence the variance associated with a study's independent variable(s), we need to distinguish between two basic approaches to studying a phenomenon—experimental and nonexperimental. In experimental studies, we actually manipulate the study's independent variable(s). In the case of the job redesign study, the autonomy dimension is manipulated through actually changing this job characteristic. In the case of a nonexperimental study we simply measure the present level of the independent variable (autonomy) for existing jobs that differ on this task characteristic. (The distinction between experimental and nonexperimental study designs is more fully described below and in chapter 7.)

As previously mentioned, in the case of an experimental study we actively manipulate a study's independent variable. Pursuing our job design study example, we might take an existing job in an organization and redesign it so as to increase its autonomy. Scores on the study's dependent variable, measured both before and after the job redesign intervention, could then be compared to assess the impact, if any, the change in job design produced. Another strategy would be to randomly assign a number of individuals to jobs that differed on only one dimension—job autonomy. By comparing the experienced job satisfaction levels for the individuals on the several jobs, we could determine how, if at all, job autonomy was related to job satisfaction.

The above should make clear the aim of independent-variable variance control: maximize variability on a study's independent variable. This can be done by (a) selecting individuals, groups, tasks, etc., for study that we know differ greatly on the study's independent variable(s), or (b) creating experimental conditions that result in high variability of the study's independent variable(s). **89**

All else constant, we would expect that if an independent variable and a dependent variable are related to one another, the greater the extent to which the independent variable varies the greater will be the impact on the dependent variable. The rule to follow is simple: *maximize* the variance of a study's independent variable (Kerlinger, 1973).

## Nuisance Variable Variance

In the case of the job design study described at the beginning of this chapter, "pay" was mentioned as one possible "nuisance variable" in the study of the job autonomy–job satisfaction relationship. *Nuisance variables* produce "undesired sources of variation in an experiment [or nonexperiment] that may affect the dependent variable" (Kirk, 1968, p. 7). Nuisance variables are also called "extraneous variables" (Kerlinger, 1973, p. 309) or "confounding variables" (Underwood, 1957, p. 90).

In designing research our objective should be to control variance associated with nuisance variables. Control can be accomplished in one or more of the following ways: First, such extraneous variance may be held constant by choosing subjects that have similar standing on the nuisance variable. For example, in the job design study we might want to select jobs for study that have differing autonomy levels but identical or nearly identical levels of pay. Second, such extraneous variance may be controlled through including it in the set of measured variables and later statistically removing its effects from the dependent variable. For example, in the job autonomy–job satisfaction study we could measure pay in addition to our two major variables of interest and remove the effects, if any, of pay-level differences among jobs through statistical means (e.g., partial correlational analyses). Third, in the case of an experimental investigation of the relationship between job autonomy and job satisfaction we could control extraneous variance by randomly assigning subjects to jobs with different levels of autonomy. Random assignment of subjects to groups that differ on a study's independent variable is an *extremely effective* means for controlling variance associated with nuisance variables.

## Error Variance

The final type of variance we need to control in a study is error variance. Error variance stems from two sources. First, the measures used in a study may not be reliable. To reduce error variance caused by unreliable measures, we simply take steps to increase the reliability of such measures. (These were discussed in chapter 3.)

Second, error variance results from any and all factors that reduce the potential of an otherwise reliable measure to accurately measure a variable. Consider these examples. If we administer an otherwise reliable measure of "intelligence" to individuals who are hungry, sleepy, physically tired, etc., we would expect the resulting scores to contain more error variance than if the test had been administered to the same subjects when their physical condition was superior. If we measure some phenomenon in a hot, noisy, crowded, or otherwise "unpleasant" environment we might expect more errors in measurement (e.g., random responses to questionnaire items) than if the same phenomenon had been measured in a more pleasant milieu. There are numerous other factors that can adversely affect the ability of an otherwise reliable measure to accurately measure some phenomenon. (For a list of these, see Thorndike, 1949).

To control this second source of error variance, we should arrange for measuring variables under as ideal conditions as possible: That is, respondents should be in "good" physical and psychological condition, environmental influences (e.g., noise, extreme temperatures, distractions, etc.) that may have an adverse impact on the measurement process should be eliminated or minimized, etc. In general, we should attempt to measure under as controlled conditions as our study permits.

## Maxmincon Principle

The effective control of variance in any study results from designing the study in accord with what has been called (Kerlinger, 1973) the "Maxmincon principle." The principle directs us to (a) *max*imize systematic variance, (b) *min*imize error variance, and (c) *con*trol extraneous variance. When the maxmincon principle is employed in designing a study the researcher maximizes the probability that the study will provide answers to the research question(s) he or she has formulated. Since the purpose of research is to answer research questions, strategies that maximize the potential of a study to accomplish this objective should be chosen over those having a lower probability of accomplishing the objective.

## BASIC RESEARCH DESIGNS

There are three major types of research designs: (a) experimental designs, (b) quasi-experimental designs, and (c) nonexperimental or preexperimental designs. These three types of designs are discussed in the paragraphs that follow.

**91**

### Experimental Designs

*Experimental designs* are those which allow for the manipulation of a study's independent variable and the subsequent assessment of the impact, if any, such manipulation has had on the study's dependent variable. In the case of the job design study mentioned at the beginning of this chapter, performing an experimental study to test the impact of autonomy on satisfaction would involve our active manipulation of the independent variable under study. Let us consider one possible way a study such as this might actually take place. The study in question employs a preexperimental research design. We use this design as a vehicle for introducing a number of problems that may arise in making valid inferences from a study's results. After covering the problems associated with this preexperimental design, we'll consider a number of methodologically superior designs.

The preexperimental design in question (i.e., the one group pretest post-test design) involves the following steps. First, we obtain observations, O's, (using questionnaires, interviews, etc.) on the current job satisfaction level of the individuals under study. We then introduce the experimental or treatment variable, X. In this case it would be increasing the level of autonomy associated with the job or jobs being studied. Subsequent to this we again measure job satisfaction. A diagram of this design is shown below:

$$\underrightarrow{O_1 \quad X \quad O_2}$$

Time

Note that if we detect a change in the level of job satisfaction between the first ($O_1$) and second ($O_2$) observations we might *tentatively* conclude that it was the treatment (i.e., increased autonomy) that produced the change. We purposely indicated that such a detected difference between $O_1$ and $O_2$ would only justify a tentative conclusion about the reason for the change, since there are several factors other than the treatment that may have had an impact on the measured levels of job satisfaction. These include:[1]

1. History: Events that occurred between $O_1$ and $O_2$ other than X which may have been responsible for the observed difference between $O_1$ and $O_2$. For example, if the job design study were being conducted in an industrial organization, the workers might have had their salary increased between $O_1$ and $O_2$. This

[1] See Campbell (1957), Campbell and Stanley (1966), and Cook and Campbell (1976).

salary change (as opposed to the job design change) may be responsible for the observed difference between $O_1$ and $O_2$.

2. Maturation: These are effects that occur systematically with the passage of time. In our hypothetical study, for instance, the workers may have become more proficient at doing their jobs. Greater proficiency could have resulted in both increased task performance and job satisfaction (assuming that workers react to greater performance with increased satisfaction). Note that the difference between history and maturation is that the effects of history result from factors outside of the subject, while the effects of maturation stem from changes within the subject.

3. Testing: Observed differences between $O_1$ and $O_2$ may be a function of simply being exposed to a measure at two periods in time. In the case of our hypothetical study, for example, job satisfaction levels measured at $O_2$ may be greater than those measured at $O_1$ simply because individuals experienced $O_1$.

4. Instrumentation: Here the ability of our measure to accurately index the measured variable changes over time. If, for example, the job satisfaction levels in our hypothetical study had been assessed through interviews, the accuracy with which the interviewer obtains and records satisfaction data may differ between $O_1$ and $O_2$ (some reasons for this were mentioned in chapter 4). Instrumentation problems (as opposed to autonomy changes) might thus be responsible for observed $O_1$-$O_2$ differences.

5. Statistical Regression: If individuals are selected for a treatment because of extreme scores on a pretest[2] that is less than perfectly reliable, it is likely that those with extreme observed scores actually have true scores that are nearer to the mean of the score distribution for all measured subjects. If the individuals with the extreme scores are measured a second time,[3] their observed scores will probably be nearer to that mean. Thus, even though an experimental treatment has no effect on a dependent variable, a group that is treated because of low scores on $O_1$ is likely to have higher scores on $O_2$, and a group that is treated because of high scores on $O_1$ is likely to have lower scores on $O_2$. With respect to our hypothetical study, statistical regression might be responsible for observed $O_1$-$O_2$ satisfaction differences if the individuals exposed to the treatment had been selected for it because they had extremely low (unreliably measured) levels of job satisfaction.

---

[2] A pretest is a measure of a dependent variable that is obtained prior to the time an experimental variable is introduced in a study.

[3] A measure of a dependent variable obtained after the time an experimental variable is introduced is known as a post-test.

6. Selection: If post-test scores for a group that has received some treatment differ from scores on the same variable for a group that has not been treated, the inequality may be due to initial differences that existed between the two groups and not the effects of the treatment. Consider the following example. We perform our hypothetical job redesign study in a company with several similarly organized branches (e.g., different stores in a retail food merchandising chain). Although we would like to randomize branches to treatment and control conditions so as to control extraneous sources of variance, the company has insisted that it will determine the assignment of branches to these conditions. The company has also insisted that no pretest measure be used in the study.

Jobs in branches in the treatment condition are redesigned so as to increase autonomy levels. Jobs in branches in the control condition are left unchanged. A few weeks after the treatment has been administered, job satisfaction levels are measured in both treatment and control branches. The data show that job satisfaction levels are higher in branches in the treatment condition than they are in branches in the control condition. Since, however, branches were not randomly assigned to conditions and we have no pretest measures of job satisfaction, we cannot rule out the hypothesis that differences revealed on the post-test existed all along and that the treatment had no effect on satisfaction.

7. Mortality: Here, observed $O_1$-$O_2$ differences are the results of individuals dropping out of a study between pretest and post-test periods. For example, suppose we did our job redesign study in a single organization and that a one group pretest post-test design is used in the study. Assume also that analysis of the study's data revealed that post-test levels of job satisfaction were higher than pretest levels of the same variable. One possible explanation of this finding is that the treatment worked: that is, increasing job autonomy led to increased job satisfaction. An equally plausible explanation, however, is that those individuals who had low levels of job satisfaction quit their jobs after the pretest, but before the post-test. And because there were fewer individuals with "low" levels of satisfaction completing the post-test than the pretest, the average level of the variable differed between the two periods.

8. Interactive Effects: It is possible that two or more of the above-mentioned phenomena may be responsible for $O_1$-$O_2$ differences. The interested reader should see Campbell (1957), Campbell and Stanley (1966), or Cook and Campbell (1976) for a discussion of such interactive effects.

The eight factors just mentioned are known as threats to the

**94**   *internal validity* of an experiment. An experiment is internally valid

FIGURE 6-1    The Solomon Four Group Experimental Design

| Group A | R* | $O_{1A}$ | X | $O_{2A}$ |
| Group B | R | $O_{1B}$ | | $O_{2B}$ |
| Group C | R | | X | $O_{2C}$ |
| Group D | R | | | $O_{2D}$ |

Time

*Subjects are assumed to have been assigned to groups A, B, C, and D randomly.

when we as researchers are able to conclude that an experimental treatment has indeed had an effect. To reach such a conclusion we must have an experimental design that allows us to rule out the effects of the numerous confounding factors (e.g., history, maturation, testing, etc.) we have just listed and described. One design that allows us to rule out *all* threats to internal validity is shown in figure 6-1. It is known as the Solomon Four Group design. Let's consider this design and its power to rule out rival hypotheses concerning pretest–post-test differences for the treated group.

In figure 6-1 subjects have been randomly assigned to groups A, B, C, and D. Through random assignment we maximize the probability that the various groups will be as equal as possible with respect to all (measured and unmeasured) variables. It is important that groups be as alike as possible at the pretest period since the absence of such equality would leave us in a position of being unable to claim with certainty that our treatment had an effect.

The reader will recall that one objective of research design is to control for the effects of nuisance variables on our dependent variable. The random assignment of subjects to groups getting various combinations of the pretest, treatment, and the post-test is *the most effective* way of controlling such variance.

Having actually randomly assigned individuals to groups A through D, we can test for the effectiveness of this by comparing measures $O_{1A}$ and $O_{2B}$. If these are equal we are reasonably safe in assuming that groups C and D are not dissimilar to groups A and B at the pretest period with respect to the variable under study and other unmeasured variables. Thus the random assignment of individuals to groups A, B, C, and D allows us to rule out selection as a threat to the internal validity of the study.

Note next in figure 6-1 that the four groups get different combinations of the pretest, post-test, and the experimental manipulation.

**95**

FIGURE 6-2    Testing and Treatment Differences for Groups in a Four Group Design

| | | Treatment | |
|---|---|---|---|
| | | Yes | No |
| Pretest | Yes | Group A:<br><br>Experimental Group | Group B:<br><br>Control Group |
| | No | Group C:<br><br>Control Group | Group D:<br><br>Control Group |

Group A receives the pretest, the experimental treatment or manipulation, and the post-test. This group is commonly referred to as either a *treatment group* or an *experimental group*. Groups B, C, and D all get the post-test, but differ from one another and from group A in that none of these other groups gets both the pretest and the treatment. This is shown in figure 6-2.

Groups B, C, and D are used to rule out numerous rival hypotheses that would serve to invalidate the claim that an observed $O_{1A}$-$O_{2A}$ difference is a function of the experimental treatment alone. Because they serve various control purposes in the research design shown in figures 6-1 and 6-2, groups B, C, and D are known as *control groups*. The control function of these various groups is described below.

Group B controls for the history, maturation, testing, instrumentation, regression, selection, and mortality threats to validity. A few examples should suffice to show the logic underlying the use of group B to control for such threats. History is controlled in that if $O_{1B}$ and $O_{2B}$ do not differ from one another it can be asserted that no historical factor influenced the dependent variable. Maturation is also controlled, for if it can be shown that $O_{1B}$ equals $O_{2B}$ then maturation could not have had an impact on the dependent variable. The same logic can be used to rule out several other threats to internal validity (i.e., testing, instrumentation, regression, selection, and mortality).

Group C is used to rule out a threat to validity we have not yet discussed: the interaction of the pretest and the experimental variable. Suppose that we are interested in determining the effectiveness of an advertising campaign aimed at increasing auto seat belt usage. Our research strategy calls for the establishment of a treatment group and three control groups. The design is that shown in figure 6-1. Our pretest is a measure of seat belt usage.

**96**    The treatment is exposure to the advertising campaign. The post-test is a measure of seat belt usage. If the treatment has the hypothesized effect, then an $O_{1A}$-$O_{2A}$ difference should be detected. We should, in addition, find that $O_{2A}$ equals $O_{2C}$ since group C also received the treatment. If we find that $O_{2A}$ is greater (or less) than $O_{2C}$ the reason may be that the pretest interacted with the treatment. That is, taking the pretest somehow sensitized (or desensitized) individuals to the treatment. If this is the case, then the treatment in the absence of the pretest would not have the same effect as the treatment coupled with the pretest. The findings of a study where such pretest-treatment interaction was detected would be of questionable validity. Having control group C in our design allows us to argue that pretest-treatment interaction is not present *if* it can be shown that $O_{2A}$ equals $O_{2C}$.

The interaction of testing and the experimental treatment represents a threat to the *external validity* of an experiment. Briefly stated, an experiment lacks external validity when the findings that result from it cannot be generalized to other subjects, measures, and study conditions.

There are several other threats to external validity that the careful researcher should consider. These include the interaction of selection and the experimental treatment, reactive experimental arrangements, and multiple treatment interference. See Campbell and Stanley (1966) or Cook and Campbell (1976) for detailed discussions of the control procedures required to rule out such threats.

Group D serves a purpose that we mention here without elaboration. Briefly stated, group D allows us to look at whether or not change scores for our experimental group are a function of the combined effects of history and maturation. Full development of the logic underlying the use of the post-test only control group is provided by Solomon (1949, pp. 147–148) and/or Campbell and Stanley (1966, pp. 24–25).

The Solomon Four Group design is a highly effective means for demonstrating that an experimental variable has had a hypothesized effect and that a number of rival hypotheses (selection, maturation, etc.) are not plausible explanations of the observed effect. The high degree of internal validity associated with this design, however, is not achieved without cost. One such "cost" is the need for a large enough number of subjects (i.e., individuals, groups, organizations, etc.) to assign to the four conditions to allow for relatively powerful statistical analyses of the data produced by a study. If there are too few subjects available to enable the use of the Solomon Four Group design and the researcher wants to employ a true (as opposed to a quasi-experimental or nonexperimental) design, an alternative, i.e., the post-test only **97** control group design, should be considered. A diagram of this latter design is shown below:[4]

$$R \quad X \quad O_{I_A}$$
$$R \qquad O_{I_B}$$
$$\overline{\qquad\qquad} \longrightarrow$$
Time

As can be seen in the diagram, this design involves only two groups, a treatment group and a control group. It requires, therefore, only half the number of subjects that are required by the Solomon Four Group design. Moreover, this design controls for all of the previously mentioned threats to internal validity (cf. Campbell & Stanley, 1966, p. 8). It is a very attractive alternative to the Solomon Four Group design.

There are many other true experimental designs than the two just discussed. The interested reader should consult any of a number of excellent sources of information on such other experimental designs.[5]

## True Experiments and Organizational Behavior Research

The reader should note that in order to use any true experimental design we must be in a position to do things such as randomly assign subjects to treatment and control conditions and introduce the treatment variable at an appropriate time. This high degree of control may be possible for studies conducted in the laboratory (especially studies dealing with physical processes using infrahuman subjects). Such control is seldom possible outside of the laboratory. As a consequence, pure experimental studies done in real-world (i.e., field) organizational settings are extremely limited in number.

There are numerous factors which militate against the use of pure experimental designs in organizational research conducted in field settings (cf. Cook & Campbell, 1976). These factors are:

a. Withholding the treatment from no-treatment control groups. Although a researcher may wish to randomly assign subjects to treatment and control conditions and withhold the treatment from those in one or more control groups, it may not be possible to do so for one or more reasons. One is that the organization in which research is being conducted may not consent to there being no-treatment control groups. Another is that the

---

[4] The letter R is used to indicate that subjects have been randomly assigned to conditions.

[5] See, for example, Campbell and Stanley (1966), Edwards (1968), Fisher (1966), Kempthorne (1952), Kirk (1968), and Winer (1962).

use of such groups may be unethical if the treatment is known to have some therapeutic value (see chapter 8).

*b.* Ineffective randomization procedures. The appropriate use of a true experimental design requires that subjects be randomly assigned to treatment and control groups. Randomization procedures, however, are not always effective. One reason for this is that there may be too few subjects associated with a study to allow randomization to be an effective procedure for insuring the pretreatment equality of groups on the study's dependent variable(s). Another reason is that the mechanical procedures used in the randomization process (e.g., drawing names from an urn) may not produce groups that are initially equivalent in terms of a study's dependent variable(s).

*c.* Treatment-related refusals to participate in a planned experiment. Assuming that a researcher has effectively used randomization to establish treatment and control groups that are equivalent at the outset of a study, he or she may still not be able to properly conduct a true experiment. The reason for this is that subjects may refuse to cooperate with the researcher (in terms of receiving a given treatment or keeping themselves isolated from the treatment variable).

*d.* Treatment-related attrition from the experiment. Over the course of a study individuals may differentially drop out of treatment and/or control groups. (This is the experimental mortality problem mentioned earlier in this chapter).

*e.* Heterogeneity in the extent of treatment implementation. Unless treatments are mechanically administered, it may not be possible to insure that all subjects receive the same level of a given treatment. One reason for this is that individuals may unevenly expose themselves to the treatment (e.g., be absent from differing numbers of training sessions in a training program spanning an extended period of time). Another reason is that the individuals in charge of administering a treatment (e.g., organizational managers) may not expose each and every subject in a treatment condition to the same level of the experimental variable.

*f.* Treatment in the no-treatment control condition. In spite of the fact that subjects in control groups are supposed to serve as no-treatment (baseline type) controls, they may not effectively do so. One reason for this is that while these individuals may not be exposed to a study's experimental variable, they receive other types of "treatments." For example, if individuals in control groups know that those in treatment groups are experiencing an "attractive" treatment of some type, they (the controls) may experience a sense of being mistreated or neglected and thus experience a "resentment treatment." **99** *g.* Treatment contamination. The fact that organizational members interact with one another may lead to problems of treatment contamination: a decrease in the "purity" of an experimental treatment caused by individuals in treatment and control conditions interacting with one another.

*h.* Unobtrusive treatment implementation. In some instances the researcher may introduce an experimental variable in such a way that individuals in treatment groups do not realize that they are the subject of an experiment and that they are being observed (see examples cited in chapter 8). In research of this type the researcher faces at least two problems. One is that unobtrusive experimentation results in subjects participating in research without their knowledge and/or consent. It thus raises legal and ethical issues (see chapter 8). Another problem is that it is often difficult, if not impossible, in such research to assess whether or not subjects have experienced the treatment in the fashion the researcher intends (cf. Cook & Campbell, 1976, pp. 307–309 for more on this).

## Quasi-Experimental Designs

As should be clear from material presented in the preceding section, true experiments are generally quite difficult to successfully carry out in field settings. This fact does not doom the researcher to performing studies that are totally devoid of internal validity, since a number of quasi-experimental designs can often be employed in research conducted in real-world organizational settings.

Quasi-experimental designs allow the researcher to control two major factors—who gets measured and when such measurement takes place. They offer a lesser degree of control than experimental designs, which allow the researcher to control the former two factors as well as who gets the experimental treatment and when the treatment is administered.

A number of quasi-experimental designs are introduced and discussed in this section. These include the nonequivalent control group design, the time series design, and the repeated treatment design.[6]

*Nonequivalent control group design.* Assume that a firm has asked you to assess whether allowing lower-level employees to participate in job-related decision making will increase their level of expressed job involvement. The organization has two similarly organized operating units (A and B) which must be kept intact. This means that while it will be possible to randomly assign units

---

[6] There are a number of other quasi-experimental designs that are not dealt with here. The interested reader should see Campbell and Stanley (1966) and Cook and Campbell (1976) for more on such designs.

A and B to treatment and control conditions, it will not be possible to randomly assign employees to each of the units.

Given the constraints facing us, the nonequivalent control group design is a likely candidate for use in our study. A diagram of this design is shown below:[7]

$$\tilde{R} \quad O_{1A} \quad X \quad O_{2A}$$
$$\tilde{R} \quad O_{1B} \qquad O_{2B}$$

Time

Note that this design requires only two groups, a treatment group and a control group. Since the assignment of individuals to these two groups has been nonrandom in nature, pretest values of the dependent variable (i.e., job involvement) are needed. Had subjects been randomly assigned to the two units, the pretreatment measures would not be needed since the units could be assumed to be equivalent on job involvement (as well as other variables).

The nonequivalent control group design allows for the control of several threats to validity (e.g., history, maturation, and testing). A number of threats to validity, however, are left uncontrolled by this design (e.g., interaction of testing and the experimental variable). In spite of the fact that this design is not as effective in dealing with threats to validity as, for example, the post-test only control group design, it is more frequently employed because organizations seldom permit a researcher to randomly assign subjects to treatment and control conditions.

*Time series design.* Assume that you've been asked by a small organization to determine the impact of a yearly bonus on the organizational commitment of the firm's employees. The firm is giving the bonus for the first time. The company's president has indicated that setting up treatment (i.e., bonus) and control (i.e., no bonus) groups will not be possible. As a consequence, you are only in a position to determine when the organizational commitment measure will be administered and who will complete it.

Faced with these constraints, the time series design is a reasonable choice for use in the study. A diagram of this design is shown below:

$$O_1\, O_2\, O_3\, O_4\, O_5\, O_6\, X\, O_7\, O_8\, O_9\, O_{10}\, O_{11}\, O_{12}$$

Time

The design calls for periodic observations of organizational commitment both before and after bonus distribution.

The effect of the bonus would be determined by examining values of the dependent variable prior to and following the in-

---

[7] The $\tilde{R}$ symbol is used to indicate that subjects have not been randomly assigned to groups.   **101**

FIGURE 6-3   Four Possible Outcomes of a Study Employing a Time Series Design

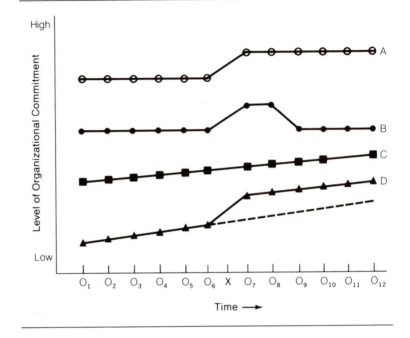

troduction of the experimental variable. Four possible outcomes are shown in figure 6-3.[8] Let's briefly consider how each of these outcomes might be interpreted.[9]

Outcome A in figure 6-3 represents fairly strong evidence that the bonus has had an effect, and that the effect was a lasting one. The average level of organizational commitment was constant prior to the introduction of the bonus, rose markedly after the bonus was introduced, and remained at the higher level for all succeeding observations.

Outcome B again shows that the treatment has had an effect. In this case, however, the effect has endured for only two periods subsequent to the presentation of the treatment.

Outcome C shows no evidence of a treatment effect. Although the level of organizational commitment is higher for post-treatment than for pretreatment periods, the post-treatment values of the variable appear to be nothing more than the result of a general upward trend evident in the pretreatment periods. The post-treatment levels of organizational commitment would have manifested themselves even in the absence of the treatment. Stated somewhat

[8] Other outcomes and their interpretation are covered in Campbell and Stanley (1966) and Cook and Campbell (1976).

[9] For more extensive coverage of the interpretations associated with these outcomes see Campbell and Stanley (1966) and Cook and Campbell (1976).

differently, the post-treatment levels of the variable could be perfectly predicted by a knowledge of pretreatment levels.

Finally, outcome D shows evidence of a treatment effect. Although there is a general upward trend in the level of organizational commitment for both pre- and post-treatment periods, the post-treatment levels are higher than the levels that would have been seen had the treatment not been introduced. In the absence of the treatment the levels of organizational commitment for periods 7 through 12 probably would have fallen along the dashed line. Since the actual post-treatment values are well above the dashed line, it is reasonably safe to conclude that the treatment has had an effect.

The time series design allows for the control of several different threats to validity (e.g., maturation, testing, regression, selection, and mortality). Other threats (e.g., history and instrumentation) are uncontrolled or poorly controlled by this design.

The reader should note that the time series design is an example of what is commonly called longitudinal research (cf., for example, Campbell & Stanley, 1966, and Helmstadter, 1970). In longitudinal studies data are collected from study participants over several time periods in an attempt to assess changes in levels of measured variables.

*Repeated treatment design.* Assume that you are faced with the assignment of determining whether or not periodic, unexpected telephone calls to individuals working as observers of a production process (e.g., individuals monitoring a gasoline production process) increase the alertness levels of such individuals. Only one work unit is available for study. In addition, the nature of the work done by the unit precludes the creation of treatment and control groups. Moreover, the effects of the telephone calls on alertness levels are assumed to be transitory (i.e., of brief duration).

The constraints facing you rule out the use of a pure experimental design. They also preclude the use of a number of quasi-experimental designs (e.g., the nonequivalent control group design) and make the use of others (e.g., the time series design) less than ideal. Faced with these constraints a viable design for use in the research is the repeated treatment design (cf. Cook & Campbell, 1976). A diagram of this design is shown below:

$$O_1 \ X \ O_2 \qquad O_3 \ X \ O_4$$
Time

The design calls for two or more cycles in which a pretest is followed by a treatment and a post-test. To the extent that the researcher can show that (a) $O_1$ differs from $O_2$, (b) $O_3$ differs **103** from $O_4$, and (c) these two differences are in the same direction, the results of a study employing this design can be interpreted as tentative evidence that the treatment has had an effect. (See Cook & Campbell, 1976, for an enumeration of factors threatening the validity of conclusions based upon research employing this design.)

## Nonexperimental Designs

The final group of designs that will be considered in this chapter is the nonexperimental or ex post facto design. In ex post facto research the investigator has virtually no control over the study's independent variable(s). Two factors may be responsible for this lack of control. First, the independent variable(s) may act upon a study's subjects before the investigator is in a position to determine who will get the treatment and when they will get it. For example, a researcher studying industrial accidents generally has no control over who will have an accident on the job and when the accident will happen. In addition, the researcher has little or no relevant pretest data on those who have accidents.

Second, the study's independent variable may not be manipulable. For example, a researcher concerned with male-female differences in absenteeism in a certain organization must take the study's participants as they come. The study's independent variable (sex or gender) cannot be manipulated by the researcher. As a second example, consider the situation confronting a researcher interested in determining what impact, if any, variations along some personality dimension have for job and organizational choice. Here again, the researcher has no control over the study's independent variable.

In nonexperimental studies the investigator concomitantly measures both the independent and the dependent variables. If the two are found to be related to one another, the conclusion that the "independent" variable is responsible for changes in the "dependent" variable is often advanced. Since the researcher often knows little or nothing about numerous other variables that may be impacting upon either or both of the study's "independent" and "dependent" variables, the conclusion of a causal relationship between the two is *totally unjustified*.

Nonexperimental research generally takes two forms: (a) the cross-sectional study and (b) the correlational study. These are briefly described below.

*Cross-Sectional Studies.* In cross-sectional research the investigator compares scores on the study's dependent variable(s) for groups that the researcher *assumes* have been differentially exposed to the study's independent variable(s). For example, a number of previous research efforts (e.g. Lenski, 1963) have sought to determine whether or not Catholics differ from Protestants on work-related values, occupational situs, educational attainment, and a number of other variables. Any detected differences may or may not be attributable to the study's "independent" variable (i.e., religious preference), since the researcher has no idea how the groups may differ apart from religious preference.

This example should serve to make the logic of a cross-sectional study clear. There are, of course, a vast number of other examples of cross-sectional studies that might have been mentioned here. Inherent in all such studies is the problem of lack of control over independent variables. As a consequence, statements about causal relationships between independent and dependent variables cannot be safely made.

*Correlational Studies.* In correlational research the investigator obtains data on the study's independent and dependent variables. These data are then used to assess strength of relationship between the two variables. (The Pearson product-moment correlation coefficient [r] is one commonly used index of association.)

Let us look at a couple of examples of correlational research. One relationship that has been examined extensively in the past using a correlational strategy is that between job satisfaction and job performance (for reviews see Brayfield & Crockett, 1955; Schwab & Cummings, 1970). A number of studies have shown that job performance is positively related to job satisfaction. (All studies have not shown such a relationship.) From the observed relationship it was often argued that satisfaction causes performance (see Schwab & Cummings, 1970). This argument has been shown to have little support. In fact, studies using experimental designs have shown support for the hypothesis that performance causes satisfaction—especially when rewards are contingent on performance (see, for example, Cherrington, Reitz, & Scott, 1971; and Staw, 1975).

As a second example, consider the hypothesis that "considerate leader behavior" causes increases in subordinate performance. This was once a popular hypothesis and correlational research was often used to support the hypothesis (e.g., Katz, Maccoby, Gurin, & Floor, 1951). Research studies using experimental designs have shown an equally plausible rival hypothesis—that leaders will increase their "considerate behavior" when employees show "high levels of performance" (see Lowin & Craig, 1968).

It should be obvious from these two examples that correlation alone cannot be used to support arguments of causality: that is, just because two variables can be shown to be related to one another, the argument that one causes the other is not justified. **105**

If, for example, we're dealing with an observed correlation between variables x and y, it is possible that: (*a*) x causes y, (*b*) y causes x, (*c*) both x and y are determined by one or more other variables, or (*d*) x and y reciprocally influence each other.

An observed relationship between x and y allows us no basis for making statements about causality; it also leaves us in a position of not being able to assert that the observed relationship is a legitimate one (i.e., one not resulting from the effects of one or more other variables). Consider the following example. A researcher collects from members of a large work organization data on coffee consumption and the incidence of heart disease. The sample consists of workers at several job levels (operatives, semi-skilled workers, skilled workers, first-level supervisors, etc.) in the organization. A correlational analysis (cf. the Statistical Methods Appendix) reveals that coffee consumption and incidence of heart disease are highly related to one another. On the basis of this evidence the investigator argues that coffee consumption *causes* heart disease. The model is:

One of a number of equally plausible rival hypotheses that the researcher may not have considered is that the relationship between coffee consumption and heart disease is spurious. The observed correlation between these two variables exists only because of relationships that coffee consumption and heart disease share with a third variable, job level. To be more specific, as job level increases: (*a*) access to coffee, and thus the amount of coffee consumed increases, and (*b*) job stress increases, thus the incidence of heart disease increases. Viewed diagrammatically:

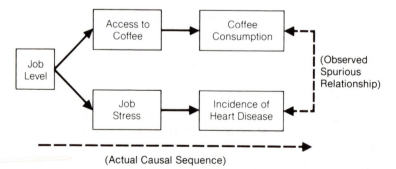

The *true* causal relationships might be as pictured here. The rela-
**106** tionship we detected in the study (i.e., one between coffee

consumption and heart disease) may be *spurious*. That is, if we somehow controlled for job level or job stress, the observed relationship between coffee consumption and heart disease would vanish.

FIGURE 6-4    Observed Relationship Between Coffee Consumption and Heart Disease

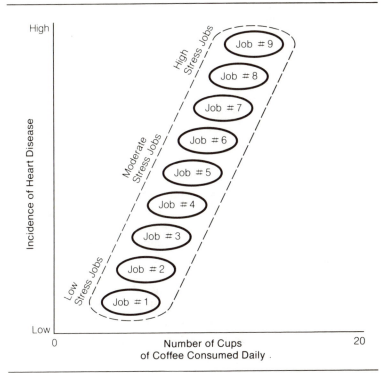

Figure 6-4 shows this clearly. Each of the small ellipses shows data points for one job. Moving upward and to the right in the diagram takes us from jobs that are low on level (and thus on stress) to jobs that are high on level (and high on stress). When we look at all jobs simultaneously we can see that numbers of cups of coffee and incidence of heart disease are related to one another. When, however, we control for job level (e.g., by looking at the coffee-disease relationship on a within-job basis), the relationship vanishes.

The examples given above suggest the weaknesses that accompany ex post facto research designs. In view of these weaknesses, we recommend that stronger, more experimentally oriented designs be employed when and where possible. If the contraints facing a researcher preclude the use of an experimental or a quasi-experimental design then the researcher should plan **107** to collect data on not only what he considers to be the study's independent and dependent variables, but also on numerous other, possibly confounding, variables as well. The researcher who uses an ex post facto or nonexperimental design must be in a position to rule out numerous rival hypotheses for any relationship he or she uncovers. Data on potential confounding or nuisance variables are critical in ruling out such competing hypotheses. Such data allow us to hold constant, through various means, the effects of measured, potentially confounding variables.

Note, however, that in the case of ex post facto research we are only able to rule out competing hypotheses associated with potentially confounding variables that we've measured. We have no idea as to how numerous other unmeasured variables may be influencing our results. In sum, nonexperimental studies leave us in the uncomfortable position of not being able to state with any degree of certainty whether two variables are causally related to one another *or* whether an observed relationship between two variables is a legitimate one (i.e., not spurious).[10]

In spite of the weaknesses of nonexperimental research, this type of study strategy has been and continues to be widely used in organizational research. Such studies help to extend our knowledge about human behavior in organizations in several ways. First, ex post facto studies may result in hypotheses that can be tested in a more rigorous fashion (i.e., quasi-experimental and experimental research). Second, the findings of experimental studies are made more credible to the extent that they can be corroborated in less rigorously controlled field research. Third, and finally, in many instances we cannot manipulate independent variables. If we relied exclusively on experimental and quasi-experimental research for generating knowledge, numerous important relationships uncovered in the behavioral, biological, and physical sciences would not be a part of the current body of knowledge.

## INTERNAL AND EXTERNAL VALIDITY

Internal validity was discussed at an earlier point in this chapter. We pointed out that in considering whether or not a study has internal validity one is, in effect, asking the question, "Did the study's treatment variable have the hypothesized effect?" This is an important consideration in any study. An equally important consideration is external validity. A given study has external validity

---

[10] It should, however, be noted that there are techniques (e.g., cross-lagged correlation and path analysis) that allow one to examine the plausability of causal connections among variables using data from non-experimental research. For more on these techniques and problems with their use see Asher (1976), Blalock (1964, 1971), Blalock and Blalock (1968), Duncan (1966, 1969), Feldman (1975), Heise (1969), Kenny (1975), Kerlinger and Pedhazur (1973), Pelz and Andrews (1964), Rozelle and Campbell (1969), and Simon (1954).

to the extent that its results are generalizable beyond the measures, subjects, and other conditions associated with the study. Let's look at each of these factors in greater detail.

First, if a study has external validity its findings should be obtained if different measures of the variables under study are used. One popular theory of job satisfaction (Herzberg, Mausner, & Snyderman, 1959) has come under fire recently. One reason for this is that the findings reported by Herzberg and his associates could not be replicated when measures different from those used in the original study were employed (see House & Wigdor, 1967; King, 1970).

Second, if a study has external validity then the results demonstrated for one set of subjects should be generalizable to other sets of subjects. To the extent that a study's subjects represent a random sample of any one population (e.g., male, blue-collar workers in the United States), the results of a study employing these subjects should generalize to at least the associated population. If the study's findings have a high degree of external validity we might expect the findings to be reproducible with samples from other populations (e.g., female, white-collar workers in the United States). The greater the diversity of subject populations to which our findings generalize, the greater the study's external validity.

Third, if a study has external validity, then its findings should be reproducible in various settings. For example, if in a laboratory setting (cf. chapter 7) we detect a positive relationship between the amount of an incentive offered study participants and the amount of effort they exert on a task, the same relationship should be capable of being established in an actual organizational setting. To the extent that a relationship uncovered in one setting holds in various other settings in which it is tested, the findings of the study have external validity.

Fourth, and finally, for a study to have external validity the strength and range of variables associated with the study should approximate the strength and range of variables in other "situations" to which the study's results are to be generalized. Consider, for example, the relationship between activation level (i.e., general level of arousal of a person) and task performance shown in figure 6-5. As the level of activation increases, task performance increases in a near linear fashion between points a and b, increases more slowly thereafter until it reaches a maximum at c, falls slowly between points c and d, and decreases in a near linear fashion between points d and e.

If the range of activation associated with a study extended only from a to b, but the range of the same variable extended from a to e in a setting to which the study's results were to be generalized (i.e., the criterion setting), the study would lack exter- **109**

FIGURE 6-5   Hypothesized Relationship Between Activation Level and Task
Performance

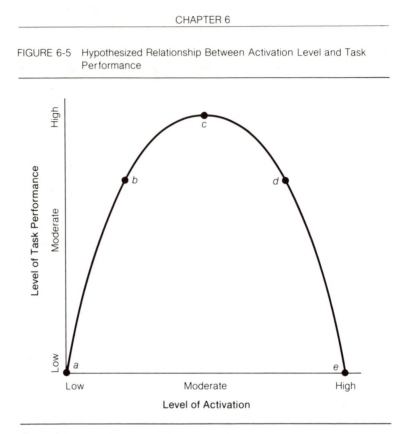

nal validity. A study would similarly lack external validity whenever the strength and range of variables connected with it were unlike the strength and range of the variables in the criterion setting.

The reader should note that for a study to have external validity it must be internally valid. As Campbell and Stanley (1966) have put it, "*internal validity* is the *sine qua non* of research design" (p. 5).

# EMPIRICAL RESEARCH STRATEGIES 7

In previous chapters dealing with various aspects of the research process we alluded to a number of strategies a researcher might employ in studying a phenomenon. In chapter 6, for example, it was noted that the impact of a job design change could be assessed through experimental or nonexperimental means. If our concern is simply to examine whether job autonomy and job satisfaction are related to one another, a nonexperimental study could be conducted. If, on the other hand, our concern is with assessing whether changes in job autonomy *cause* changes in job satisfaction, then an experimental or quasi-experimental design would be appropriate.

## DIMENSIONS ALONG WHICH STRATEGIES DIFFER

While the experimental, quasi-experimental, and nonexperimental designations are useful ones, they tell us little or nothing about a number of other dimensions along which research strategies differ from one another. These include:[1]

*a. Naturalness of the Research Setting.* In some instances the phenomenon of interest is studied in the setting where it occurs naturally. Roethlisberger and Dickson (1939), for example, studied the impact of a number of variables (level of illumination, length of workday, etc.) on worker productivity by manipulating these variables in an actual factory.

---

[1] These dimensions were derived from such sources as Helmstadter (1970), Runkel and McGrath (1972), and Selltiz, Wrightsman, and Cook (1976).

In other instances the phenomenon of interest is studied in a setting that has been created specifically for the research in question. Lowin and Craig (1968), for example, studied the influence of subordinate productivity on managerial behavior in a simulated work environment. The "subordinates" were actually confederates of the researchers, while the "supervisors" were college students who had been recruited for a "part-time" temporary supervisory position.

In still other instances the phenomenon of interest is assumed to be relatively independent of the setting in which it is studied. A researcher concerned with the ability of individuals to solve simple algebra problems could assess this in classrooms, homes, offices, etc. The setting in which the individual performs the work should not greatly influence performance at the task.

*b. Generalizability.* In some cases a researcher is more interested in demonstrating the existence of a phenomenon than in generalizing a study's results to any particular population. Stone and Porter (1975), for example, studied relationships among job characteristics and job attitudes among employees of a telephone company. The concern of the researchers was the degree to which individuals' job attitudes differed systematically across various jobs—not with the degree to which the observed relationships were common to all organizational roles and role incumbents.

In other cases the intent of the researcher is to obtain data relevant to some phenomenon from a subset (i.e., sample) of some population in such a way as to enable subsequent generalizations about the population to be made from the sample data. National studies of job satisfaction by the Survey Research Center of the University of Michigan (e.g., Quinn, Seashore, Kahn, Mangione, Campbell, Staines, & McCullough, 1971) are conducted with this generalizability criterion in mind.

*c. Control.* To the extent that a researcher is interested in demonstrating causal relationship between or among variables he or she must have control over independent and nuisance variables that impact upon a study's dependent variable(s). Some settings allow the researcher to tightly control factors that may have an influence on a study's dependent variable(s). A study by Lowin and Craig (1968) is an example. In this study the independent variable, "subordinate" behavior, was systematically varied to determine its impact on various aspects of leader behavior.

Other settings allow the researcher some degree of control over independent variables and little or no control over nuisance variables. An example is a job redesign experiment conducted by Lawler, Hackman, and Kaufman (1973). In this study Lawler et al. experimentally varied the job characteristics of toll and directory assistance operators employed by a New England telephone company. Interest centered upon the extent to which these changes would impact upon several dependent variables (job satisfaction, satisfaction with supervision, etc.). Nuisance variables (e.g., reactions of supervisors to the job changes) were beyond the direct control of the investigators.

Still other studies allow no control over independent, nuisance, and dependent variables. The researcher is limited to the measurement of what are presumed to be independent, nuisance, and dependent variables. A study by Stone (1976) is an example of such research. In this study data on job characteristics, work-related values, satisfaction with the work itself, etc., were collected (via questionnaire) from individuals in a variety of nonmanagerial jobs. None of the study's variables was actually manipulated by the researcher. Instead the researcher assumed that study participants provided valid data on job characteristics, work-related values, etc.

*d. Artifacts.* At times the values of a study's dependent variables are influenced either in part or totally by the researcher's methodology instead of by a study's measured or manipulated independent variables. The confounding of methodological factors with a study's independent variables results in systematic sources of error known as "artifacts." Among the artifacts that may confound a study's results are experimenter expectancy effects, demand characteristics, and evaluation apprehension.[2]

The experimenter's hypotheses represent expectations about the outcomes of a study. These expectations may influence relationships between the researcher and the subjects of a study in such a way as to lead subjects to behave so as to confirm the researcher's hyphotheses.[3] The by-products of such expectations are known as *experimenter expectancy effects*.

Demand characteristics are a second source of confounding effects. *Demand characteristics* in a study are those factors which lead the subject to behave in ways they perceive they are expected to behave.[4] Often subjects attempt to intuit the researcher's hypotheses and behave in such a way as to confirm them. The motivation to behave so as to confirm the researcher's hypotheses is thought to stem from the desire to appear as a "good subject," i.e., one who provides data that will aid the scientist and science. It should be noted here that not all persons are motivated to appear

---

[2] For more on the general issue of artifacts see Carlsmith, Ellsworth, and Aronson (1976), Cook and Campbell (1976), Fromkin and Streufert (1976), and Webb, Campbell, Schwartz, and Sechrest (1966).

[3] Issues associated with experimenter expectancy effects are more fully covered in such works as McGuigan (1963), Rosenthal (1963, 1964, 1966, 1976), and Rosenthal and Rosnow (1969).

[4] For additional information on demand characteristics see Orne (1962), Sigall, Aronson, and Van Hoose (1970), Weber and Cook (1972), Cook and Campbell (1976), and Fromkin and Streufert (1976).

as "good subjects." Some subjects may intentionally behave so as to disconfirm the researcher's hypotheses.[5]

The third artifactual variable that may influence a study's results is evaluation apprehension. *Evaluation apprehension* leads the study participant to behave in such a way as to cause the researcher to evaluate him or her favorably: The subject attempts to appear intelligent, psychologically healthy, normal, mature, etc.

Different research strategies lead to varying degrees of contamination of a study's results by these artifacts. The laboratory experiment has been singled out by many writers as a strategy that is accompanied by high levels of these artifacts. As has been noted elsewhere (Fromkin & Streufert, 1976), however, *all* research strategies are subject to the influence of evaluation apprehension, demand characteristics, and experimenter expectancy effects.

*e. Study Induced Changes in the Researcher.* Various study strategies call for differing degrees of contact between the researcher and the system being studied. To the extent that a research strategy requires the investigator to maintain prolonged contact with a studied system, his or her objectivity in studying the system may suffer. Some research strategies (e.g., the case study and the field experiment) would appear to be more subject to this problem than other strategies (e.g., the laboratory experiment or the sample survey).

*f. Strength and Range of Studied Variables.* The strength of variables is *generally* greater in naturally occurring settings than in contrived settings. For example, the level of role-related stress found in "real-world" settings (studied by field study and sample survey strategies) is much greater than the level of stress that might be induced by the actions of a researcher studying this phenomenon in a contrived setting (e.g., a laboratory experiment or a simulation).

Not only are variables generally stronger in naturally occurring settings than in those created for research purposes, but the range of most variables is greater in the former as opposed to the latter settings. A researcher interested in assessing the impact of task characteristics on worker attitudes, for example, would probably find a much greater range of task characteristics if naturally occurring work organizations were studied (e.g., using a field study strategy) than if task characteristics were studied in a researcher-created setting (e.g., using a simulation strategy).

The greater range of variables associated with some strategies has implications for the degree of relationship a researcher is likely to find between any two studied variables. As was pointed out

[5] See, for example, Carlsmith et al. (1976), Fromkin and Streufert (1976), and Orne (1962).

in chapter 3, the size of the correlation coefficient (as well as other measures of association) is lawfully related to the ranges of the variables being correlated; all else equal, the greater the range of two variables the stronger will be the relationship between them.

*g. Costs.* Research strategies differ greatly in terms of costs. There are two types of costs that merit consideration: (1) the initial costs of "setting up" a study, and (2) the managerial costs of collecting data from each study participant. In some cases (e.g., sample surveys) both the set-up cost and the cost of additional observations may be high (especially when interviews are the source of data). In other cases (e.g., laboratory experiments) both set-up and marginal data collection costs may be quite low.

## COMPARISON OF RESEARCH STRATEGIES

Table 7-1 lists a number of dimensions along which research strategies vary. Also shown in the table are ratings of six research strategies on these dimensions. It should be noted that the ratings should be considered only rough approximations of the actual standing of each strategy vis-à-vis the rated dimensions. It should also be noted that no single strategy has "favorable" ratings on all dimensions. The implication of this latter point is that in deciding to use one research strategy as opposed to others, the researcher always makes trade-offs: the selection of a strategy that maximizes naturalness of the research setting entials a loss of control over independent and confounding variables; the selection of a strategy that allows for rigorous control over confounding variables entails a concomitant loss in the generality of a study's findings, etc. The choice of one strategy as opposed to another at any given stage in the study of some phenomenon (formulation of hypotheses, testing of hypotheses, establishing the external validity of a detected relationship, etc.) should be guided by the purpose of the research, the resources available to the researcher, and other considerations that are addressed in chapters 6 and 8. In the following sections the six research strategies listed in table 7-1 are discussed.[6] Coverage of each strategy includes (a) a brief review of an empirical study that employed the strategy in the investigation of some phenomenon, (b) a description of major characteristics of the strategy, and (c) a representative listing of advantages and disadvantages commonly associated with the use of the strategy.

---

[6] Research strategies covered in this chapter are limited to those that deal with the collection of empirical data from human subjects; nonempirical strategies (e.g., library research and computer simulations) are not considered.

TABLE 7-1　Comparison of Empirical Research Strategies*

| Rated Dimension | Laboratory Experiment | Simulation | Field Experiment | Field Study | Sample Survey | Case Study |
|---|---|---|---|---|---|---|
| *COST:* | | | | | | |
| Initial "Set-up" | M | L-H | M-H | M-H | H | L-H |
| Marginal Cost per Subject | L | L-H | M | M | L-M | L-H |
| *VARIABLES:* | | | | | | |
| Strength of Independent Variables | L | L-M | M | H | H | H |
| Range of Variables | L | M | M | H | H | L-H |
| Potential to Manipulate Independent Variables | H | M-H | M | N | N | N |
| *CONTROL:* | | | | | | |
| Potential for Testing Causal Hypotheses | H | M-H | M | L | L | N |
| Potential for Study to Change Researcher | L | L | M | M | L | H |
| Potential for Controlling Confounding Variables | H | M-H | L-M | L | L | N |
| *ARTIFACTS:* | | | | | | |
| Potential for Experimenter Expectancy Effects | H | M | M-H | M | L | H |
| Potential for Demand Characteristics | H | M | M-H | M | L | H |
| Potential for Evaluation Apprehension | H | M-H | M-H | M | L | H |
| *SETTING:* | | | | | | |
| Naturalness of Setting | L | M-H | H | H | H | H |
| Degree to which Behavior Is Setting-Dependent | H | L-M | H | H | L | H |
| *GENERALIZABILITY:* | | | | | | |
| Applicability of Study's Results to Different Populations | L-H | L-H | L | L | H | N |

*N: None　　L: Low　　M: Moderate　　H: High

## SPECIFIC EMPIRICAL RESEARCH STRATEGIES

### Laboratory Experiments

*An Example of the Strategy's Use.* Staw (1975), after examining numerous correlational studies relating organizational attributes to member performance levels, reasoned that the results of such studies might just as well be accounted for by the explanation that knowledge of performance causes systematic changes in perceived organizational attributes as by the explanation that these attributes cause systematic changes in performance. That is, "questionnaire measures [of individual, group, and organizational characteristics] considered by organizational researchers to be

**116**

indicators of the determinants of performance, may actually constitute the consequences of performance" (p. 417).

To examine the validity of the "performance causes differential attributions" hypothesis, Staw randomly assigned 60 students to groups of three. Each group was asked to participate in a "Financial Puzzle Task." Data on the financial history of a firm (1965-1969) were given to each group. Group members were then given 30 minutes to study these data, hold discussions, and prepare group estimates of the firm's sales and earnings per share for the year 1970.

After each group had generated its estimates, Staw randomly assigned them one of two types of performance feedback: (a) the group had done "quite well" since the sales figure was only off by $10,000, the earnings estimate was accurate within $.05 per share, and the group's performance was in the top 20% of three-person groups that had previously made the required estimates; or (b) the group had "not done too well" since the sales estimate was off by $10,000,000, the earnings estimate was off by $1.00 per share, and the group's performance was in the bottom 20% of three-person groups that had previously made the required estimates.

Performance feedback (high vs. low) was the manipulated independent variable in this study. Because subjects had been randomly assigned to groups and the groups had been randomly assigned to the "high" and "low" performance feedback conditions, Staw was relatively confident that the only variable that differed between "high" and "low" groups was performance feedback.

To assess whether differences in such feedback influenced self reports of individual, group, and organizational attributes Staw had group members complete questionnaire measures of cohesiveness, influence, communication, task conflict, openness to change, satisfaction, motivation, ability, and role clarity. These measures were completed *after* subjects had been given the "false" feedback on their performance.

The study's results showed that while actual performance levels of the two groups did not differ, those who had been assigned "high" as opposed to "low" performance feedback had higher scores on the self-report type measures of ability, cohesiveness, influence, communication, and openness to change, motivation, satisfaction, and role clarity. Staw concluded that the study's results provided support for the notion that "individuals attribute one set of characteristics to a work group they believe is effective and another, different set of characteristics to an ineffective work group" (p. 424). This conclusion appears well justified by the study's results. **117**

*Description of the Strategy.* A laboratory experiment is a re-search strategy characterized by the following attributes: *(a)* the researcher creates a setting for the study of some phenomenon; *(b)* the experimenter has control over the assignment of experimental subjects to treatment and control conditions (cf. chapter 6); *(c)* the experimenter has control over virtually all independent variables that may have an impact on the dependent variable; and *(d)* the experimenter manipulates one or more independent variables of interest.[7] Each of these points is more fully developed below.

Laboratory experiments take place in laboratories as opposed to organizations or other naturally occurring systems. A laboratory may be defined as any setting in which the experimenter has a high degree of control over the stimuli to which experimental subjects are exposed and the conditions associated with the observation of behavior (Zelditch & Hopkins, 1961). In creating this setting the experimenter's objective is not to duplicate some naturally occurring behavioral system (e.g., a work organization), but rather to highlight selected aspects of such a system (Runkel & McGrath, 1972). In the study by Staw (1975), for example, it was not necessary to create an entire work organization to study the hypothesis that feedback about performance influences self reports of individual, group, and organizational attributes. It was, however, vital that the laboratory environment approximate certain aspects of a naturally occurring organization (allow individuals to perform a task, provide them with performance feedback, etc.). Processes that would be found in work organizations (e.g., performance feedback and attitude measurement) were as characteristic of the experimental setting as they were of some actual organizational settings.

Stated somewhat differently, a laboratory experiment should be designed so as to mirror one or more conditions found in some criterion setting and to have none of the features that would never be found in the criterion setting (Fromkin & Streufert, 1976). A criterion setting is one for which the results of our research are assumed to have relevance. In the case of the study by Staw the criterion setting would be any naturally occurring organization where performance-attitude relationships are studied.

In the laboratory experiment the experimenter has control over the assignment of subjects to treatment and control conditions. It was noted earlier (cf. chapter 6) that the most effective method for minimizing the effects of nuisance variables is the random assignment of subjects to various groups associated with a study's design. Since the experimenter has control over the assignment

[7] See Carlsmith et al. (1976), Fromkin and Streufert (1976), and Runkel and McGrath (1972).

of subjects, the minimization of nuisance variable variance is better accomplished with laboratory experiments than with any other research strategy. It should, however, be noted that it is *impossible* to design an experiment in which no variables other than the manipulated independent variables affect the experiment's results (Carlsmith et al., 1976). At best, the influence of nuisance (confounding) variables can be held to a minimum through adequate experimental design.

In laboratory experiments the researcher manipulates one or more independent variables while controlling for the effects of virtually all other independent variables. In the study by Staw "level of performance" for each group was manipulated by the assignment of either "high" or "low" performance feedback. And because of the randomization of subjects to groups and feedback to groups the experimenter was relatively safe in assuming that performance feedback was the only variable that could have influenced the self-report measures of individual, group, and organizational attributes.

*Advantages and Disadvantages of the Strategy.* As is the case with all research strategies, laboratory experiments have both advantages and disadvantages. Among the advantages of laboratory experiments are:

a. Measurement is generally more precise with laboratory experiments than with other research strategies because measurement in the laboratory takes place under highly controlled conditions. This minimizes the degree of error variance in measures (caused by such factors as filling out the questionnaires in environments with many distractions) and minimizes the extent to which the systematic variance of confounding variables influences our measures.

b. Causality can be inferred from the results of a laboratory experiment since threats to internal validity can be reduced or eliminated through the use of control groups (cf. chapter 6).

c. The experimenter controls the assignment of subjects to treatment and control conditions.

d. The independent variable(s) of a study can be precisely and unambiguously defined by the experimenter through the manipulations used to produce them.

e. Laboratory experiments can be replicated (i.e., results of one study reproduced in a later study) because experimenters other than the one first reporting an experiment's results can, with generally little difficulty, closely approximate the laboratory setting, manipulations, measures, etc., of a study they are attempting to replicate.

Among the disadvantages of laboratory experiments are:[8]

a. Some phenomena cannot be studied in the laboratory (e.g., natural disasters and the behavior that accompanies them).

---

[8] See Festinger (1953), Fromkin and Streufert (1976), and Weick (1967).

b. A number of variables cannot be manipulated by experimenters (age, race, intelligence, etc.).

c. There are ethical and moral concerns with the manipulations associated with some experiments (i.e., subjects may experience psychological and / or physical harm).

d. The generality (i.e., external validity) of results produced through laboratory experimentation may be limited, that is, the range of criterion settings may be restricted.[9]

e. A number of artifacts (i.e., demand characteristics, evaluation apprehension, and experimenter expectancy effects) may influence the results obtained from laboratory experiments.

f. Laboratory settings may lack ''realism'' (i.e., a high degree of correspondence between the laboratory setting and naturally occurring organizational settings).

g. The strength of independent variables produced by experimental manipulations is, in general, very low when compared to the strength of these same variables in ''real-life'' situations.

h. It is difficult to successfully manipulate more than three or four independent variables in any given experiment.

i. Performing laboratory experiments successfully requires highly skilled and creative experimenters (in Weick's [1967] term, ''artisans'').

j. Subjects may substitute their own tasks for those they are asked to perform by the experimenter.

k. An independent variable that is shown, through laboratory experimentation, to influence a dependent variable may have little or no impact on the same variable in a field setting because the independent variable may have little or no prominence in a setting where a myriad of other independent variables impact upon subjects.

l. Subjects may react more to the perceived harm (e.g., esteem losses and degradation) that accompanies some experimental manipulations than they do to the study's real independent variable(s).

## Simulation[10]

*An example of the strategy's use.* The behavior of inmates and guards in penal institutions might be viewed from two perspectives. One is what Haney, Banks, and Zimbardo (1973) refer to as a dispositional hypothesis: the state of prisons is a function of *(a)*

---

[9] Some critics of laboratory experimentation take the position that the findings of laboratory experiments are totally devoid of external validity and are not in general relevant to the solution of real-world problems. We reject this rather extreme view in favor of the position expressed by Fromkin and Streufert (1976) that instead of laboratory experiments never or seldom yielding data relevant to the solution of real-world problems, such studies *''merely impose identifiable limitations upon the range of criterion situations to which a particular set of laboratory findings may be applied''* (p. 442).

The interested reader should consult Fromkin and Streufert (1976) and Weick (1967) for more on the defense of laboratory experimentation as a mode of solving ''real-world'' problems.

[10] The presentation associated with the simulation strategy is limited to those studies in which human behavior (as opposed to computer-simulated behavior) is the focus. Those interested in computer simulation of individual, group, and organizational behavior should consult such sources as Abelson (1968), Borko (1962), Cohen and Cyert (1965), Green (1963), Roby (1967), and Tompkins and Messick (1963).

the nature of prison inmates, (b) the nature of prison administrators, or (c) the nature of both inmates and administrators. The second perspective is what Haney et al. term a situational hypothesis: the state of prisons is a function of the organizational environments of inmates and administrators. An individual subscribing to the former view would argue that "prison reform" is difficult, if not impossible, since the basic nature of inmates and administrators is relatively fixed. On the other hand, a person subscribing to the second explanation would reason that if we wish to change the behavior of inmates and administrators (in bringing about reform) then the environment of prisons should be changed.

Haney et al. wanted to assess the validity of the situational hypothesis. In order to do so they planned an investigation in which a simulated prison setting would be used to study the behavior of individuals functioning in the roles of either "inmate" or "guard." The researchers chose a simulated (rather than an actual) prison setting because a simulation would allow them to randomly assign study participants to guard or inmate roles. The researchers felt it critical to have the inmates and guards as comparable to one another and as "psychologically healthy" as possible at the outset of the simulation. Had the study been done in an actual prison, environmental effects would be confounded with "chronic characteristics" of inmates and guards.

The investigators built a prison-like complex in a basement corridor of the psychology building at Stanford University. The "prison" had actual cells, a room for solitary confinement of inmates, living quarters for guards, and other features aimed at making it approximate as closely as possible a real prison. Subjects were recruited for the study by a newspaper advertisement calling for male volunteers to participate in a psychological study of prison life. They were informed that the pay was $15 per day and that the study would last about two weeks. Of 75 individuals who responded to the advertisement 22 were ultimately selected for participation in the study. The researchers randomly assigned half the subjects the guard role and the other half the role of inmate. Inmates were actually arrested (at their homes) by officers from a local police department, accused of a crime, booked, and finally transported (while blindfolded) to the simulated prison. Upon arriving at the prison the inmates were issued numbered smocks, minimal toilet supplies, assigned to cells, etc. They encountered uniformed guards who carried wooden nightsticks and had a great deal of control over the activities of inmates. The prisoners remained in the simulated prison for the duration of the experiment. The guards worked eight-hour shifts and were free to leave the prison at the end of each shift. **121**

Data were collected by a number of means (i.e., videotaping, audio recording, questionnaires, and personal observation) on *(a)* transactions between and among the inmates and guards, *(b)* affective responses to the prison environment, and *(c)* a number of other dependent variables.

Results of the study showed that the simulated prison environment had a "great impact upon the affective states of both guards and prisoners as well as upon the interpersonal processes between and within those role-groups" (p. 80). In the case of prisoners, for example, it was found that self-evaluations deteriorated, intentions to do harm to others increased, emotional depression set in, and responses to others were marked by passiveness. With respect to the guards it was found that commands pervaded verbal interchanges with prisoners, aggressiveness toward inmates (e.g., verbal affronts) was frequent, and inmates were generally treated in an impersonal fashion. Haney et al. concluded that "the negative, antisocial reactions observed [in the behavior of inmates and guards] were not the product of an environment created by combining a collection of deviant personalities [such as might characterize a real prison system] but rather the result of an intrinsically pathological situation which could distort and rechannel the behavior of essentially normal individuals. The abnormality here clearly resided in the psychological nature of the situation and not in those who passed through it" (p. 90). Stated somewhat differently, the researchers contended that the results of their study showed support for the "situational hypothesis."

*Description of the Strategy.* Simulations are research strategies with the following features:[11] *(a)* the simulation settings are created so as to replicate, to varying degrees, the attributes of naturally occurring systems; *(b)* participants (i.e., subjects) are exposed to a number of "real-world-like" events; *(c)* participants are free to behave within the constraints of the established rules of the simulation; *(d)* participation in the simulation is generally for protracted time periods; *(e)* depending upon the type of simulation ("free" vs. "experimental") the researcher exerts varying degrees of control over (1) the assignment of subjects to various simulation conditions, and (2) the stimuli to which the participants are exposed; and *(f)* the dependent variables of the simulation are the behaviors exhibited by the participants.

The simulation setting is created so as to mirror important dimensions of some naturally occurring system. As in the case of the laboratory experiment, the simulation setting is deliberately structured for the purposes of a study. Unlike the setting of the

---

[11] See Crano and Brewer (1973), Fromkin and Streufert (1976), and Runkel and McGrath (1972).

laboratory experiment (which is created so as to have properties common to a *generic class* of systems), the setting of the simulation is designed so as to be like a specific class of behavior systems (Runkel & McGrath, 1972). In the study by Haney et al., for example, the setting was designed so as to mirror the attributes of a prison—a specific type of formal organization— rather than formal organizations in general.

The simulated environment is created in such a way as to maximize the degree of mundane realism associated with a study. At the same time the researcher often maintains a high degree of control over the events to which participants are exposed. Thus, simulation may be looked upon as a strategy falling somewhere between the laboratory experiment on the one hand and the field study on the other (Crano & Brewer, 1973). In the study by Haney et al. the researchers enjoyed the realism of a simulated prison environment and the controls generally associated with laboratory experiments (e.g., randomization of participants to guard and inmate roles).

Simulation participants are exposed to a number of events that parallel those found in naturally occurring systems. In the *experimental simulation* (cf. Fromkin & Streufert, 1976) the nature and timing of these events is completely determined by the researcher. In the free simulation, on the other hand, events and their timing are determined by both researcher-established simulation rules and the behavior of simulation participants. The experimental simulation thus more closely resembles the laboratory experiment than the *free simulation* as far as degree of control is concerned. The study by Haney et al. would appear to be of the free simulation variety in that with the exception of randomization of subjects to roles and the specification of general rules to be followed by inmates and guards, the events that occurred were largely determined by interactions among the study participants.

Simulations generally require participants to remain in the simulation setting for considerable time periods (ranging from a few hours to several days). The research by Haney et al. was designed to involve participants in the simulated prison setting for up to two weeks. High subject attrition (i.e., experimental mortality) and other factors, however, resulted in the study being terminated after only six days.

Depending upon the form (i.e., free vs. experimental) taken by the simulation, causal hypotheses may be tested using this research strategy. The greater the degree to which the simulation approximates the experimental form (e.g., allows the researcher to randomly assign subjects to various conditions and control the stimuli to which subjects are exposed), the greater the potential **123** for the testing of causal hypotheses. Where a study takes the form a free simulation, the assessment of causality is more risky since the behavior of participants is determined not only by the rules established by the researcher, but also by interactions among the subjects.

The dependent variables of a simulation are the measured behaviors of study participants. (Behavior here implies not only observable acts, but also expressed attitudes, opinions, etc.) The measurement of such behavior may take a number of forms (observation, questionnaires, interviews, etc.). In the study by Haney et al. behaviors of study participants were assessed using videotapes, audio recordings, observation, and several different types of paper-and-pencil type measures.

*Advantages and Disadvantages of the Strategy.* Included in the advantages of the simulation strategy are:

> *a.* Realism is high because the setting mirrors some "real-world" setting and the events that take place in the simulation are "real-world-like";
> *b.* Subject involvement generally tends to be high;
> *c.* Causal hypotheses may be tested in simulations that are of the experimental variety;
> *d.* Demand characteristics (Orne, 1962) are generally lower in simulations than in laboratory experiments;
> *e.* Control over extraneous sources of variance is generally higher than in field studies, especially in the case of the experimental simulation; and
> *f.* Simulations allow for the manipulation of independent variables. The researcher's ability to manipulate independent variables is, of course, greater in experimental than free simulations.

Among the disadvantages of the simulation strategy are:

> *a.* Simulations are expensive. This expense results mainly from the costs associated with creation of the setting for the simulation;
> *b.* To the extent that the simulation is of the free (as opposed to the experimental) variety the study's independent variables are harder to identify, the possibility of confounding factors in influencing dependent variables increases, and the opportunity to test causal hypotheses decreases; and
> *c.* The high degree of participant involvement in the simulation increases the risk of subjects being psychologically harmed in the course of the study (cf. for example, Haney et al., 1973, or Milgram, 1963, 1965).[12]

### Field Experiments

*An Example of the Strategy's Use.* Latham and Kinne (1974) were interested in assessing the impact of goal setting on job performance in a natural work setting. A number of previous field studies indicated that goal setting was positively correlated with employee productivity. However, causality could not be inferred

---

[12] It should be pointed out that several of the disadvantages of laboratory experimentation (e.g., items *a* and *c*) also apply to simulations—especially to those of the experimental variety.

from these field studies. Latham and Kinne. therefore, undertook a study in which goal setting was experimentally varied to determine its impact on a number of performance measures.

The research was conducted among the crews of 20 producers of pulpwood. These were randomly assigned to treatment and control conditions in a post-test-only control group design (cf. chapter 6). A diagram of the design is shown below:

$$R \ X \ O_T$$
$$R \ \ \ \ O_C$$

Sawyers in the 10 treatment groups operated under moderately difficult production goals provided them by the researchers. Sawyers in the 10 control groups, on the other hand, operated in the absence of such goals. Observations were made over a 14-week period of cords cut per sawhand-hour, cords cut per crew-hour, turnover, absenteeism, and injury rates.

Analysis of the study's data revealed that those in the treatment (compared to those in the control) condition had higher levels of cords produced per sawhand hour and cords produced per crew-hour. In addition, absenteeism was significantly lower in the treatment groups than in the control groups. The researchers concluded that goal setting can lead to an increase in production and a decrease in absenteeism. Of particular importance was that in this study, as opposed to previous research that had been conducted on goal setting in real-world organizations, causal inferences were justified.

*Description of the Strategy.* A field experiment is a research strategy characterized by the following features: *(a)* the research takes place in a natural setting (i.e., one that subjects do not perceive as having been set up primarily for the conduct of research); *(b)* the experimenter manipulates one or more independent variables while exerting as much control as the situation permits over other, possibly confounding variables; and *(c)* the effect of the manipulations on one or more dependent variables is systematically observed.

Field experiments take place in naturally occurring systems rather than in settings that subjects perceive as having been created specifically for research purposes (Cook & Campbell, 1976). In the study by Latham and Kinne (1974), for example, the field experiment was conducted in the forests where sawyers typically work. The study of "natural" groupings of subjects in naturally occurring social systems *may* lead to greater generalizability of research findings (Meyers & Grossen, 1974; Lin, 1976).

A researcher employing this strategy manipulates one or more independent variables and attempts to exert as much control as is possible over nuisance variables. In the study by Latham and **125**

Kinne, for instance, the "goal setting" variable was manipulated by the researchers to determine its impact upon the study's dependent variables. In previously conducted field studies of goal setting no such manipulations were made.

Control over nuisance variables is accomplished by the use of experimental designs (e.g., the Solomon Four Group and the post-test-only control group designs), the use of quasi-experimental designs (e.g., the time-series design), or through less effective means (e.g., statistically removing the effects of suspected confounding variables from discovered independent-dependent variable relationships). In the study by Latham and Kinne nuisance variables were controlled by the use of an experimental design (i.e., the post-test-only control group design) that controls for all but a few threats to internal validity (cf. Campbell & Stanley, 1966; and Cook & Campbell, 1976).

The reader should note that organizational field experiments need not (and generally do not) employ true experimental designs. Both quasi-experimental and preexperimental designs are commonly used in field experiments. A study to test the effects of changes in job design on workers' attitudes (Lawler, Hackman, & Kaufman, 1973), for example, used a one group pretest-post-test preexperimental design. And a study to test the effects of participation in decision making on employee absenteeism (Lawler & Hackman, 1969) employed a time-series design. To the extent that an investigation deviates from a true experimental design the results of a study become progressively more difficult to interpret unambiguously.

In field experiments the effect of the independent variable on the dependent variable is systematically observed. In the study by Latham and Kinne such observation took the form of measuring the values of the study's dependent variables in the treatment and control groups for a 14-week period following the introduction of the treatment. Since groups had been randomly assigned to treatment and control conditions it was not necessary to measure the pretreatment values of dependent variables.

*Advantages and Disadvantages of the Strategy.* The advantages of a field experiment are as follows:

  a. Assuming that the researcher employs an experimental design or one of the better (in terms of control) quasi-experimental designs, causal inferences from field experimental data may be justified;
  b. As a consequence of the fact that field experiments involve studying phenomena in "natural settings" the external validity of results of such studies may be greater than that of data from laboratory experiments;
  c. The manipulation of independent variables (as opposed to the simple measurement of their values) allows the researcher to clearly identify antecedents of observed effects. Stated differently, the independent variables have greater construct validity (cf. Cook & Campbell, 1976).

d. Randomization of individuals, groups, and organizations is sometimes possible, allowing for improved control of nuisance variables;

e. Field experiments are useful for not only the development of theory, but also for the solution of applied problems;

f. If the investigator chooses to do so, both the short- and long-term effects of manipulated variables can be addressed using the field experimental strategy;

g. The logic of the field experiment can be applied in the analysis of many naturally occurring changes (cf. Campbell, 1969; Cook & Campbell, 1976). The strength of the independent variable in naturally occurring experiments is often greater than the strength of researchers' manipulations; and

h. Field experiments allow for the testing of "broad" hypotheses dealing with complex social processes in lifelike situations (Kerlinger, 1973). In the case of the Latham and Kinne (1974) study, for example, the effect of goal setting on a number of performance criteria was assessed. In a laboratory experiment the focus of the study would generally have been much narrower (e.g., a study by Chapanis [1964] dealing with the effects of differing levels of task feedback on task productivity).

Among the disadvantages of field experiments as research strategies are:[13]

a. The degree of control associated with most field experiments is insufficient to allow for unequivocal claims of causality;

b. The manipulation of variables in field settings may result in legal and/or ethical problems;

c. The precise measurement of dependent variables possible in laboratory settings, in general, cannot be attained in field settings;

d. Field experiments are generally much more expensive to conduct than laboratory experiments;

e. The greater the strength of the manipulation employed by the experimenter the greater the degree to which the "naturalness" of the original setting is disrupted (Runkel & McGrath, 1972);

f. In general, too few units agree to participate in a field experiment for randomization to be an effective control procedure;

g. The intentional manipulation of one variable in field experiments often results in the unintentional manipulation of others;

h. Field experimenters must be highly skilled "social operators" to gain and maintain access to social systems they desire to study (Kerlinger, 1973);

i. To the extent that a field experiment requires the researcher to maintain prolonged contact with a system, the experimenter's objectivity in studying the system may suffer;

j. If the researcher acts as the change agent (i.e., the person effecting the change), his or her presence may alter the values of the variables measured in the study;

k. Gaining access to social systems generally requires the approval of "top management personnel" in such systems. "Lower-level" participants may come to associate the researcher with top management, and, therefore, data the lower-level personnel supply may be biased;

l. Organizational officials are often reluctant to withhold desirable treatments from no-treatment control groups;

m. Even if randomization of individuals, groups, work units, etc., is initially

---

[13] See Cook and Campbell (1976), Festinger (1953), Scott (1965), and Seashore (1964).

effective, processes occurring within the system studied (inter-unit transfer of personnel, merger, etc.) may destroy its effectiveness;

n. Some individuals, groups, or other units may refuse to accept the treatment they are scheduled to receive;

o. Control groups not receiving what is perceived to be a desirable treatment may resent their status and experience a "resentment treatment" (Cook & Campbell, 1976); and

p. If individuals in groups that are supposed to be experiencing different treatments communicate with one another the purity of the various treatments may suffer.

While extensive, the above mentioned points do not exhaust the disadvantages that could be listed for field experiments.

Although field experiments are difficult to perform successfully their value as a research strategy should not be underestimated. Only through the field experiment can findings of rigorous, well-controlled laboratory experiments be tested for their applicability to naturally occurring systems.

Those contemplating the use of the field experimental strategy should carefully study a number of published works on the subject.[14] One source (i.e., Cook & Campbell, 1976) offers a thorough treatment of field experiments in organizational settings.

## Field Studies

*An Example of the Strategy's Use.* A number of researchers (e.g., Hulin, 1971; Hulin & Blood, 1968; Turner & Lawrence, 1965) have taken the position that a positive relationship between job size (i.e., job scope or degree of job enrichment) and job satisfaction cannot be assumed to be general, but that the nature of this relationship depends upon the degree to which the individuals under study have internalized "middle class" work norms and values (i.e., the work or Protestant ethic). Specifically, it has been argued that the job scope–job satisfaction relationship will be positive for those with a strong belief in the ethic, zero for those who view the ethic neutrally, and negative for those who are alienated from the ethic.

A review of the empirical literature (Stone, 1976) on job design, individual differences, and job satisfaction (that included studies performed up to and including 1975) revealed that no methodologically acceptable tests of the aforementioned hypothesis had ever been made. As a consequence the reviewer (Stone, 1976) designed and executed a study to assess the impact individual differences (in belief in Protestant ethic) have on the relationship between job scope and job satisfaction.

---

[14] See, for example, Campbell (1969), Cook and Campbell (1976), Festinger (1953), Scott (1965), and Seashore (1964).

A number of organizations in southern California were contacted by the researcher and asked to provide participants for the study. The study's sample ultimately consisted of 594 individuals in one of 13 different jobs (ranging from automobile assembler to electrician).

Study participants completed questionnaire measures of job characteristics, Protestant ethic, satisfaction with the work itself, several other satisfaction facets, and demographic variables. Questionnaires were completed anonymously in group administration sessions. Participation in the study was voluntary.

Correlational analysis of the study's data revealed that the relationship between job scope (a linear combination of several job characteristics) and satisfaction with the work itself was positive for the total sample ($N = 594$). It was also positive for subsamples created by trichotomizing the total sample based upon their scores on the Protestant ethic measure.

Additional analyses showed that the observed relationship between job scope and satisfaction with the work itself was not spurious: statistically controlling for the influence of work-related values, various satisfaction facets, and several demographic items did not measurably alter the strength of the job scope-satisfaction with the work itself relationship. Stone concluded that Protestant ethic is *not* an important individual differences variable to consider if the researcher or practitioner is concerned with how satisfaction with the work itself covaries with job scope.

*Description of the Strategy.* The field study strategy can be characterized in the following way:[15] (a) the research is ex post facto in nature (cf. chapter 6), no independent variables are manipulated by the researcher; (b) intact, naturally occurring systems are the object of study; (c) variables are systematically measured; (d) the investigator attempts to minimize his or her intrusion upon the system being studied; and (e) the focus of such research may be exploratory, descriptive, or hypothesis testing.

The field study strategy comes under the general heading of ex post facto research, which, as was discussed in chapter 6, is nonexperimental in nature. (Campbell & Stanley, 1966, label such research as "pre-experimental.") The researcher has no control whatsoever over the independent variable(s) of a study. Instead, the investigator relies upon self-reports of subjects or some other (nonmanipulation based) measure of the extent to which subjects have received some treatment as a mode for assigning independent variable values to subjects. In the research by Stone, for example, levels of job scope (the independent variable) and Protestant ethic (the "moderator" variable) were not ma-

---

[15] See Bouchard (1976), Kerlinger (1973), Runkel and McGrath (1972), and Scott (1965).  **129**

nipulated, but were instead inferred from the responses of individuals to items in questionnaires. While Stone provided some evidence as to the validity of the job scope measure, inferences of job scope levels based upon questionnaire data are less satisfying than are inferences stemming from the experimental manipulation of job scope.

Field studies deal with intact, naturally occurring systems as opposed to those created for research purposes (as, for example, the setting of a laboratory experiment). As Scott (1965, p. 262) has said, field studies are used to study "human beings 'on the hoof'—as opposed to studies of *ad hoc* groups conducted in the laboratory." In the research by Stone, for example, employees of a number of "real-world" organizations served as subjects, and measurement of the study's variables took place in surroundings familiar to the subjects. As a consequence "realism" is heightened.[16]

Field studies employ systematic means for obtaining and recording the value of studied variables. Other research strategies (e.g., the case study) involve far less systematic data-gathering techniques. In most instances field study data are obtained through questionnaires or interviews. In the study by Stone, for instance, all study participants completed questionnaire measures of job characteristics, work-related values, satisfaction facets, and demographic variables.

A key consideration of the researcher employing the field study strategy is to intrude as little as possible upon the system being studied. The consequence of this is that the investigator ends up collecting a weaker form of data than could be collected from more intrusive methods (e.g., a field experiment). Collecting data at only one point in time means that only correlational or cross-sectional analyses (cf. chapter 6) of the data are possible. If the investigator collects data longitudinally the data base is strengthened but there is an increased probability that data collection efforts will modify the system under study (Runkel & McGrath, 1972). It should be noted here that even in instances of "one-shot" data collection efforts in field studies, intrusiveness is never eliminated.

Field studies have several purposes.[17] One variant of the field study has as its goal the gaining of familiarity with a system (e.g., a work organization). Increased familiarity might enable the researcher to define a research problem or develop hypotheses about some process associated with the system. A second variant of the field study has as its objective the description of a system.

---

[16] See Kerlinger (1973), Runkel and McGrath (1972), and Selltiz et al. (1976).

[17] See Katz (1953), Kerlinger (1973), and Selltiz et al. (1976).

This might include measurement of a number of characteristics of system elements (e.g., organizational members) or recording the frequency of certain system occurrences (e.g., rates of message flow among organizational units). The final variant of the field study has as its aim the "testing of hypotheses." The term hypothesis testing is used loosely here since as Campbell and Stanley (1966) have noted, data from correlational and/or cross sectional studies are relevant for hypothesis testing only in that they expose causal hypotheses to opportunities for disconfirmation. The study by Stone (1976), for example, provided disconfirming evidence concerning the validity of the Hulin and Blood model. The study also showed that for the jobs studied variations in job scope were systematically related to variations in satisfaction with the work itself. These results, however, *do not* imply confirmation of the hypothesis that changes in job scope *cause* changes in satisfaction with the work itself. They simply indicate that the study's data did not disconfirm the validity of this hypothesis.

*Advantages and Disadvantages of the Strategy.* The field study strategy has a number of advantages, including:[18]

a. Field studies are high on realism since they are conducted in naturally occurring systems;
b. The intrusiveness of this strategy is relatively low compared with that of others (e.g., the field experiment);
c. Data on a large number of variables can be obtained from subjects;
d. Complex phenomena can be studied;
e. Socially significant (i.e., applications-oriented) problems are amenable to study by this strategy;
f. Field studies are often valuable for their heuristic qualities; and
g. The strengths of independent, intervening, and dependent variables are generally greater than would be found in a laboratory experiment.

### Disadvantages of the field study strategy include:

a. The cooperation of organizations is often difficult to obtain;
b. The effects of any given variable upon another are difficult, if not impossible, to assess with data from field studies. Causal inferences from field study data, therefore, are highly tenuous;
c. Data from most field studies are likely to contain unknown sampling biases;
d. There are usually limits on the number of variables that can be measured in a field study. As a result, many variables that may be relevant to a phenomenon under study are simply ignored by the researcher;
e. Independent variables are not manipulated in field studies;
f. Measurement is not as precise as it is in the laboratory because of increased error variance and the influence of confounding variables;
g. Field studies are generally very expensive to conduct and, as has been recently noted (Bouchard, 1976, p. 367), "with the development of sophisticated instrumentation and more extensive and powerful research designs . . . [the field study] will get even more expensive"; and

---

[18] See Bouchard (1976), Kerlinger (1973), and Scott (1965).

*h.* The "dross rate" or proportion of irrelevant data yielded by measures (cf. Webb et al., 1966) may be high in field studies (for a conflicting view see Bouchard, 1976).

It should be noted here that despite all the problems associated with field studies, "most of what we know today about organizations and the behavior of their members is known on the basis of field studies" (Scott, 1965, p. 261). But as Runkel and McGrath have observed so aptly, ". . . with the field study strategy the investigator ends up learning a lot about complex and meaningful behavior systems, but he [or she] does not know with high confidence just what he [or she] has learned" (1972, p. 94). Fortunately for those interested in organizational behavior phenomena, recent years have seen an increase in the practice of testing propositions stemming from field studies in the laboratory and vice-versa. The study of goal setting (cf. Steers & Porter, 1974) is an area where laboratory experimentation, field experimentation, and field study have been used complementarily in the investigation of a phenomenon.

## Sample Surveys

*An Example of the Strategy's Use.* Kahn, Wolfe, Quinn, Snoek, and Rosenthal (1964) conducted a two phase study dealing with role conflict and role ambiguity in industrial organizations. The first phase involved the intensive study of 53 role incumbents and members of their role sets (cf. Kahn et al., 1964, for additional information on the "intensive study."). The second phase of the study consisted of interviewing members of the United States labor force who were employed during the spring of 1961.

The investigators used a multi-stage probability sampling strategy to select an initial sample of 1,300 individuals to be interviewed. Of those interviewed 725 reported that they usually worked for pay and that they were working more than 20 hours per week at the time the survey was conducted. These individuals constituted the study's final sample. (Since the study's focus was job-related tension, it was appropriate to exclude "nonworkers" from the initial sample in arriving at the final sample.) Members of the final sample were all working adults who lived in private households.

The variable of greatest interest to the researchers was job-related tension. Data on this variable, its assumed "causes" (i.e., demographic and organizational variables), and its assumed consequences (e.g., self-reports of health and absence from work) were obtained from each respondent through interviews. Items comprising the interview are presented in appendices of the Kahn et al. (1964) publication.

**132**

Among the numerous findings of the study were: (*a*) the greater the degree to which a person was engaged in interdepartmental contacts (i.e., spanned departmental boundaries), the greater the degree of experienced tension; (*b*) the greater the person's occupational status the better the individual's health; (*c*) the greater the respondent's occupational status the greater the level of reported job satisfaction; (*d*) the greater one's occupational status the greater the degree of experienced tension; and (*e*) the greater the degree of supervisory responsibility an individual has the greater the degree of tension. The interested reader should consult the original text (Kahn et al., 1964) for additional findings of the study.

*Description of the strategy.* The sample survey strategy involves research in which (*a*) data are collected from members of a sample that represents a known population; (*b*) a systematic technique (e.g., questionnaires or interviews) is used to collect data; (*c*) the researcher manipulates no independent variables; (*d*) data are sought directly from respondents; (*e*) subjects provide data in natural settings; (*f*) responses of subjects are assumed to be largely unaffected by the context in which they are elicited; (*g*) influences of confounding variables are "controlled" statistically; and (*h*) the purpose of the research may range from exploration of phenomena to hypothesis testing.

The sampling strategy used in the sample survey allows the researcher to generalize a study's results to a known population. in the case of the study by Kahn et al. (1964) a multi-stage probability sampling strategy was employed to achieve a sample of individuals who were representative of the population of working adults living in private households in the United States. (In the typical field study the sample is not a random one, and the population to which generalizations might be made is left unspecified.)

A researcher using the sample survey strategy collects data directly from respondents in a systematic fashion. The setting in which the data are obtained is natural and assumed to not influence the values of measured variables. In the study by Kahn et al. (1964) interviewing was used to obtain data from respondents. Other means (e.g., questionnaires and observation) have been employed by other researchers at various times. The important criterion is that the method by systematic (i.e., each study participant provide responses to a constant set of stimulus materials).

Data collection takes place in settings that are natural and assumed to have no measurable impact upon the levels of measured variables. Kahn et al. interviewed subjects in their homes. The researchers presumed that the measurement of job satisfaction, job-related tension, etc., would be as reliably and validly accomplished in this setting as in alternate settings (offices, facto-

**133**

ries, street corners, etc.). This assumption appears reasonable.

The sample survey is a form of ex post facto research. The researcher manipulates no independent variables. Instead, such variables are simply measured by the researcher. In the study by Kahn et al., such ''independent'' variables as interdepartmental boundary spanning, occupational status, and supervisory responsibility were all assumed to have been manipulated by the organizations for which respondents worked.

If the investigator suspects that confounding influences may be present in the data obtained from a survey then the potentially confounding variables are measured and statistical techniques (partial correlation, hierarchial correlation, etc.) are used to ''control'' their effects. The study by Kahn et al., for example, used statistical means for assessing the degree to which sex, age, education, and type of employment had confounding influences on studied relationships.

As was the case with the field study strategy, a researcher doing a sample survey might be concerned with gaining familiarity with a population, describing a population, or the testing of hypotheses. The study by Kahn et al. appears to have concentrated its attention largely on the latter two purposes. Work on gaining familiarity with the job-related tension phenomenon was done in the intensive study (of 53 focal persons) that preceded the national survey.

Apart from the purposes mentioned above, the sample survey may also be used to predict future conditions (e.g., the outcome of an election or consumer buying behavior), to evaluate social programs (e.g., assess the effects of a guaranteed income program), or to develop social indicators (e.g., data upon which to base the unemployment rate, the consumer price index, and the wholesale price index). (Warwick & Lininger, 1975, provide detailed coverage of the various purposes served by the sample survey.)

*Advantages and Disadvantages of the Strategy.* Among the advantages associated with the sample survey strategy are:

a. The sample is chosen in such a way as to allow for generalizations to a defined population;
b. Results are accurate because of large sample sizes and generally low sampling error;
c. Random sampling procedures reduce or eliminate problems of sample bias;
d. Data collection takes place in ''natural'' settings;
e. Data are obtained directly from respondents;
f. Surveys often yield data that suggest new hypotheses;
g. If mailed questionnaires are used to collect data, the per subject cost of data is relatively low (compared, for example, to interview data); and

*h.* A variety of systematic data collection methods (e.g., interviews, question-naires, and observation) can be used alone or in combination.

Disadvantages of this strategy include:

*a.* Decreased willingness of people to respond to sample survey probes. As Warwick and Lininger have observed: "Sample surveys and even the 1970 census in the United States have been plagued by refusals and omissions because of suspicions, fear, and other forms of resistance, particularly in central city areas" (p. 5);

*b.* Most surveys are "one-shot" (as opposed to the panel type in which repeated measures are taken on the same sample). As a result their capacity for generating data with which to test causal connections among variables is limited;

*c.* In terms of total costs, the sample survey is an extremely expensive re-search strategy because of large administrative and/or personnel costs;

*d.* The standardized response formats of many sample survey measures (e.g., questionnaires and structured interviews) may force respondents to subscribe to statements they don't fully endorse. (Note that this is more an indictment of the measurement mode than it is of the sample survey research strategy.);

*e.* If questionnaires are used to collect data, the proportion of returned ques-tionnaires may be low;

*f.* Questionnaire and/or interview measures may be "poor" indicants of the constructs studied by a researcher using the sample survey strategy. Information gleaned from sample surveys generally is "shallow" in nature;

*g.* Control over nuisance or confounding variables is poor. If such variables are controlled at all it must be through statistical means; and

*h.* No independent variables are manipulated by the researcher using this strategy. As a result, causal inferences from sample survey-generated data are difficult to justify.

## The Case Study

*An Example of the Strategy's Use.* Gouldner's (1954) interest in bureaucratization processes in organizations led to the intense study of a gypsum factory. The overall aim of the study was "to clarify some of the social processes leading to different degrees of bureaucratization, to identify some of the crucial variables, and to formulate tentative propositions (hypotheses) concerning their inter-connections" (p. 27).

Gouldner noted that in conducting the research itself, "No effort has been made to specify metrically or quantify these vari-ables or their interrelations." Instead, qualitative data were obtained through a number of means: First, the researchers conducted a total of 174 formal interviews (generally nondirective in nature) with plant employees during normal working hours. In addition, the research team conducted numerous informal interviews on and off the plant's premises. A second means for obtaining data was observation. As Gouldner noted, "We spent a good deal of time just walking around or standing with a worker and talking **135** with him casually as he worked. The small size of the plant enabled us to 'see' it as a *whole* fairly quickly'' (p. 250). A third source of data was what the investigator described as documentary material (newspaper clippings, interoffice memoranda, company reports, government reports, union contracts, etc.).

As the study progressed Gouldner formed ''provisional generalizations'' about phenomena associated with bureaucratization of the plant. These provisional generalizations were discussed by members of the research team and subsequent observations and interviews were directed at assessing the validity of these tentative hypotheses.

Among the final set of hypotheses offered by the investigator were: (*a*) bureaucratic rules arise when organizational members perceive others as failing to meet their role obligations; (*b*) efforts will be made to formulate or enforce bureaucratic rules only when such rules are both ''expedient'' and ''legitimate,'' and (*c*) the extent to which efforts at bureaucratization will result in stable bureaucratic routines depends, at least in part, upon the degree to which individuals subject to increased bureaucratization resist such efforts.

*Description of the Strategy.* The case study approach to research can be described as follows: (*a*) the researcher intensely examines a single unit (e.g., person, group, or organization); (*b*) data are often collected by multiple means; (*c*) no attempt is made to exercise experimental or statistical controls; (*d*) phenomena are studied in natural settings; and (*e*) the strategy is suited more to the generation of hypotheses than their testing.

Whereas other research strategies such as the sample survey involve the study of multiple elements of a defined population, the case study restricts attention to but one. The element may be a person, group, organization, or a larger entity. In the case of the study by Gouldner (1954), for example, the element selected for study was a gypsum plant. Even though data were obtained from multiple sources (i.e., numerous interviewees, reports of observers, and documentary material) the unit of analysis was a single plant.

As the reader is well aware by now, data on a single unit cannot be used as a base for generalizations about larger populations. Gouldner, in recognition of this fact, wrote: ''As a case history [i.e., case study] of only one factory, this study can offer no conclusions about the 'state' of American industry at large, or about the forces that make for bureaucratization in general. It is the function of a case history to develop hypotheses which may be shown, on further investigation, to have broader application'' (p. 231). Results of a case study are useful inductive or hypothesis generating vehicles; they are not appropriate for deductive or hypothesis testing purposes.

Not only is generalization (i.e., external validity) problematic with the case study, but the certainty of what one has really discovered (internal validity) using this research strategy is also dubious. As Campbell and Stanley (1966) have observed in their seminal work on research design: "Basic to scientific evidence. . .is the process of comparison, of recording differences, or of contrast. Any appearance of absolute knowledge, or intrinsic knowledge about singular isolated objects, is found to be illusory upon analysis" (p. 6). Since the study of the gypsum plant by Gouldner involved no comparisons, its internal validity would appear to be open to debate.

The case study allows for "flexibility" in data collection. The researcher has considerable discretion over not only the type of data gathered, but also over sources from which information is obtained. Gouldner's study used data collected from multiple sources (interviews, observations, documentary material, etc.). Gouldner noted that one technique used to get a "crude" overall picture of the community in which workers lived was for members of the research team to spend evenings "at one of the workers' favorite taverns, playing cards or drinking beer with the men" (p. 252). While such methods allow for the gathering of data in natural settings, they also open the possibility for the investigator to alter the setting under study and vice versa. While some would argue that the case study minimally interferes with the natural setting under study, this appears to be an overly optimistic view of the strategy.

Several purposes might be served by the case study approach; these include (Shontz, 1965): (a) presentation of "evidence" on what the researcher considers to be a rare, remarkable, or atypical instance of some phenomenon; (b) exemplifying or illustrating a concept that would be difficult to describe using solely abstract theoretical language; (c) demonstrating the use of a technique (e.g., the conduct of a "team building" exercise); (d) establishing a pool of data that may be useful at a future point in time; (e) challenging existing modes of thought by showing case study evidence that cannot be explained adequately by existing theory; and (f) "confirming" theories or hypotheses by the presentation of supporting case study data.

*Advantages and Disadvantages of the Strategy*. Advantages of the case study strategy are:

a. The full compexity of the unit under study can be taken into consideration;
b. Data collection is flexible;

c. The case study is a useful vehicle for the generation of hypotheses and insights;
d. Data are collected in natural settings; and
e. Case studies are generallly less expensive research strategies than others (e.g., laboratory experiments, field experiments, field studies, and sample surveys).

Included in the set of disadvantages of the case study strategy are:

a. It is the least systematic of all research strategies;
b. Causal inferences from case study data are impossible since there are no controls over confounding variables;
c. Data collection may alter the setting under study;
d. Hypothesis testing is not possible using case study data;
e. Results of case studies are likely to have substantial amounts of bias because of nonsystematic collection, condensation, and interpretation of data;
f. Generalization from a case study's findings is not possible; and
g. Case studies are more time-consuming than other strategies (e.g., laboratory experiments, and field studies).

## INTEGRATION OF RESEARCH STRATEGIES

A researcher contemplating the study of some phenomenon can employ one or more of several different research strategies. Each strategy has a unique set of advantages and disadvantages. Case studies while useful in the formulation of hypotheses are of little use in the testing of hypotheses. Laboratory experiments are ideal strategies for maximizing internal validity but leave unanswered questions of external validity. No strategy is more appropriate than others for *all* research purposes!

A researcher investigating any phenomenon would be well advised to carry out not a single study or a series of studies employing one research strategy, but instead a series of studies using multiple strategies. What is being advocated here is a programmatic approach to research.[19] While their number is limited, several organizational behavior phenomena have been studied recently using a more or less programmatic mode. Motivation, job design, goal setting, role-related tension, and communication are among them.

Runkel and McGrath (1972, p. 116) observed: "Too often in behavioral science [research] the choice of a strategy is made first, based on the investigator's previous experience, preference, and resources and then the problem is chosen and formulated

---

[19] For more on programmatic research see Evan (1971, p. 4), Fromkin and Streufert (1976, p. 457), and Runkel and McGrath (1972, p. 103).

to fit the selected strategy rather than the other way around.''
This is indeed a lamentable state of affairs. Clearly, the nature
of the problem being dealt with should be the major determinant
of the strategy used by the researcher.

# 8 ETHICAL, LEGAL, AND OTHER CONSIDERATIONS IN RESEARCH

The preceding chapters have introduced the reader to the importance of research, the organization of a research project, measurement and properties of measures, sampling, research design, and a number of potentially useful empirical research strategies. At this point the reader should be familiar enough with these technical aspects of research to design and execute his or her own empirical study. A study designed and executed in accordance with the guidelines offered in previous chapters, while technically sound, may be unacceptable or unworthy of execution for other reasons. Specifically, the study may be unethical, illegal, or unwarranted given the costs and benefits that are expected to result from its execution.

In this final chapter we consider a potpourri of topics aimed at supplementing the reader's knowledge of previously presented technical material. Among the issues covered are ethical considerations in research, legal aspects of research, cost/benefit analysis of a proposed study, and the competing values that face the researcher.

Before presenting material on ethical issues in research, two points deserve mention. First, as a consequence of numerous factors, the solution of ethical problems in research may be more problematic than a casual reading of the material in the next section suggests. One reason for this is that in any given study it may not be possible to implement easily the procedures we recommend for dealing with ethical issues. Another reason is that any given reader's opinion about what is and is not ethical may differ

**140**    from positions taken in this book. Still another reason is that ethical issues are often not as clear cut in organizational research as they are in other types of research (e.g., pharmaceutical and medical research). In view of the possible difficulties associated with resolving ethical issues in research, we recommend that you approach the material in this chapter not only with the aim of familiarizing yourself with the various ethical issues, but also with the objective of considering what your own position is vis-à-vis such issues.

The second point that should be considered in advance of reading the following material is that in the course of discussing various ethical issues we make reference to a number of studies (and their attendant problems) that are outside the mainstream of organizational behavior research (e.g., research in medicine and social psychology). There are two reasons for doing this. One is that while we know of no published organizational behavior studies that exemplify each of the several ethical issues dealt with in the next section, this does not mean that such issues have not previously arisen in such studies or that they will not arise in future studies. Since there is some likelihood that each of the issues discussed has been or someday may be the concern of a researcher interested in organizational behavior phenomena, we present as complete a sampling as this book permits. The second reason for introducing material outside the mainstream of organizational behavior is that in doing so we are able to provide the reader with a number of specific examples of previously conducted research that is ethically controversial.

## ETHICAL CONSIDERATIONS IN RESEARCH

In conducting an empirical investigation the researcher faces ethical questions when one or more of the following practices are employed:[1]

- Individuals participate in research without their knowledge or consent;
- Individuals are coerced into being study participants.
- Individuals are not told about the true nature of the research in which they are to participate.
- Individuals are deceived about various aspects of a study.
- Individuals are led to perform acts which have the potential for harming them psychologically.
- Individuals are subjected to physical harm in the course of a study.
- The attitudes, opinions, behaviors, etc., of individuals are modified without their consent.
- The individual's privacy is invaded.

---

[1] Mention of these and other ethically questionable practices is made by Cook (1976), the American Psychological Association or APA (1972, 1973), Baumrind (1971), Kelman (1967, 1968, 1972), Runkel and McGrath (1972), and the U.S. Public Health Service or USPHS (1969).

**141**

- As a result of being placed in a control group, the individual is denied benefits that accrue to those in treatment groups.
- Following participation in a study, individuals are not adequately debriefed (i.e., told about any deception that may have been employed by the researcher and told about the reasons for their behavior as study participants).
- Data obtained from study participants are not treated confidentially.
- A study's results are reported in such a way that participants and/or groups to which they belong experience negative post-study consequences.

## Participation Without Knowledge or Consent

Ethical research practice requires that the researcher obtain the "informed consent" of a potential research participant before involving him or her in a study (APA, 1972, 1973; USPHS, 1969). The basic elements of informed consent are (USPHS, 1969, p. 7):

a. The individual is given a fair explanation of the procedures that are to be followed in a study, including the identification of any procedures that are considered "experimental" in nature;

b. The individual is offered a full description of all the discomforts and/or risks associated with research participation;

c. The individual is provided with a description of the benefits that are associated with participation in the study;

d. The individual is informed about appropriate alternative procedures that would be advantageous;

e. The individual is afforded the opportunity to ask (and have adequately answered) any questions concerning the procedures that are to be used in a study;

f. The individual is informed that he or she is free to withdraw his or her consent and to discontinue participation in the study at any time; and

g. The individual, in assenting to participate in a study, is not asked (or appeared to be asked) to waive any legal rights or to release the researcher and the organization he or she represents from liability for negligence. (The details of many aspects of informed consent are more fully described at various points in the chapter.)

Obtaining the informed consent of individuals prior to involving them in a study is an ideal that should be pursued by all researchers. There are, however, a number of situations in which individuals can be "caused to" participate in research without having given their informed consent. One such situation is where the researcher collects data via participant observation (cf. chapter 4) among individuals who are unaware of the researcher's motives (e.g., a study by Festinger, Riecken, & Schachter, 1956, in which the researchers joined a group that had prophesied the end of the world to observe activities of group members). A second example is where the investigator operating from a "hidden" location observes the behavior of individuals engaged in some activities (e.g., a study by Zimbardo, 1969, in which the investigator stationed himself in a building near an automobile that looked as

**142**

if it had been abandoned and watched unsuspecting individuals vandalize the car). A third situation is where the researcher conducts a field experiment in a public place (e.g., a study by Piliavin & Piliavin, 1972, in which the experimenter, walking with a cane in a subway car, collapses with "stage blood" trickling from his mouth in an attempt to determine peoples' reactions to the event). In all such instances the researcher structures the situation in such a way that those participating in the research are unaware that they are doing so and, thus, have not had an opportunity to decline participation in the research.

## Forced Participation

An individual's decision to participate in a study should be one that is made voluntarily. There are situations, however, where individuals are coerced into participating in research. An employer may, for example, require employees to participate in a study. Forced participation may also result if potential participants are offered such strong incentives for being a participant that they are unable to resist (e.g., prisoners are coerced into being research subjects by the hope of an early parole for cooperating in institutionally sanctioned research efforts). Still another example of forced participation is that of the university student enrolled in a course where research participation is required (e.g., subject pools composed of students in introductory psychology classes). All of the above situations have the potential of causing individuals to participate in research that, given free choice, they would not have agreed to do so. As a consequence, all such situations present the researcher with ethical concerns.

The reader should note that there are many organizational research situations in which ethics are not an issue. An organization may rearrange elements on an assembly line in the hopes of improving productivity. Such an intervention would appear to present no ethical problems. Research ethics, similarly, would not be an issue where a firm had job applicants take a series of preemployment tests aimed at predicting job performance. (The assumption here is that such tests actually have predictive validity and do not *unfairly* discriminate against minority group members protected by Title VII of the 1964 Civil Rights Act.) There are, in addition, a multitude of other organizational research efforts that do not raise ethical issues.

## Participation Without Full Knowledge
## of the Nature of a Study

Ethical research practices require the researcher to inform potential study participants of all features of a study that would rea- **143** sonably be expected to influence the individuals' decisions to participate in the study. In addition, the researcher is ethically bound to answer any questions that participants may have about a study (APA, 1973).

An example should help to clarify why less than full knowledge of the nature of a study may be a cause for concern from the standpoint of ethics. Suppose that individuals are approached at their homes by a researcher who asks them to respond to items in an interview schedule that deals with work-related attitudes. There would be no ethical issue if the researcher were collecting the data anonymously and had no connection with the organization(s) employing the study's participants. Ethical concerns would arise, however, if the researcher actually happened to be an agent of the organization(s) that employed the study's participants and failed to reveal this fact to the participants. The decision to participate in the study would reasonably be expected to be influenced by the nature of the relationship the researcher had with the organization(s) for which study participants worked. If the interviewer failed to reveal this relationship to interviewees, the ethics of the study would most certainly be subject to question.

In some instances methodological considerations (e.g., the desire not to communicate hypotheses to study participants) necessitate that some information about a study be withheld from participants. Where and when this occurs, the investigator is ethically bound to (a) explain the reasons for less than full disclosure to participants prior to involving them in the research, and (b) restore an "open and honest" relationship with participants once the research has been completed (cf. APA, 1972, 1973).

## Participation in Studies Involving Deception

Some research studies (especially those performed by experimental social psychologists) involve the purposeful deception of the research participant. Such deception can take several forms in any given study.[2] One example of the use of deception in organizationally relevant research is a study by Staw (1975) in which the researcher provided individuals with false feedback about their performance on a "Financial Puzzle Task" to determine the impact of knowledge of level of performance on a number of task-related attitudes (see chapter 7 of this book for a more detailed description of the research by Staw). This deception was relatively mild compared to deception employed in other previously conducted research (e.g., telling study participants that a personality test has revealed that they have latent homosexual

---

[2] For examples of deception employed in research see Carlsmith, Ellsworth, and Aronson (1976), Cook (1976), Crano and Brewer (1973), Kelman (1967), and Seeman (1969).

tendencies, or leading subjects to believe that they have administered potentially lethal levels of electrical shock to others).

The use of deception, no matter how mild, is viewed as unethical by a number of methodologists.[3] There are others who view deception as legitimate if the scientific advances that result from a study outweigh the potential harm that subjects may experience as a consequence of being deceived.[4]

The position taken in this book is that deception should not be employed in research if alternative strategies can be productively employed to investigate the phenomenon under study. One alternative is role-playing or role-enactment.[5] There are, in addition, numerous other strategies for conducting research without deceiving study participants (Argyris, 1968, 1975; Haney, Banks, & Zimbardo, 1973).

## Participants Experience Psychological Harm

A researcher has an ethical obligation to prevent the research participant from experiencing mental discomfort during a study.[6] Research participants may be psychologically stressed and/or harmed in numerous ways during the course of a study: the demands of a study may lead participants to lie, cheat, steal, harm others, or engage in other forms of reprehensible behavior. Harm may also come from study participants being pressured to deny their own convictions, beliefs, or perceptions. Participants may also experience psychological discomfort if in the course of a study they behave in nonhumanitarian ways toward others (cf. Cook, 1976).

It has been argued (see, for example, Baumrind, 1971; Runkel & McGrath, 1972) that there are *no* circumstances under which it is ethically appropriate to place research participants in a position where they may be subject to psychological harm or discomfort without (a) the participants being fully apprised of the harm that may come to them in the study and (b) the participants having the right to withdraw from the study at any time they choose. Where there is *any* potential for lasting and serious psychological distress in a study, it should in all likelihood not be conducted (APA, 1972, 1973).

---

[3] Examples are the positions on deception taken by Argyris (1968), Baumrind (1971), Kelman (1967, 1968, 1971), Rubin (1970), and Warwick (1975).

[4] See, for example, APA (1972, 1973), Cooper (1976), Gergen (1973), Holmes (1976a, 1976b), and Holmes and Bennett (1974).

[5] Note, however, that role-enactment is viewed by some (e.g., Cooper, 1976) as inadequate for research concerned with hypothesis testing.

[6] For detailed discussions see APA (1972, 1973), Baumrind, (1971), Carlsmith et al. (1976), U.S. Department of Health, Education, and Welfare or USDHEW (1971), and Runkel and McGrath (1972). **145**

## Participants Experience Physical Harm

There are several examples of research in which participants have experienced various degrees of physical harm, including death. The most opprobrious example is the medical research done on inmates in Nazi concentration camps in World War II. Another example is the medical research done on the inmates of prisons and asylums in the United States. Still another example is the experimentation with LSD and/or other hallucinogenic drugs using members of the armed services as subjects (often without their knowledge or consent).

Where there is any potential whatsoever for a person to be physically harmed in the course of a study, ethical practices require that (a) the potential participant be fully informed as to the risks associated with participating in the study, (b) the potential participant voluntarily provide his or her consent to participate in the research, (c) the researcher take whatever steps necessary to minimize physical distress, and (d) the researcher do whatever possible to remove any harmful effects from participants once the research has been completed.[7] Another crucial feature of research in which there is the potential for physically harming participants is that the gains in knowledge that are likely to accrue from a study outweigh the potential harm that might be experienced by participants (USDHEW, 1971; APA, 1972, 1973).

It is important to note that some view any research in which there is the potential for participants to be harmed as ethically unacceptable. Baumrind (1971), for example, writes: "*Scientific ends, however laudable these may be, do not by themselves justify the use of means* [deception, physical harm, etc.] *that in ordinary transactions would be regarded as reprehensible*" (p. 890). With respect to the question of a researcher balancing the risks of a study against its potential benefits, she goes on to state: "*The risk/benefit assessment justifies the sacrifice of the welfare of* [research] *subjects in the name of science, thus creating moral dilemmas for the investigator, and,* [it] *as such is not moral*" (p. 890).

## Individuals Are Changed Without Their Consent

In a cogent discussion of ethical issues in research Cook (1976) raises the questions, "Do scientists have the right—even if they have the power—to produce significant changes in the behavior or the personalities of other people? Or, in doing so are they

---

[7] See APA (1972, 1973), USDHEW (1971), and Katz (1967) for more on the responsibility of the researcher in studies where there is the possibility of participants suffering physical harm.

violating the individual's own right to self-determination in action and character?'' (p. 219). Ethical questions might be raised each and every time a work organization attempts to change the attitudes (e.g., job satisfaction, organizational identification, and performance motivation) and/or behaviors (e.g., productivity, attendance, and turnover) of its members without first obtaining their consent. Where the attitudes and/or behaviors of organizational members are the object of change efforts and the individuals involved have assented to participate in change programs, ethics are not an issue.

An example of research where ethics might be questionable is a study in which individuals are required by their employing organization to participate in a training program aimed at increasing their level of need for achievement. Even though many would regard such a change as beneficial, some persons might not, and subjecting unwilling persons to such training would be unethical. However, there would be no ethical problems in such a training program if participation were restricted to volunteers (e.g., McClelland & Winter, 1969).

**Invasion of the Individual's Privacy**

The right to privacy may be looked upon as the right of the individual to decide the extent to which attitudes, opinions, behaviors, and personal facts will be shared with others.[8] Ethical questions are raised whenever research practices have the intent or effect of abridging this right. (For a dissenting view see Bennett, 1967).

There are several ways in which individuals' right to privacy may be violated in research (Cook, 1976). One is for the researcher to operate as a participant observer in a setting without others in the setting being aware that they are being observed (e.g., the previously cited study by Festinger, Riecken, & Schachter, 1956). A second ethically questionable practice is for the researcher to observe others from a ''hidden'' location (e.g., the previously mentioned research of Zimbardo, 1969). A third way in which privacy may be invaded is to ask questions of a highly personal nature in questionnaires or interviews (e.g., asking questions about intimate relationships, personal habits, and illegal or immoral practices). A fourth ethically questionable activity is the collection of data using projective tests or other instruments to assess variables in a disguised or indirect fashion (e.g., the Thematic Apperception Test, the Rorschach Test, and pupilo-

---

[8] For additional discussion on the ''right to privacy'' see Ernst and Schwartz (1962), Panel on Privacy and Behavioral Research (1967), Ruebhausen and Brim (1965, 1966), and Sears (1967).

metric devices). A fifth ethically questionable procedure is for the researcher to obtain data about research participants from third parties without first securing the consent of the participants to such inquiry (e.g., conducting background checks on job applicants without their knowledge and/or consent).

The reader should note that, in general, the greater the degree to which measurement is of the unobtrusive variety, the greater the degree to which privacy is invaded by such data collection. This is not meant to imply that researchers should abandon the use of such measurement methods. Rather, the implication is that where unobtrusive measures are employed in a study the investigator must be especially sensitive to ethical considerations. The researcher must consider whether or not individuals subject to measurement through unobtrusive means intend for their behavior, opinions, attitudes, etc., to be public or private. If there is no question but that these are public, then the use of unobtrusive measures would appear legitimate.

There are those who would argue that at times the scientific ends associated with a study (e.g., contributing to the body of knowledge) justify means that would under normal circumstances be considered less than ethically sound. Others (e.g., Runkel & McGrath, 1972) argue that it is "a serious invasion of privacy to obtain and use, even for the purest of scientific purposes, records of behavior the actor intended to be private and had every reason to expect to be private" (p. 236). The position taken in this book is that if a study's design opens the possibility for the invasion of individuals' rights to privacy, in all likelihood it should not be conducted.

### Control Group Members Denied Benefits of Treatment

As mentioned in chapter 7, the design of true experiments and many quasi-experiments calls for individuals in a certain group (treatment group) to receive a treatment that is withheld from individuals in other groups (control groups). Where the treatment (a) is known to have beneficial effects and (b) individuals in control groups would have otherwise been exposed to the treatment, then (c) placing individuals in control groups is an ethically questionable practice. Consider, for example, a (fictitious) study in which an organization interested in studying the frequency and severity of industrial accidents installed safety equipment on machines in one of its plants (treatment group), but not on machines in another plant (control group). If the safety equipment had known value in reducing accidents and in the absence of the study such equipment would have been installed in all plants in the organization, the research would be unethical.

**148**

While there is seemingly no organizational research in which a beneficial treatment that would otherwise have been offered control group members is withheld from them, there are other areas of research where this has taken place. Cook (1976), for example, cites medical research in which individuals with syphilis were assigned to either a treatment condition (in which they received a therapeutic drug) or a control condition (in which the therapeutic drug was withheld). As a consequence of not receiving the drug, the health of those in the control group deteriorated markedly during the course of and following the termination of the study. This is a clear example of ethically unacceptable research.

## Inadequate Debriefing

After data have been collected in a study, ethical practice requires the researcher to provide the research participant with a full explanation of the nature of the study and to remove any misconceptions that may have arisen in the minds of participants as a result of having been involved in the study. Post-study meetings in which the researcher attempts to accomplish these purposes are known as "debriefing" sessions. According to Holmes (1976a, 1976b), debriefing activities have as their focus "dehoaxing" and/or "desensitizing." Participants are *dehoaxed* in order to explain any deception that may have been used by the researcher in the course of a study (e.g., being supplied with false feedback on performance of an experimental task). *Desensitization,* on the other hand, is used to alter participants' feelings about attitudes they may have expressed or behavior they may have exhibited during a study. The need to desensitize, for example, would present itself in a study in which participants were led to believe that they, upon the urging of the experimenter, had administered potentially lethal shocks to others (cf. Milgram, 1963).

If participants are not properly debriefed, they may suffer undesirable aftereffects of having been involved in a study. An individual who, for example, participates in a study in which he or she is supplied with false feedback that his or her scores on a personality test indicate "maladjustment" may have long-term doubts about personal emotional adjustment. It would clearly be unethical to not debrief the individual.

It should be noted here that recent reviews of the literature (Holmes, 1976a, 1976b) suggest that both dehoaxing and desensitizing procedures are effective as post-study techniques for averting long-term harm from research participation. Holmes (1976b) notes that: ". . . it appears that when debriefing is done properly it is possible both to eliminate the misinformation a sub- **149** ject receives in the course of an experiment involving a deception and to eliminate the arousal and concern a subject may experience as a consequence of insights about himself he obtained in the course of an experiment'' (p. 875).

## Data Are Not Confidentially Treated

Ethical practices require the researcher to treat all data secured from research participants in a confidential manner. One mode for guaranteeing confidentiality is for the researcher to have research participants anonymously respond to questionnaires, interviews, etc. Where the research requires that participants provide data non-anonymously the investigator must take whatever steps necessary to insure the confidentiality of such data.

Organizational research requires special precautions to protect the anonymity or confidentiality of data secured from individuals in the course of a study. If such data are collected by an individual who is not a member of the organization in which the research is being conducted, the researcher may find himself faced with requests for the data from administrative personnel of the organization. Reasons behind such requests may range from wanting the data to provide organizational members with some type of help (e.g., counseling) or to help the organization itself (e.g., helping the organization to identify ''troublemakers''). The researcher must resist all such organizational requests for data.

If research is carried out by an individual who is a member of the organization being studied, the researcher may find other organizational members (e.g., his or her superiors) demanding access to the data. Cook (1976) recommends that the prudent organizational researcher anticipate this possibility and make advance arrangements with organizational administrators to protect the confidentiality of data collected from study participants. However, when such advance arrangements cannot be worked out, the researcher has an obligation to inform participants of an inability to protect the confidentiality of data obtained from them.

Confidentiality is not an issue if individuals *voluntarily* provide data to others with full awareness that such data will be revealed to others (e.g., colleagues of a researcher, data banks, organizational officials, government agencies, etc.). For example, individuals who complete and submit federal Income Tax returns do so with the knowledge that information contained in such returns will be shared with the Department of Justice, the states, etc. Individuals who take the Graduate Record Examination do so with an awareness that scores on the exam will be shared with educational institutions to which individuals have applied for admission. There are many other examples of individuals consenting to the dissemination of data they provide to others. Whenever such consent is given, information collected in a study may ethically be shared with others.

## Injudicious Reporting of a Study's Results

If the study results are to be disseminated in any fashion (e.g., public talks, technical reports, journal articles, and books), the researcher has an ethical obligation to report such results in a way that precludes the possibility of negative consequences accruing to individuals, groups, or organizations that have participated in the study. In general, this implies that research reports be prepared in such a way as to preclude the possibility of participant identification.

Ethical research practices also require the researcher to make study participants aware of the uses that will be made of data obtained from them (results will be published in professional journals, results will be fed back to the organization, etc.). If individuals are less than comfortable about providing a researcher with data that will subsequently serve as a basis for a semi-public or public report, they should be given the option of withdrawing from the study.

## Other Ethical Issues

The aforementioned ethical issues are among the critical ones facing the researcher. There are other ethical questions that might arise in a given study. If such questions present themselves, what should the researcher do? One solution would be for the individual conducting a study to analyze it in terms of his·or her own ethical standards. This strategy is less than optimal since (as will be pointed out later in this chapter) there are often marked differences among individuals' values. As a result, what would appear as an ethically responsible research practice to one individual may not be similarly perceived by another. Nazi doctors in charge of medical experiments on concentration camp inmates may not have perceived their research as unethical. The highly immoral nature of these experiments, however, was widely recognized at the Nuremberg trials that followed World War II.

Another solution to resolving ethical issues in research is to have a "human subjects research committee" review a proposed study. Such committees may be found on the campuses of most colleges and universities. If an individual is a faculty member, a university-based researcher, or a student engaged in research, access to such a committee's services is generally not difficult. An organizational researcher who has no affiliation with an academic institution, however, may find it difficult to get research proposals reviewed by a "human subjects research committee."    **151**

A third and more viable option available to the organizational researcher is for him or her to consult any one of a number of existing codes of research ethics. Such codes have been issued by the American Psychological Association (APA, 1972, 1973), the American Medical Association (AMA, 1966), the American Personnel and Guidance Association (no date), the Nuremberg Military Tribunals (Nuremberg Code, 1949), the National Association of Social Workers (NASW, 1968), the American Anthropological Association (AAA, 1971), the American Sociological Association (ASA, 1971), the U.S. Department of Health, Education, and Welfare (1971), and numerous other organizations or associations. Ethical principles listed in such codes should greatly facilitate answering questions about the ethicality of any given study plan.[9]

Only after the researcher has consulted one or more codes of research ethics and found that a proposed study appears not to violate *any* principles contained therein, should he or she actually carry out a planned study. Where there are any questions whatsoever about the ethics of a study the researcher has a moral obligation to seek the advice of others on whether or not the study should be conducted. Depending upon the nature of the research being considered, the investigator may seek counsel from members of the clergy, psychologists, psychiatrists, attorneys, sociologists, research methodologists, and other professionals.

## ADDITIONAL ISSUES

### Legal Considerations in Research

In the past several decades a number of organizational research practices have been successfully contested in the courts (cf. U.S. Civil Service Commission, 1974; National Employment Law Project, 1973). The focus of much of this litigation has been the organizational practice of using data from application blanks, tests of various types, background checks, references, and numerous other sources in selection, placement, promotion, and several other personnel-related decisions.

Looking beyond the specific realm of organizational research, one finds legal challenges to other research activities. For example, there has been recent court action on a medical study in which cancer cells were injected into the systems of sick and debilitated, but noncancerous patients in a Jewish hospital

---

[9] It should be noted that there are those who have serious doubts about the promulgation of ethical research standards (e.g., Gergen, 1973).

(Hyman vs. Jewish Chronic Disease Hospital, 21 A.D. 495, 251 NYS 2d 818 [1964]; 15 N.Y. 2d 317, 206 N.E. 2d 388 [1965]). And, there have been numerous suits concerned with the alleged invasion of individuals' right to privacy (cf. the cases cited in Ruebhausen & Brim, 1965).

In short, the researcher must be highly sensitive to the legal ramifications of a study. Practices that have often been employed in social science research (e.g., unobtrusive measurement, deception, and involving individuals in research without their consent) may be illegal.[10] Depending upon the research in question, and the nature and extent of damage suffered by a research participant, civil and/or criminal charges could be brought against a researcher.

In a recent study by Wilson and Donnerstein (1976) data were obtained from 174 persons on the perceived ethicality, legality, etc., of a number of previously conducted social science research studies. Results of the study showed that substantial percentages of those asked to evaluate the previously conducted research felt that they would be harassed by the procedures used in the studies; their privacy would be invaded by the studies; they would mind participating in the studies; and the studies were unethical.

Sizable percentages also felt that such experiments should not be performed by social science researchers; the studies were not justified by their potential scientific contributions; and such studies lowered public trust in social scientists and social science research.

Finally, substantial percentages felt that the actions of the researchers in question were *against the law;* if they discovered the research was illegal they would see a lawyer and press charges; and in a select group of studies trespassing had been committed. While the limited number of individuals interviewed and the nonrandom nature of the sample associated with the Wilson and Donnerstein study make the generalizability of their results suspect, the study is nevertheless worthy of note in that it suggests that social science research practices may not be viewed neutrally by individuals in society.

## Cost-Benefit Analysis of a Proposed Study

An important consideration in deciding whether or not to execute a proposed study is the cost of it relative to the benefits expected to result from it. Thus, even though a study may be methodologically sound (i.e., possess internal and external validity) and have no legal or ethical problems, it should not be conducted

---

[10] See, for example, Conrad (1967), King and Spector (1963), Nash (1975), Ruebhausen and Brim (1965, 1966), Silverman (1975), and Wilson and Donnerstein (1976).

unless the benefits expected to accrue from it outweigh the costs of conducting it.

Among the costs of conducting a study are (a) the initial costs of setting up a study, (b) the costs of collecting data from each research participant, and (c) the "costs" experienced by research participants (e.g., short and/or long-term physical and/or psychological harm, discomfort, and loss of right to self-determination). Dollar values can be assigned to the first and second of these three groups of costs. The costs experienced by research participants, however, must be determined subjectively. (See Farr & Seaver, 1975, for ratings of perceived physical and psychological discomfort associated with a number of research procedures.)

Among the benefits of a study are: (a) contributing to the general body of knowledge associated with a topic, (b) contributing to the solution of applied problems, and (c) contributing to the welfare of research participants. While it may be possible to assign specific dollar values to the benefits connected with the solution of applied problems (e.g., the dollar savings of a management by objectives program), the monetary value of the other two classes of benefits, in general, would require subjective determination.

It should be noted here that the researcher should not be the sole evaluator of the costs and benefits associated with a proposed study if there is any potential for research participants to suffer any negative consequences (e.g., physical pain, psychological harm, and discomfort) as a result of their involvement in a study. In such instances the assessment of costs and benefits should probably be the responsibility of a "human subjects research committee" or a group of independent professionals competent to perform such an assessment (cf. USPHS, 1969; APA, 1972, 1973). An independent review of a proposed study is critical, since as M. Brewster Smith (1967) has recently noted, when scientific values are in conflict with humanitarian, libertarian, or legal values the scientist/researcher "may underestimate or rationalize away the costs and risks to his subjects" (p. 379). As a result, the decision to conduct a study in which there are value conflicts "can no longer be left to the unaided conscience of the individual investigator" (p. 379).

## Competing Values in Research

Research in organizations and other settings is generally guided by multiple, sometimes conflicting values. Values influence whether or not empirical research will be used to investigate a phenomenon of interest, the context in which a study takes place,

**154**

the variables that will be studied, the composition and size of a study's sample, the modes that will be employed to collect data, the analytical strategy applied to such data, and the manner in which a study's results will be reported. In sum, values influence decision making in virtually all phases of the research cycle.

The pursuit of knowledge is a value that motivates virtually all empirical research. Humanitarian values demand that research participants never be harmed as a result of involvement in a study. Libertarian values require the researcher to respect the autonomy and privacy of research participants. Legal values prohibit conducting a study in such a way as to violate civil or criminal laws (Smith, 1967).

Apart from these values, the behavior of the researcher is also guided by a concern for achieving the goals of individuals, agencies, and organizations that sponsor his or her research. Research sponsors often have considerable influence over such matters as the formulation of research questions, the strategies used to investigate a phenomenon, and the uses that are to be made of a study's results. This influence is likely to be especially strong when the researcher is an employee of the organization sponsoring an investigation. Where such a relationship exists, the researcher must take special precautions to insure that the values of the organization do not lead to the displacement of humanitarian, libertarian, legal, and scientific values.

## CLOSING COMMENTS

In the course of conducting an empirical study the researcher is faced with a series of questions: What is the problem? What hypotheses should be tested? How should relevant variables be operationalized? What methods should be used to assess the reliability and validity of measures? What sampling strategy should be used? What overall research strategy (field study, laboratory experiment, etc.) should be employed? How will ethical and/or legal issues be resolved? The answers to these questions may vary from one study to the next. And depending upon the answers selected, the researcher gains certain benefits and suffers certain costs. No one set of answers—under all circumstances—will be any more or any less right than any other set. In sum, what we advocate is that the researcher employ a wide variety of empirical research strategies, measurement methods, etc. It is only through such an approach that meaningful additions will be made to our fund of knowledge of organizational behavior phenomena.

We close this book with the hope that the reader's increased knowledge of research methods will be effectively applied in the solution of organizational behavior or other real-world problems. **155**

# APPENDIX: STATISTICAL METHODS

Understanding a number of issues dealt with in this book requires familiarity with some univariate (i.e., one variable) and bivariate (i.e., two variable) statistical notions. Among the statistical concepts that will prove useful in understanding the material are:

a. Measures of Central Tendency. These include the mean, median, and mode. Such measures indicate what the "average" or "typical" value is for a set (group) of scores;

b. Measures of Dispersion. These include the range, variance, and standard deviation. Such measures denote how "spread out" or "far from the typical value" a set of scores are; and

c. Measures of Association. These include the correlation coefficient and numerous other indices not covered in this appendix. Such measures signify how strongly two (or more) variables are related to one another.

Many readers of this book at some point in their educational development have been exposed to elementary statistical concepts. Others may not have had such exposure. The material contained in this appendix is directed primarily to this latter group of individuals. It is suggested that they study the Appendix before tackling other sections of the book.

The reader should note that statistical methods can be grouped under two headings: descriptive statistics and inferential statistics. If our concern is simply with the effective organization and communication of data from a sample of individuals, groups, organizations, etc., then descriptive statistics are employed. If, on the other hand, our interest is in extending findings of data from a sample to a larger group (i.e., a population), then inferential statistics are used. (See chapter 5 for distinctions between

samples and populations.)

The paragraphs that follow deal only with descriptive statistics. Given the purpose of this book (i.e., presentation of research methods useful in the study of organizational behavior), only a superficial treatment of statistical techniques is possible. While cursory, the material should facilitate the reader's understanding of issues covered in other parts of this book.

## Data from a Fictitious Study

In the sections that follow formulas for computing various sample statistics are presented. To further the reader's understanding we also show applications of these formulas to a set of data from a fictitious study. In this "study" five individuals who applied for a job at a firm were administered a test to predict performance on the job. The range of possible scores on the test was 0 (low job aptitude) to 10 (high job aptitude). Actual scores for the five individuals are shown in column 2 of table A-1.

The company hired all five workers since it was unsure of the test's value in predicting job performance. Three months later the supervisor in charge of the five new employees rated their job performance. The range of possible scores on the performance rating was 0 (extremely poor performance) to 10 (extremely good performance). The supervisor's ratings are shown in column 3 of table A-1.

## Notational System

The formulas presented in this appendix employ the following notational conventions:

i: subscript used to identify individual cases

$X_i$: score of individual i on variable X

$Y_i$: score of individual i on variable Y

$\Sigma$: summation sign

For the first worker's data (i = 1) the aptitude test score, $X_1$, equals 5 and the performance rating score, $Y_1$, equals 5; for the second worker (i = 2), $X_2$ equals 6 and $Y_2$ equals 9; etc.

The Greek letter $\Sigma$ (capital sigma) is a shortcut way of saying "the sum of a set of values." (It is formally known as a summation operator.) For example, $\Sigma X$ means the sum of all values of X and $\Sigma Y$ means the sum of all values of Y. For the aptitude test data shown in table A-1:

$$\begin{aligned} \Sigma X &= X_1 + X_2 + X_3 + X_4 + X_5 \\ &= 5 + 6 + 8 + 5 + 7 \\ &= 31. \end{aligned}$$

And, for the performance rating data:

$$\begin{aligned} \Sigma Y &= Y_1 + Y_2 + Y_3 + Y_4 + Y_5 \\ \Sigma Y &= 5 + 9 + 10 + 6 + 8 \\ &= 38. \end{aligned}$$

**157**

Table A-1

Data Used in Computations Covered in the Appendix

| (1) Individual Number | (2) Test Score | (3) Performance Score | (4) Deviate Scores | (5) Deviate Scores | (6) Squared Deviate Scores | (7) Squared Deviate Scores | (8) Standardized (Z) Scores | (9) Standardized (Z) Scores | (10) Z-Score Cross Products | (11) Squared $X_i$ Values | (12) Squared $Y_i$ Values | (13) Cross Products of $X_i$ and $Y_i$ Values |
|---|---|---|---|---|---|---|---|---|---|---|---|---|
| $i$ | $X_i$ | $Y_i$ | $(X_i-\bar{X})$ | $(Y_i-\bar{Y})$ | $(X_i-\bar{X})^2$ | $(Y_i-\bar{Y})^2$ | $Z_x$ | $Z_y$ | $Z_x \cdot Z_y$ | $X_i^2$ | $Y_i^2$ | $X_i \cdot Y_i$ |
| 1 | 5 | 5 | -1.2 | -2.6 | 1.44 | 6.76 | -1.03 | -1.41 | 1.45 | 25 | 25 | 25 |
| 2 | 6 | 9 | -0.2 | 1.4 | 0.04 | 1.96 | -0.17 | 0.76 | -0.13 | 36 | 81 | 54 |
| 3 | 8 | 10 | 1.8 | 2.4 | 3.24 | 5.76 | 1.54 | 1.30 | 2.00 | 64 | 100 | 80 |
| 4 | 5 | 6 | -1.2 | -1.6 | 1.44 | 2.56 | -1.03 | -0.86 | 0.89 | 25 | 36 | 30 |
| 5 | 7 | 8 | 0.8 | 0.4 | 0.64 | 0.16 | 0.68 | 0.22 | 0.15 | 49 | 64 | 56 |
| $\Sigma$ | 31 | 38 | 0 | 0 | 6.80 | 17.2 | 0 | 0 | 4.36 | 199 | 306 | 245 |

## MEASURES OF CENTRAL TENDENCY

Measures of central tendency are useful in describing the "average" or "typical" value of a set of scores. Three measures of central tendency are considered here: the mean, the median, and the mode.

### The Mean

The arithmetic mean of a set of scores is simply the sum of the individual values in the set divided by the number ($N$) of such elements. For values of X the mean ($\overline{X}$) is:

$$\overline{X} = \frac{\Sigma X_i}{N} \qquad [1]$$

And for values of Y the mean ($\overline{Y}$) is:

$$\overline{Y} = \frac{\Sigma Y_i}{N} \qquad [2]$$

For the data in table A-1 the mean value for the aptitude test scores ($\overline{X}$) is $(5 + 6 + 8 + 5 + 7)/5$ or 6.2. And the mean value for the performance ratings ($\overline{Y}$) is $(5 + 9 + 10 + 6 + 8)/5$ or 7.6.

### The Median

The median is another measure of central tendency. Determination of the median requires that a set of scores first be arrayed.[1] If there are an odd number of elements in the set of scores the median (Mn) is that value midway between the two extreme values in the array. For an array with $N$ cases Mn is the value associated with the element numbered $(N + 1)/2$.

For the aptitude test data in table A-1 the arrayed values are 5, 5, 6, 7, and 8. Since $N = 5$, $(N + 1)/2 = (5 + 1)/2 = 3$. The Mn is thus the third value in the array, or 6.

For a set of scores having an even number of elements the Mn is the arithmetic mean of the scores for elements numbered $(N/2)$ and $(N/2) + 1$ in the array.

### The Mode

The final measure of central tendency considered here is the mode. For any given set of scores the mode (Mo) is defined as the value of the element that appears with the greatest frequency. For the

---

[1] Scores are arrayed by placing them in ascending or descending order.

aptitude test data of table A-1 the mode is 5 since it appears twice, while all other values appear only once. Note that the performance rating data have no mode. It is also possible for a set of scores to have two, three, or more modes.

## MEASURES OF DISPERSION

Measures of dispersion indicate the extent to which: (a) extreme elements in a set of arrayed scores differ from one another or (b) the extent to which elements in a set of scores deviate from a central tendency value. Three measures of dispersion are covered here: the range, the variance, and the standard deviation.

### The Range

The range of a set of scores is the difference between the largest and smallest values in a set of arrayed scores. In the case of the aptitude test data the range is 3 (i.e., 8 – 5). And for the performance rating data the range is 5 (i.e., 10 – 5).

### The Variance

Before formally defining variance, deviate scores need to be introduced. A deviate score is the difference between a given element in a set of scores and the mean of such scores. Deviate scores for person 1 on aptitude test and performance rating scores are, respectively, – 1.2 (i.e., 5 – 6.2) and – 2.6 (i.e., 5 – 7.6). Deviate scores for individuals 2 thru 5 are shown in columns 4 and 5 of table A-1. Also shown in the table (cf. columns 6 and 7) are squared deviate scores for each individual. These will be used in the computation of the variance and standard deviation.

The variance of a set of scores reflects the degree to which elements in the set deviate from the mean of the set. More precisely, the variance of a set of scores equals the average squared deviation of the set of scores. For scores on the variable X, the variance ($S_x^2$) is:

$$S_x^2 = \frac{\Sigma(X_i - \overline{X})^2}{N} \qquad [3]$$

And for the variable Y, the variance ($S_y^2$) is:

$$S_y^2 = \frac{\Sigma(Y_i - \overline{Y})^2}{N} \qquad [4]$$

For the data shown in table A-1 the variance of scores on the **160** aptitude test ($S_x^2$) is found by dividing the sum of the squared deviations about the mean of the set of scores (see the last value in column 6 of table A-1) by the number of elements in the set:

$$S_x^2 = \frac{\Sigma(X_i - \bar{X})^2}{N} = \frac{6.80}{5} = 1.36$$

And the variance of scores on the performance ratings is:

$$S_y^2 = \frac{\Sigma(Y_i - \bar{Y})^2}{N} = \frac{17.2}{5} = 3.44.$$

## The Standard Deviation

The standard deviation is the square root of the variance of a set of scores. For scores on X the standard deviation ($S_x$) is:

$$S_x = \sqrt{S_x^2} \qquad [5]$$

And for scores on Y, the standard deviation ($S_y$) is:

$$S_y = \sqrt{S_y^2} \qquad [6]$$

For the data in table A-1 the standard deviations for variables X and Y are, respectively, 1.17 (i.e., $\sqrt{1.36}$) and 1.85 (i.e., $\sqrt{3.44}$).

Having values for the standard deviations of variables X and Y we are in a position to determine standardized (Z) scores for each individual in the score distribution. Z scores, as will be shown below, are useful in the computation of the correlation coefficient, a measure of association between variables.[2]

Computation of Z scores involves simply the division of each individual's deviate score on a variable by the standard deviation of the same variable:

$$Z_x = \frac{(X_i - \bar{X})}{S_x} \qquad [7] \qquad \text{and} \qquad Z_y = \frac{(Y_i - \bar{Y})}{S_y} \qquad [8]$$

Standardized (Z) scores for person 1 on variables X and Y are, respectively, −1.03 (i.e., −1.2/1.17) and −1.41 (i.e., −2.6/1.85). Z scores for persons 1 thru 5 on variables X and Y are shown, respectively, in columns 8 and 9 of table A-1.

## MEASURE OF ASSOCIATION

At the beginning of this statistical appendix we noted that the purpose of the firm's collecting aptitude test and performance data was to assess the extent to which scores on these two vari-

---

[2] Standardized scores are also useful in that they are more easily interpreted than raw (non-standardized scores). By knowing a standardized score, for example, one knows how "far" a given score is from the mean of a set of scores. Raw scores, by themselves, do not convey this information. Two common uses of standardized scores are (a) comparing the performance of a person on tests with different means and standard deviations, and (b) comparing ratings of workers by different raters. For more on the use of standardized scores see Nunnally (1967, 1972), Ghiselli (1964), and Schneider (1976).

ables were related to one another. Inspection of the two sets of scores (cf. table A-1) suggests that they are, in fact, highly related: the greater the aptitude test score (X), the greater the value of the performance rating (Y). The relationship between the two sets of scores can be depicted in what is called a bivariate (i.e., two variable) scatterplot. Such a scatterplot, using the original scores, is shown in figure A-1.

FIGURE A-1    Bivariate Plot of Aptitude Test and Performance Rating Scores

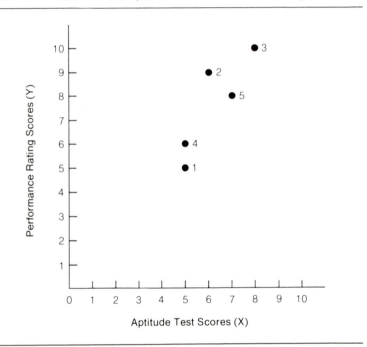

Aptitude Test Scores (X)

Scatterplots are useful in depicting the degree of association between two variables. If data for only a few cases (i.e., individuals, groups, etc.) are involved such scatterplots are not difficult to prepare. They thus provide us with one option for organizing and presenting data to others. Scatterplots, however, present us with two problems: First, short of showing a scatterplot to another person it is impossible to communicate the degree to which two variables are related to one another. And second, individuals may disagree on the strength of association they ascribe to any given scatterplot. One person, for example, may characterize the association between variables X and Y in figure A-1 as ''extremely high,'' while another may view it as only ''moderate.''

A quantitative index of the degree to which two variables are related to one another would solve both problems of communication and interpretation. Luckily such an index exists. It is known as the (Pearson) product-moment correlation coefficient ($r$).[3]

This coefficient ($r$) varies between $-1.0$ and $+1.0$. When two variables are negatively related to one another and scores on one can be perfectly predicted by knowing scores on the other, $r$ takes on a value of $-1.0$. A bivariate scatterplot for which $r = -1.0$ is shown in ($a$) of figure A-2.

When scores on two variables are positively related to one another and scores on one variable allow for the perfect prediction of scores on the other variable, $r$ assumes a value of $+1.0$. In figure A-2, ($b$) shows a bivariate scatterplot for which $r = 1.0$. Note that when $r$ equals either $+1.0$ or $-1.0$ all points lie on a straight line.

The correlation coefficient takes on a value of 0 when scores on one variable are completely unrelated to scores on another. This situation is depicted in ($c$), ($d$), and ($e$) of figure A-2. In the case of ($c$) in figure A-2 scores on both variables X and Y vary, but knowledge of scores on one variable does nothing to aid our prediction of scores on the other. In the cases of both ($d$) and ($e$) in figure A-2 scores on one variable vary while scores on the other have no variance.

Bivariate scatterplots for data sets having correlations of .2, .5, and .7 are shown in figure A-2 ($f$) through ($h$). Note that the greater the degree to which the data points fall along a straight line (assuming greater than zero variance on both variables) the greater the (absolute) value of the correlation coefficient.

The reader should note that the product-moment correlation coefficient is an appropriate index of how strongly variables are related to one another *only* when such variables are linearly related to one another (i.e., a straight line best describes the relationship). This index should not be used if there is a curvilinear relationship between two variables (i.e., a curved line best describes the relationship). The product-moment correlation coefficient would, thus, be appropriate for indexing the relationships shown in figure A-2, ($a$) through ($h$). It would not be appropriate, on the other hand, for indexing the relationships depicted in ($i$) and ($j$). Note that if the product-moment correlation were computed for either of these relationships its value would be zero, in spite of the fact that both relationships are extremely strong (but are curvilinear).

Determining the value of the correlation coefficient ($r$) is a simple task. If we have computed standardized scores on two

---

[3] The reader should note that this measure of association is but one of many that can be used to quantitatively index the degree of association between two variables. For information on others see Hays (1973), Guilford and Fruchter (1974), Glass and Stanley (1970), Cohen and Cohen (1975), Cooley and Lohnes (1971), and Overall and Klett (1972).

FIGURE A-2   Scatterplots Showing Various Levels of Correlation

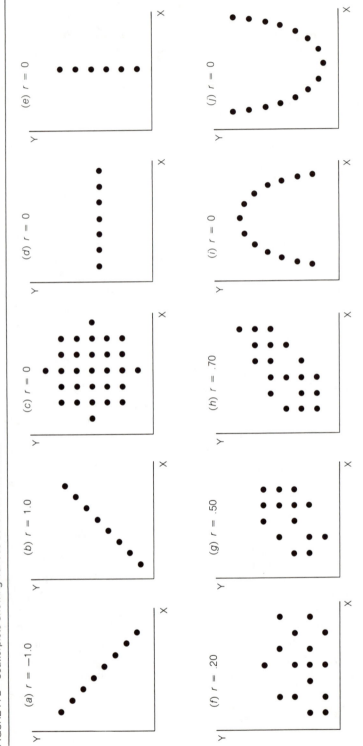

variables we simply form the product of such scores for each case, sum the products, and divide the sum by the number of cases:

$$r = \frac{\Sigma(Z_x Z_y)}{N} \qquad [9]$$

For the data in table A-1, standardized score cross products are shown in column 13. The sum of these cross-products, $\Sigma Z_x Z_y$, is 4.36. The correlation coefficient therefore equals (4.36)/5 or .87.

Assuming that we had not computed standardized scores for variables X and Y, the correlation coefficient could have been computed as follows:

$$r = \frac{N(\Sigma X_i Y_i) - (\Sigma X_i)(\Sigma Y_i)}{\sqrt{[N(\Sigma X_i^2) - (\Sigma X_i)^2][N(\Sigma Y_i^2) - (\Sigma Y_i)^2]}} \qquad [10]$$

The various values needed to compute the correlation coefficient with this formula are shown in the bottom row of table A-1. Substituting these values in the formula we have:

$$r = \frac{5(245) - (31)(38)}{\sqrt{[5(199) - (31)^2][5(306) - (38)^2]}}$$

$$= .87$$

Note that the value of r computed using formula 10 is precisely the same as that obtained using formula 9. The advantage of formula 10 is that to compute r we do not first have to compute means, standard deviations, and standardized scores for two variables; thus formula 10 is easier to use with raw (i.e., unstandardized) data than is formula 9.

## CLOSING WORD

The reader should find the concepts dealt with in this appendix useful in the study of realiability, validity, and other topics considered in various chapters of this book. As indicated earlier, only a brief overview of useful statistical notions can accompany a book having the major purpose of describing research methods. For more complete treatments of useful statistical methods the reader may consult any one of a number of excellent works (Hays, 1973; Glass & Stanley, 1970; Marascuilo, 1971).

# References

Abelson, R.P. "Simulation of Social Behavior." In G. Lindzey and E. Aronson, eds., *Handbook of Social Psychology*, vol. 2. Reading, Mass.: Addison-Wesley, 1968, 274–356.

Allport, G., Vernon, P., and Lindzey, G. *Study of Values,* rev. ed. Boston: Houghton-Mifflin, 1951.

American Anthropological Association. *Principles of Professional Responsibility.* Washington, D.C.: AAA, 1971.

American Medical Association. *AMA Ethical Guidelines for Clinical Investigation.* Chicago: AMA, Nov. 1966.

American Personnel and Guidance Association. *Code of Ethical Standards.* Washington, D.C.: APGA, No Date.

American Psychological Association. *Ethical Standards of Psychologists.* Washington, D.C.: APA, 1972.

American Psychological Association. *Ethical Principles in the Conduct of Research with Human Participants.* Washington, D.C.: APA, 1973.

American Psychological Association. *Standards for Educational and Psychological Tests.* Washington, D.C.: APA, 1974.

American Sociological Association. *Code of Ethics.* Washington, D.C.: ASA, Sept. 1971.

Argyris, C. "Dangers in Applying Results from Experimental Social Psychology." *American Psychologist,* 30(1975), 469–485.

Argyris, C. "Some Unintended Consequences of Rigorous Research." *Psychological Bulletin,* 70(1968), 185–197.

Arrington, R. "Time Sampling in Studies of Social Behavior: A Critical Review of Techniques and Results with Research Suggestions." *Psychological Bulletin,* 40(1943), 81–124.

Asher, H.B. *Causal Modeling.* Beverly Hills, Calif.: Sage Publications, 1976.

Balma, M.J. "The Concept of Synthetic Validity." *Personnel Psychology,* 12(1959), 395–396.

Barrett, G.V. "New Research Models of the Future for Industrial and Organizational Psychology." *Personnel Psychology,* 25(1972), 1–17.

Barrett, R.S. "Guide to Using Psychological Tests." *Harvard Business Review,* Sept.-Oct. 1963, 138–146.

Bass, B.M., Cascio, W.F., and O'Connor, E.J. "Magnitude Estimations of Expressions of Frequency and Amount." *Journal of Applied Psychology,* 59(1974), 313–320.

Baumrind, D. "Principles of Ethical Conduct in the Treatment of Subjects." *American Psychologist,* 26(1971), 887–896.

Bechtoldt, H.P. "Construct Validity: A Critique." *American Psychologist,* 14(1959), 619–629.

Becker, H.S., and Geer, B. "Participant Observation and Interviewing: A Comparison." *Human Organization,* 16(1957), 28–32.

Bennett, C.C. "What Price Privacy?" *American Psychologist,* 22(1967), 371–376.

Blalock, H.M. *Causal Inferences in Nonexperimental Research.* Chapel Hill, N.C.: University of North Carolina Press, 1964.

Blalock, H.M., ed. *Causal Models in the Social Sciences.* Chicago: Aldine-Atherton, 1971.

Blalock, H.M., and Blalock, A.B., eds. *Methodology in Social Research.* New York: McGraw-Hill, 1968.

Block, J. "A Comparison of Forced and Unforced Q-Sorting Procedures." *Educational and Psychological Measurement,* 16(1956), 481–493.

Blum, M., and Naylor, J.C. *Industrial Psychology: Its Theoretical and Social Foundations.* New York: Harper and Row, 1968.

Bonjean, C.M., Hill, R.J., and McLemore, S.D. *Sociological Measurement: An Inventory of Scales and Indices.* San Francisco: Chandler, 1962.

Borko, H. *Computer Applications in the Behavioral Sciences.* Englewood Cliffs, N.J.: Prentice-Hall, 1962.

Bouchard, T.J. "Field Research Methods: Interviewing, Questionnaires, Participant Observation, Systematic Observation, Unobtrusive Measures." In M.D. Dunnette, ed., *Handbook of Industrial and Organizational Psychology.* Chicago: Rand McNally, 1976, 363–413.

Brayfield, A.H., and Crockett, W. "Employee Attitudes and Employee Performance." *Psychological Bulletin,* 52(1955), 396–424.

Brayfield, A.H., and Rothe, H.F. "An Index of Job Satisfaction." *Journal of Applied Psychology,* 35(1951), 307–311.

Buros, O.K., ed. *Tests in Print: A Comprehensive Bibliography of Tests for Use in Education, Psychology, and Industry.* Highland Park, N.J.: Gryphon Press, 1961.

Buros, O.K. *Tests in Print II.* Highland Park, N.J.: Gryphon Press, 1974.

Campbell, D.T. "Factors Relevant to the Validity of Experiments in Social Settings." *Psychological Bulletin,* 54(1957), 297–312.

Campbell, D.T. "Recommendations for APA Test Standards Regarding Construct, Trait, and Discriminant Validity." *American Psychologist,* 15(1960), 546–553.

Campbell, D.T. "Reforms as Experiments." *American Psychologist,* 24(1969), 409–429.

Campbell, D.T., and Fiske, D.W. "Convergent and Discriminant Validation by the Multitrait-Multimethod Matrix." *Psychological Bulletin,* 56(1959), 81–105.

Campbell, D.T., and Stanley, J.C. *Experimental and Quasi-Experimental Designs for Research.* Chicago: Rand McNally, 1966.

Campbell, J.P. "Psychometric Theory." In M.D. Dunnette, ed., *Handbook of Industrial and Organizational Psychology.* Chicago: Rand McNally, 1976.

Carlsmith, J.M., Ellsworth, P.C., and Aronson, E. *Methods of Research in Social Psychology.* Reading, Mass.: Addison-Wesley, 1976.

**167**

Centers, R., and Bugental, D.E. "Intrinsic and Extrinsic Job Motivations Among Different Segments of the Working Population." *Journal of Applied Psychology*, 50(1966), 193–197.

Chapanis, A. "Knowledge of Performance as an Incentive in Repetitive, Monotonous Tasks." *Journal of Applied Psychology*, 48(1964), 263–267.

Chaplin, J.P. *Dictionary of Psychology*. New York: Dell Publishing, 1975.

Cherrington, D.L., Reitz, H.J., and Scott Jr., W.E. "Effects of Reward and Contingent Reinforcement on Satisfaction and Task Performance." *Journal of Applied Psychology*, 55(1971), 531–536.

Chun, K., Cobb, S., and French, J.R.P. *Measures for Psychological Assessment*. Ann Arbor, Mich.: Institute for Social Research, 1975.

Cleary, A.T., Humphreys, L.G., Kendrick, S.A., and Wesman, A. "Educational Uses of Tests with Disadvantaged Students." *American Psychologist*, 30(1975), 15–41.

Cochran, W.G. *Sampling Techniques*, 2nd ed. New York: John Wiley and Sons, 1963.

Cohen, J. *Statistical Power Analysis for the Behavioral Sciences*. New York: Academic Press, 1969.

Cohen, J., and Cohen, P. *Applied Multiple Regression/Correlation Analysis for the Behavioral Sciences*. Hillsdale, N.J.: Lawrence Erlbaum Associates, 1975.

Cohen, K.J., and Cyert, R.M. "Simulation of Organizational Behavior." In J.G. March, ed., *Handbook of Organizations*. Chicago: Rand McNally, 1965, 305–334.

Cohen, M., and Nagel, E. *An Introduction to Logic and Scientific Method*. New York: Harcourt, Brace and Co., 1934.

Conrad, H. "Clearance of Questionnaires with Respect to 'Invasion of Privacy,' Public Sensitivities, Ethical Standards, etc." *American Psychologist*, 22(1967), 356–359.

Cook, S.W. "Ethical Issues in the Conduct of Research in Social Relations." Chapter 7 in *Research Methods in Social Relations*, 3rd ed., by C. Selltiz, L.S. Wrightsman, and S.W. Cook. New York: Holt, Rinehart and Winston, 1976.

Cook, S.W., and Selltiz, C. "A Multiple Indicator Approach to Attitude Measurement." *Psychological Bulletin*, 62(1964), 36–55.

Cook, T.D., and Campbell, D.T. "The Design and Conduct of Quasi-Experiments and True Experiments in Field Settings." Chapter 7 in M.D. Dunnette, ed., *Handbook of Industrial and Organizational Psychology*. Chicago: Rand McNally, 1976, 223–326.

Cooley, W.W., and Lohnes, P.R. *Multivariate Data Analysis*. New York: John Wiley and Sons, 1971.

Cooper, J. "Deception and Role Playing: On Telling the Good Guys from the Bad Guys." *American Psychologist*, 31(1976), 605–610.

Cooper, W.W., Leavitt, H.J., and Shelly, M.W., eds. *New Perspectives in Organization Research*. New York: John Wiley and Sons, 1964.

Crano, W.D., and Brewer, M.B. *Principles of Research in Social Psychology*. New York: McGraw-Hill, 1973.

Cronbach, L.J. "Coefficient Alpha and the Internal Structure of Tests." *Psychometrika*, 16(1951), 297–334.

Cronbach, L.J. "Test Reliability: Its Meaning and Determination." *Psychometrika*, 12(1947), 1–16.

Cronbach, L.J., and Meehl, P.C. "Construct Validity in Psychological Tests." *Psychological Bulletin*, 52(1955), 281–302.

Dillman, D.A. "Increasing Mail Questionnaire Response in Large Samples of the General Public." *Public Opinion Quarterly*, 36(1972), 254–257.

Dukes, W. "Psychological Studies of Values." *Psychological Bulletin,* 52(1955), 24–50.

Duncan, O.D. "Contingencies in Constructing Causal Models." In E.F. Borgatta and G.W. Bohrnstedt, eds., *Sociological Methodology.* San Francisco: Jossey-Bass, 1969, 74–112.

Duncan, O.D. "Path Analysis: Sociological Examples." *American Journal of Sociology,* 72(1966), 1–16.

Dunnette, M.D. *Personnel Selection and Placement.* Belmont, Calif.: Brooks/Cole Publishing Co., 1966.

Dunnette, M.D., ed. *Handbook of Industrial and Organizational Psychology.* Chicago: Rand McNally, 1976.

Ebel, R. "Estimation of the Reliability of Ratings." *Psychometrika,* 16(1951), 407–424.

Ebel, R. "Obtaining and Reporting Evidence on Content Validity." *Educational and Psychological Measurement,* 16(1956), 269–282.

Edwards, A. *Experimental Design in Psychological Research,* 3rd ed. New York: Holt, Rinehart and Winston, 1968.

Einhorn, H.J., and Bass, A.R. "Methodological Considerations Relevant to Discrimination in Employment Testing." *Psychological Bulletin,* 75(1971), 261–269.

Ernst, M.L., and Schwartz, A.U. *Privacy: The Right to Be Let Alone.* New York: Macmillan, 1962.

Evan, W.M., ed. *Organizational Experiments.* New York: Harper and Row, 1971.

Farr, J.L., and Seaver, W.B. "Stress and Discomfort in Psychological Research: Subject Perceptions of Experimental Procedures." *American Psychologist,* 30(1975), 770–773.

Feldman, J. "Considerations in the Use of Causal-Correlational Techniques in Applied Psychology." *Journal of Applied Psychology,* 60(1975), 663–670.

Festinger, L. "Laboratory Experiments." In L. Festinger and D. Katz, eds., *Research Methods in the Behavioral Sciences.* New York: Dryden Press, 1953, 136–172.

Festinger, L., Riecken, H.W., and Schachter, S. *When Prophecy Fails.* Minneapolis: University of Minnesota Press, 1956.

Fishbein, M. *Readings in Attitude Theory and Measurement.* New York: John Wiley and Sons, 1967.

Fisher, R. *The Design of Experiments,* 8th ed. New York: Hafner, 1966.

Forward, J., Canter, R., and Kirsch, N. "Role Enactment and Deception Methodologies: Alternative Paradigms?" *American Psychologist,* 31(1976), 595–604.

Fromkin, H.L., and Streufert, S. "Laboratory Experimentation." In M.D. Dunnette, ed., *Handbook of Industrial and Organizational Psychology.* Chicago: Rand McNally, 1976, 415–465.

Georgopoulos, B.S., Mahoney, G.M., and Jones, N.W. "A Path-Goal Approach to Productivity." *Journal of Applied Psychology,* 41(1957), 345–353.

Gergen, K.J. "The Codification of Research Ethics: Views of a Doubting Thomas." *American Psychologist,* 28(1973), 907–912.

Ghiselli, E.E. *Theory of Psychological Measurement.* New York: McGraw-Hill, 1964.

Ghiselli, E.E. *The Validity of Occupational Aptitude Tests.* New York: John Wiley and Sons, 1966.

Gibb, C.A. "Leadership." In G. Lindzey and E. Aronson, eds., *The Handbook of Social Psychology,* 2nd ed. Reading, Mass.: Addison-Wesley, 1969, vol. 4, 216–228.

Glass, G.V., and Stanley, J.C. *Statistical Methods in Education and Psychology.* Englewood Cliffs, N.J.: Prentice-Hall, 1970.

Gouldner, A. *Patterns of Industrial Bureaucracy.* Glencoe, Ill.: Free Press, 1954.

**169**

Green, B. *Digital Computers in Research: An Introduction for Behavioral and Social Scientists.* New York: McGraw-Hill, 1963.

Guilford, J.P. *Psychometric Methods,* 2nd ed. New York: McGraw-Hill, 1954.

Guilford, J.P., and Fruchter, B. *Fundamental Statistics in Psychology and Education,* 5th ed. New York: McGraw-Hill, 1973.

Guion, R.M. "Employment Tests and Discriminatory Hiring." *Industrial Relations,* 5(1966), 20–37.

Guion, R.M. *Personnel Testing.* New York: McGraw-Hill, 1965. (a)

Guion, R.M., "Synthetic Validity in a Small Company: A Demonstration." *Personnel Psychology,* 18(1965), 49–65. (b)

Guion, R.M., and Gottier, R.F. "Validity of Personnel Measures in Personnel Selection." *Personnel Psychology,* 18(1965), 135–164.

Gulliksen, H. "Intrinsic Validity." *American Psychologist,* 5(1950), 511–517. (a)

Gulliksen, H. *Theory of Mental Tests.* New York: John Wiley and Sons, 1950. (b)

Gulliksen, H., and Messick, S., eds. *Psychological Scaling: Theory and Applications.* New York: John Wiley and Sons, 1960.

Hackman, J.R., and Lawler, E.E. "Employee Reactions to Job Characteristics." *Journal of Applied Psychology,* 55(1971), 259–286.

Hackman, J.R., and Porter, L.W. "Expectancy Theory Predictions of Work Effectiveness." *Organizational Behavior and Human Performance,* 3(1968), 417–426.

Haney, C., Banks, W.C., and Zimbardo, P.G. "Interpersonal Dynamics in a Simulated Prison." *International Journal of Criminology and Penology,* 1(1973), 69–97.

Hathaway, S.R., and McKinley, J.C. *Minnesota Multiphasic Personality Inventory,* rev. ed. New York: Psychological Corporation, 1943.

Hays, W.L. *Statistics for the Social Sciences,* 2nd ed. New York: Holt, Rinehart and Winston, 1973.

Hedluise, D.E. "A Review of the MMPI in Industry." *Psychological Reports,* 17(1965), 875–889.

Heise, D.R. "Problems in Path-Analysis and Causal Inference." In E.F. Borgatta and G.W. Bohrnstedt, eds., *Sociological Methodology.* San Francisco: Jossey-Bass, 1969, 38–73.

Helmstadter, G.C. *Research Concepts in Human Behavior.* Englewood Cliffs, N.J.: Prentice-Hall, 1970.

Hempel, C.G. *Aspects of Scientific Explanation.* New York: The Free Press, 1965.

Herzberg, F., Mausner, B., and Snyderman, B. *The Motivation to Work,* 2nd ed. New York: John Wiley and Sons, 1959.

Heyns, R.W., and Zander, A.F. "Observation of Group Behavior." Chapter 9 in L. Festinger and D. Katz, eds., *Research Methods in the Behavioral Sciences.* New York: Dryden Press, 1953.

Holmes, D.S. "Debriefing After Psychological Experiments: I. Effectiveness of Post-deception Dehoaxing." *American Psychologist,* 31(1976), 858–867. (a)

Holmes, D.S. "Debriefing After Psychological Experiments: II. Effectiveness of Post-experimental Desensitizing." *American Psychologist,* 31(1976), 868–875. (b)

Holmes, D.S., and Bennett, D.H. "Experiments to Answer Questions Raised by the Use of Deception in Psychological Research: I. Role Playing as an Alternative to Deception; II. Effectiveness of Debriefing After a Deception; III. Effect of Informed Consent on Deception." *Journal of Personality and Social Psychology,* 29(1974), 358–367.

House, R.J., and Wigdor, L.A. "Herzberg's Dual-Factor Theory of Job Satisfaction and Motivation: A Review of the Evidence and a Criticism." *Personnel Psychology,* 20(1967), 369–390.

Hoyt, C. "Test Reliability Obtained by Analysis of Variance." *Psychometrika,* 6(1941), 153–160.

Hulin, C.L. "Individual Differences and Job Enrichment: The Case Against General Treatments." In J.R. Maher, ed., *New Perspectives in Job Enrichment.* New York: Van Nostrand Reinhold, 1971.

Hulin, C.L., and Blood, M.R. "Job Enlargement, Individual Differences, and Worker Responses." *Psychological Bulletin,* 69(1968), 41–55.

Hyman, H.H. "The Value Systems of Different Classes." In R. Bendix and S.M. Lipset, eds., *Class, Status, and Power,* 2nd ed. New York: Free Press, 1966.

Hyman, H.H., Cobb, W.J., Feldman, J.J., Hart, C.W., and Stember, C.H. *Interviewing in Social Research.* Chicago: University of Chicago Press, 1954.

*Hyman vs. Jewish Chronic Disease Hospital.* 21, A.D. 495, 251, NYS 2d 818 (1964).

*Hyman vs. Jewish Chronic Disease Hospital.* 15 N.Y. 2d 317, 206 N.E. 2d 388 (1965).

Jackson, D.N. *Personality Research Form Manual.* Goshen, N.Y.: Research Psychologists Press, 1967.

Jones, A. "Distribution of Traits in Current Q-Sort Methodology." *Journal of Abnormal and Social Psychology,* 53(1956), 90–95.

Kahn, R.L., Wolfe, D.M., Quinn, R.P., Snoek, J.D., and Rosenthal, R.A. *Organizational Stress: Studies in Role Conflict and Role Ambiguity.* New York: John Wiley and Sons, 1964.

Kalleberg, A.L., and Kluegel, J.R. "Analysis of the Multitrait-Multimethod Matrix: Some Limitations and an Alternative." *Journal of Applied Psychology,* 60(1975), 1–9.

Kanuk, L., and Berenson, L. "Mail Surveys and Response Rates: A Literature Review." *Journal of Marketing Research,* 12(1975), 440–453.

Kaplan, A. *The Conduct of Inquiry.* San Francisco: Chandler Publishing Co., 1964.

Katz, D. "Field Studies." In L. Festinger and D. Katz, eds., *Research Methods in the Behavioral Sciences.* New York: Dryden Press, 1953.

Katz, D., Maccoby, N., Gurin, G., and Floor, L. *Productivity, Supervision, and Morale Among Railroad Workers.* Ann Arbor, Mich.: Survey Research Center, University of Michigan, 1951.

Katz, M. "Ethical Issues in the Use of Human Subjects in Psychopharmacologic Research." *American Psychologist,* 22(1967), 360–363.

Kelman, H.C. *A Time to Speak: On Human Values and Social Research.* San Francisco: Jossey-Bass, 1968.

Kelman, H.C. "Human Use of Human Subjects: The Problem of Deception in Social Psychological Experiments." *Psychological Bulletin,* 22(1967), 1–11.

Kelman, H.C. "The Rights of the Subject in Social Research: An Analysis in Terms of Relative Power and Legitimacy." *American Psychologist,* 27(1972), 989–1016.

Kemeny, J.G. *A Philosopher Looks at Science.* Princeton, N.J.: D. Van Nostrand, 1959.

Kempthorne, O. *The Design and Analysis of Experiments.* New York: John Wiley and Sons, 1952.

Kenny, D.A. "Cross-Lagged Panel Correlation: A Test for Spuriousness." *Psychological Bulletin,* 82(1975), 887–903.

Kerlinger, F. *Foundations of Behavioral Research,* 2nd ed. New York: Holt, Rinehart and Winston, 1973.

Kerlinger, F. "Q-Methodology in Behavioral Science Research." Chapter 1 in: S. Brown and D. Brenner, *Science, Psychology, and Communication.* New York: Teachers College Press, 1972.

**171**

Kerlinger, F., and Pedhazur, E.J. *Multiple Regression in Behavioral Research.* New York: Holt, Rinehart and Winston, 1973.

King, A.J., and Spector, A.J. "Ethical and Legal Aspects of Survey Research." *American Psychologist,* 18(1963), 204–208.

King, N. "Clarification and Evaluation of the Two-Factor Theory of Job Satisfaction." *Psychological Bulletin,* 74(1970), 18–31.

Kinslinger, H.J. "Application of Projective Techniques in Personnel Psychology Since 1940." *Psychological Bulletin,* 66(1966), 134–149.

Kirk, R. *Experimental Design: Procedures for the Behavioral Sciences.* Belmont, Calif.: Brooks/Cole, 1968.

Kish, L. "Selection of the Sample." In L. Festinger and D. Katz, eds., *Research Methods in the Behavioral Sciences.* New York: Dryden Press, 1953.

Kish L. *Survey Sampling.* New York: John Wiley and Sons, 1965.

Kohn, M.L., and Schooler, C. "Class, Occupation, and Orientation." *American Sociological Review,* 34(1969), 659–678.

Korman, A.K. *Industrial and Organizational Psychology.* Englewood Cliffs, N.J.: Prentice-Hall, 1971.

Kuder, G.F. *Kuder Preference Record—Occupational.* Chicago: Science Research Associates, 1956.

Kuder, G.F. *Kuder Preference Record—Vocational.* Chicago: Science Research Associates, 1934.

Kuder, G.F., and Richardson, M.W. "The Theory of the Estimation of Test Reliability." *Psychometrika,* 2(1937), 151–160.

Landy, F.J., and Trumbo, D.A. *Psychology of Work Behavior.* Homewood, Ill.: Dorsey Press, 1976.

Latham, G.P., and Kinne, S.B. "Improving Job Performance Through Training in Goal Setting." *Journal of Applied Psychology,* 59(1974), 187–191.

Lawler, E.E., and Hackman, J.R. "Impact of Employee Participation in the Development of Pay Incentive Plans: A Field Experiment." *Journal of Applied Psychology,* 53(1969), 467–471.

Lawler, E.E., Hackman, J.R., and Kaufman, S. "Effects of Job Redesign: A Field Experiment." *Journal of Applied Social Psychology,* 3(1973), 49–62.

Lawshe, C.H. "A Quantitative Approach to Content Validity." *Personnel Psychology,* 28(1975), 563–575.

Lawshe, C.H., and Steinberg, M.D. "Studies in Synthetic Validity, I. An Exploratory Investigation of Clerical Jobs." *Personnel Psychology,* 8(1955), 291–301.

Lennon, R.T. "Assumptions Underlying the Use of Content Validity." *Educational and Psychological Measurement,* 16(1956), 294–304.

Lenski, G. *The Religious Factor: A Sociologist's Inquiry,* rev. ed. Garden City, N.Y.: Anchor Books, 1963.

Lin, N. *Foundations of Social Research.* New York: McGraw-Hill, 1976.

Lindzey, G. "On the Classification of Projective Techniques." *Psychological Bulletin,* 56(1959), 158–168.

Lindzey, G., and Borgatta, E.F. "Sociometric Measurement." In G. Lindzey, ed., *Handbook of Social Psychology,* vol. 1. Reading, Mass.: Addison-Wesley, 1954.

Lindzey, G., and Byrne, D. "Measurement of Social Choice and Interpersonal Attractiveness." In G. Lindzey and E. Aronson, eds., *The Handbook of Social Psychology,* 2nd ed., vol. 2, Chapter 14. Reading, Mass.: Addison-Wesley, 1968.

Linsky, A.S. "Stimulating Responses to Mailed Questionnaires: A Review." *Public Opinion Quarterly,* 39(1975), 82–101.

Locke, E.A. "Toward a Theory of Task Motivation and Incentives." *Organizational Behavior and Human Performance,* 3(1968), 157–189.

Locke, E.A. "What is Job Satisfaction?" *Organizational Behavior and Human Performance,* 4(1969), 309–336.

Loevinger, J. "The Attenuation Paradox in Test Theory." *Psychological Bulletin,* 51(1954), 493–504.

Lofquist, L.H., and Dawis, R.V. *Adjustment to Work.* New York: Appleton-Century-Crofts, 1969.

Lowin, A., and Craig, J.R. "The Influence of Level of Performance on Managerial Style: An Experimental Object-Lesson in the Ambiguity of Correlational Data." *Organizational Behavior and Human Performance,* 3(1968), 440–458.

Lumsden, J. "Test Theory." *Annual Review of Psychology,* 27(1976), 251–280.

MacCorquodale, K., and Meehl, P.E. "On a Distinction Between Hypothetical Constructs and Intervening Variables." *Psychological Review,* 55(1948), 95–107.

Maier, N.R.F. *Psychology in Industrial Organizations,* 4th ed. Boston: Houghton Mifflin, 1973.

Manheim, H.L. *Sociological Research: Philosophy and Methods.* Homewood, Ill.: Dorsey Press, 1977.

Manning, S.A., and Rosenstock, E. *Classical Psychophysics and Scaling.* New York: McGraw-Hill, 1968.

Marascuilo, L.A. *Statistical Methods for Behavioral Science Research.* New York: McGraw-Hill, 1971.

McClelland, D.C., Atkinson, J.W., Clark, R.A., and Lowell, E.L. *The Achievement Motive.* New York: Appleton-Century-Crofts, 1953.

McClelland, D.C., and Winter, D.G. *Motivating Economic Achievement.* New York: The Free Press, 1969.

McCormick, E.J., and Tiffin, J. *Industrial Psychology,* 6th ed. Englewood Cliffs, N.J.: Prentice-Hall, 1974.

McGuigan, F.J. "The Experimenter: A Neglected Stimulus Object." *Psychological Bulletin,* 60(1963), 421–428.

Meyers, L.S., and Grossen, N.E. *Behavioral Research: Theory, Procedure, and Design.* San Francisco: W.H. Freeman, 1974.

Miles, M., and Lake, D. *Social Measurement Scales.* New York: Columbia Teachers Press, 1967.

Milgram, S. "Behavioral Study of Obedience." *Journal of Abnormal and Social Psychology,* 67(1963), 371–378.

Milgram, S. "Some Conditions of Obedience and Disobedience to Authority." *Human Relations,* 18(1965), 57–75.

Miller, D.C. *Handbook of Research Design and Social Measurement.* New York: David McKay, 1964.

Miner, J.B. *Personnel Psychology.* Toronto: Macmillan, Co., 1969.

Mitchell, T.R., and Biglan, A. "Instrumentality Theories: Current Uses in Psychology." *Psychological Bulletin,* 76(1971), 432–454.

Moreno, J.L. *Who Shall Survive?* rev. ed. Washington, D.C.: Nervous and Mental Disease Publishing Co., 1953.

Mosier, C.I. "A Critical Examination of the Concepts of Face Validity." *Educational and Psychological Measurement,* 7(1947), 191–205.

Murstein, B.I. *Theory and Research in Projective Techniques.* New York: John Wiley and Sons, 1963.

Nagel, E. *The Structure of Science.* New York: Harcourt, Brace and World, 1961.

Nash, M.M. "Nonreactive Methods and the Law: Additional Comments on Legal Liability in Behavior Research." *American Psychologist,* 30(1975), 777–780.

National Association of Social Workers. *NASW Code of Ethics.* New York: NASW, Oct. 1968.

National Employment Law Project. *Legal Services Manual for Title VII Litigation.* New York: NELP, 1973.

Northway, M. *A Primer of Sociometry.* Toronto: University of Toronto Press, 1952.

Nunnally, J.C. *Educational Measurement and Evaluation,* 2nd ed. New York: Mc-Graw-Hill, 1972.

Nunnally, J.C. *Psychometric Theory.* New York: McGraw-Hill, 1967.

Nuremberg Military Tribunals, "Nuremberg Code," (Text). *Trials of War Criminals Before the Nuremberg Military Tribunals,* vol. II. Washington, D.C.: U.S. Government Printing Office, 1949, 181–182.

Orne, M.T. "On the Social Psychology of the Psychological Experiments: With Particular Reference to Demand Characteristics and Their Implications." *American Psychologist,* 17(1962), 776–783.

Overall, J.C., and Klett, C.J. *Applied Multivariate Analysis.* New York: McGraw-Hill, 1972.

Panel on Privacy and Behavioral Research. "Privacy and Behavioral Research." *Science,* 155(1967), 535–538.

Patchen, M., Pelz, D.C., and Allen, C.W. *Some Questionnaire Measures of Employee Motivation and Morale.* Ann Arbor, Mich.: Institute for Social Research, 1966.

Pelz, D.C., and Andrews, F.M. "Detecting Causal Priorities in Panel Study Data." *American Sociological Review,* 29(1964), 836–848.

Piliavin, J.A., and Piliavin, I.M. "Effect of Blood on Reactions to a Victim." *Journal of Personality and Social Psychology,* 23(1972), 353–361.

Pittel, S., and Mendelsohn, G. "Measurement of Moral Values." *Psychological Bulletin,* 66(1966), 22–35.

Popper, K.R. *The Logic of Scientific Discovery.* New York: Science Editions, Inc., 1959.

Porter, L.W., and Lawler, E.E. *Managerial Attitudes and Performance.* Homewood, Ill.: Irwin-Dorsey, 1968.

Proctor, C.H., and Loomis, C.P. "Analysis of Sociometric Data." In M. Jahoda, M. Deutsch, and S.W. Cook, eds., *Research Methods in Social Relations,* vol. II. New York: Dryden, 1951.

Quinn, R., Seashore, S., Kahn, R., Mangione, T., Campbell, D., Staines, G., and McCullough, M. *Survey of Working Conditions.* Document 2916–0001. Washington, D.C.: U.S. Government Printing Office, 1971.

Robinson, J.P., Athanasiou, R., and Head, K.B. *Measures of Occupational Attitudes and Occupational Characteristics.* Ann Arbor, Mich.: Institute for Social Research, 1969.

Robinson, J.P., and Shaver, P.R. *Measures of Social Psychological Attitudes,* rev. ed. Ann Arbor, Mich.: Institute for Social Research, 1973.

Roby, T.B. "Computer Simulation Methods for Organizational Research." In V.H. Vroom, ed., *Methods of Organizational Research.* Pittsburgh: University of Pittsburgh Press, 1967, 171–211.

Roethlisberger, F.J., and Dickson, W.J. *Management and the Worker.* Cambridge: Harvard University Press, 1939.

Romney, A.K., Shepard, R.N., and Nerlove, S.B. *Multidimensional Scaling, Vol. II: Applications.* New York: Seminar Press, 1972.

Rosenthal, R. *Experimenter Effects in Behavioral Research.* New York: Appleton-Century-Crofts, 1966.

Rosenthal, R. *Experimenter Effects in Behavioral Research,* enlarged edition. New York: John Wiley and Sons, 1976.

Rosenthal, R. "Experimenter Outcome-Orientation and the Results of the Psychological Experiment." *Psychological Bulletin,* 61(1964), 405–412.

Rosenthal, R. "On the Social Psychology of the Psychological Experiment: The Experimenter's Hypothesis as Unintended Determinant of Experimental Results." *American Scientist,* 51(1963), 268–283.

Rosenthal, R., and Rosnow, R.L. *Artifacts in Behavioral Research.* New York: Academic Press, 1969.

Rozelle, R.M., and Campbell, D.T. "More Plausible Rival Hypotheses in the Cross-Lagged Panel Correlation Technique." *Psychological Bulletin,* 71(1969), 74–80.

Rubin, Z. "Jokers Wild in the Lab." *Psychology Today,* 4(1970), 18; 20; 22–24; 79.

Ruebhausen, O.M., and Brim, O.G. "Privacy and Behavioral Research." *Columbia Law Review,* 65(1965), 1184–1211.

Ruebhausen, O.M., and Brim, O.G. "Privacy and Behavioral Research," *American Psychologist,* 21(1966), 423–437.

Runkel, P.J., and McGrath, J.E. *Research on Human Behavior.* New York: Holt, Rinehart and Winston, 1972.

Sargent, H. "Projective Methods: Their Origins, Theory, and Applications in Personality Research." *Psychological Bulletin,* 42(1945), 257–293.

Saunders, D.R. "Moderator Variables in Prediction." *Educational and Psychological Measurement,* 16(1956), 209–222.

Schmidt, F.L., Hunter, J.E., and Urry, V.W. "Statistical Power in Criterion-Related Validation Studies." *Journal of Applied Psychology,* 61(1976), 473–485.

Schmitt, N. "Social and Situational Determinants of Interview Decisions: Implications for the Employment Interview." *Personnel Psychology,* 29(1976), 79–101.

Schneider, B. *Staffing Organizations.* Pacific Palisades, Calif.: Goodyear Publishing Co., 1976.

Schoenfeldt, L.F., and Gatewood, R.D. "Industrial and Organizational Psychology Through the Looking Glass of the Division 14 Dissertation Contest." *Personnel Psychology,* 27(1974), 543–554.

Schultz, D. *Psychology and Industry Today.* New York: Macmillan Co., 1973.

Schwab, D.P., and Cummings, L.L. "Theories of Performance and Satisfaction: A Review." *Industrial Relations,* 9(1970), 408–430.

Scott, W.R. "Field Methods in the Study of Organizations." In J.G. March, ed., *Handbook of Organizations.* Chicago: Rand McNally, 1965, 261–304.

Sears, R.R. *Privacy and Behavioral Research.* Washington, D.C.: Executive Office of the President, 1967.

Seashore, S.E. "Field Experiments with Formal Organizations." *Human Organization,* 23(1964), 164–170.

Sechrest, L. "Incremental Validity." *Educational and Psychological Measurement,* 23(1963), 153–158.

Seeman, J. "Deception in Psychological Research." *American Psychologist,* 24(1969), 1025–1028.

Selltiz, C., Jahoda, M., Deutsch, M., and Cook, S. *Research Methods in Social Relations,* rev. ed. New York: Holt, Rinehart and Winston, 1959.

Selltiz, C., Wrightsman, L.S., and Cook, S.W. *Research Methods in Social Relations,* 3rd ed. New York: Holt, Rinehart and Winston, 1976.

Shaw, M., and Wright, J. *Scales for the Measurement of Attitudes.* New York: McGraw-Hill, 1967.

**175**

Shontz, F.C. *Research Methods in Personality.* New York: Appleton-Century-Crofts, 1965.

Sidman, M. *Tactics of Scientific Research.* New York: Basic Books, 1960.

Sigall, H.E., Aronson, E., and Van Hoose, T. "The Cooperative Subject: Myth or Reality?" *Journal of Experimental Social Psychology,* 6(1970), 1–10.

Silverman, I. "Nonreactive Methods and the Law." *American Psychologist,* 30(1975), 764–769.

Simon, H. "Spurious Correlation: A Causal Interpretation." *Journal of the American Statistical Association,* 59(1954), 467–479.

Smith, H.L., and Hyman, H. "The Biasing Effect of Interviewer Expectations on Survey Results." *Public Opinion Quarterly,* 14(1950), 491–506.

Smith, M.B. "Conflicting Values Affecting Behavioral Research with Children." *American Psychologist,* 22(1967), 377–382.

Smith, P.C., Kendall, L.M., and Hulin, C.L. *The Measurement of Satisfaction in Work and Retirement.* Chicago: Rand McNally, 1969.

Solomon, R.L. "An Extension of Control Group Design." *Psychological Bulletin,* 46(1949), 137–150.

Spearman, C. "Correlation Computed from Faulty Data." *British Journal of Psychology,* 3(1910) 271–295.

Srinivasan, V., and Weinstein, A.G. "Effects of Curtailment on an Admissions Model for a Graduate Management Program." *Journal of Applied Psychology,* 58(1973), 339–346.

Staw, B.M. "Attribution of 'Causes' of Performance: A General Alternative Interpretation of Cross-Sectional Research on Organizations." *Organizational Behavior and Human Performance,* 13(1975), 414–432.

Steers, R.M., and Porter, L.W. "The Role of Task-Goal Attributes in Employee Performance." *Psychological Bulletin,* 81(1974), 434–452.

Steers, R.M., and Porter, L.W. *Motivation and Work Behavior.* New York: McGraw-Hill, 1975.

Stephenson, W. *The Study of Behavior.* Chicago: University of Chicago Press, 1953.

Stevens, S. "Measurement, Statistics, and the Schemapiric View." *Science,* 161(1968), 849–856.

Stevens, S. "Problems and Methods of Psychophysics." *Psychological Bulletin,* 55(1958), 177–196.

Stevens, S. "Scales of Measurement." In J.A. Steger, *Readings in Statistics for the Behavioral Scientist.* New York: Holt, Rinehart and Winston, 1971, 8–18.

Stodgill, R.M., and Coons, A.E. eds. *Leader Behavior: Its Description and Measurement.* Columbus, Ohio: Ohio State University, Bureau of Business Research Monograph, No. 88, 1957.

Stone, E.F. "The Moderating Effect of Work-Related Values on the Job Scope-Job Satisfaction Relationship." *Organizational Behavior and Human Performance,* 15(1976), 147–167.

Stone, E.F., and Porter, L.W. "Job Characteristics and Job Attitudes: A Multivariate Study." *Journal of Applied Psychology,* 60(1975), 57–64.

Strong, E.K., Jr. *Strong Vocational Interest Blank for Men, Revised.* Stanford, Calif.: Stanford University Press, 1938.

Sundland, D. "The Construction of Q Sorts: A Criticism." *Psychological Review,* 69(1962), 62–64.

Taksuoka, M.M. *Multivariate Analysis.* New York: John Wiley and Sons, 1971.

Thorndike, R.L. *Personnel Selection.* New York: John Wiley and Sons, 1949.

Thorndike, R.L. "Reliability." In D.N. Jackson and S. Messick, eds., *Problems in Human Assessment*. New York: McGraw-Hill Book Co., 1967, 217–240.

Thornton, R. "Organizational Involvement and Commitment to Organization and Profession." *Administrative Science Quarterly,* 15(1970), 417–426.

Tompkins, S.S., and Messick, S. eds. *Computer Simulation of Personality: Frontier of Psychological Theory*. New York: John Wiley and Sons, 1963.

Torgerson, W. *Theory and Methods of Scaling*. New York: John Wiley and Sons, 1958.

Tryon, R. "Reliability and Behavioral Domain Validity: Reformulation and Historical Critique." *Psychological Bulletin,* 54(1957), 229–249.

Turner, A.N., and Lawrence, P.R. *Industrial Jobs and the Worker: An Investigation of Response to Task Attributes*. Boston: Harvard University Press, 1965.

Underwood, B. *Psychological Research*. New York: Appleton, 1957.

U.S. Civil Service Commission. *Equal Employment Opportunity Court Cases*. Washington, D.C.: U.S. Civil Service Commission, Bureau of Intergovernmental Personnel Programs, March 1974.

U.S. Department of Health, Education, and Welfare. *The Institutional Guide to DHEW Policy on Protection of Human Subjects*. Washington, D.C.: U.S. Government Printing Office, 1971.

U.S. Public Health Service. *Protection of the Individual as a Research Subject*. Washington, D.C.: U.S. Government Printing Office, 1969.

Vroom, V.H. *Work and Motivation*. New York: John Wiley and Sons, 1964.

Warwick, D.P. "Social Scientists Ought to Stop Lying." *Psychology Today,* Feb. 1975, 38, 40, 105–106.

Warwick, D.P., and Lininger, C.A. *The Sample Survey: Theory and Practice*. New York: McGraw-Hill, 1975.

Webb, E.J., Campbell, D.T., Schwartz, R.D., and Sechrest, L. *Unobtrusive Measures: Nonreactive Research in the Social Sciences*. Chicago: Rand McNally, 1966.

Weber, S.J., and Cook, T.D. "Subject Effects in Laboratory Research: An Examination of Subject Roles, Demand Characteristics, and Valid Inference." *Psychological Bulletin,* 77(1972), 273–295.

Weick, K.E. "Organizations in the Laboratory." In V.H. Vroom, ed., *Methods of Organizational Research*. Pittsburgh: University of Pittsburgh Press, 1967, 1–56.

Williams, E., and Raush, H., eds. *Naturalistic Viewpoints in Psychological Research*. New York: Holt, Rinehart and Winston, 1969.

Williams, J.A., Jr. "Interviewer-Respondent Interaction: A Study of Bias in the Information Interview." *Sociometry,* 27(1964), 338–352.

Williams, L.K., Seybolt, J.W., and Pinder, C.C. "On Administering Questionnaires in Organizational Settings." *Personnel Psychology,* 28(1975), 93–103.

Wilson, D.W., and Donnerstein, E. "Legal and Ethical Aspects of Nonreactive Social Psychological Research: An Excursion into the Public Mind." *American Psychologist,* 31(1976), 765–773.

Winer, B.J. *Statistical Principles in Experimental Design*. New York: McGraw-Hill, 1962.

Wittenborn, J. "Contributions and Current Status of Q-Methodology." *Psychological Bulletin,* 58(1961), 132–142.

Wollack, S., Goodale, J.G., Wijting, J.P., and Smith, P.C. "Development of the Survey of Work Values." *Journal of Applied Psychology,* 55(1971), 331–338.

Woodward, J. *Management and Technology*. London: Her Majesty's Stationery Office, 1958.

**177**

Woodward, J. *Industrial Organization: Theory and Practice.* London: Oxford University Press, 1965.

Woolf, H.B., ed. *Webster's New Collegiate Dictionary.* Springfield, Mass.: G. and C. Merriam Company, 1975.

Yule, G.U. *An Introduction to the Theory of Statistics.* London: Griffin, 1922.

Zedeck, S. "Problems with the Use of Moderator Variables." *Psychological Bulletin,* 76(1971), 295–310.

Zedeck, S., and Blood, M.R. *Foundations of Behavioral Science Research in Organizations.* Monterey, Calif.: Brooks/Cole, 1974.

Zelditch, M., and Hopkins, T.K. "Laboratory Experiments with Organizations." In A. Etzioni, ed., *Complex Organizations: A Sociological Reader.* New York: Holt, Rinehart, and Winston, 1961, 464–478.

Zimbardo, P. "The Human Choice: Individuation, Reason and Order Versus Deindividuation, Impulse and Chaos." In W.J. Arnold and D. Levine, eds., *Nebraska Symposium on Motivation,* vol. 17. Lincoln, Neb.: University of Nebraska Press, 1969.

# NAME INDEX

**179**

**181**

# SUBJECT INDEX

**185**